I0793730

IMAGES
of America

WALNUT

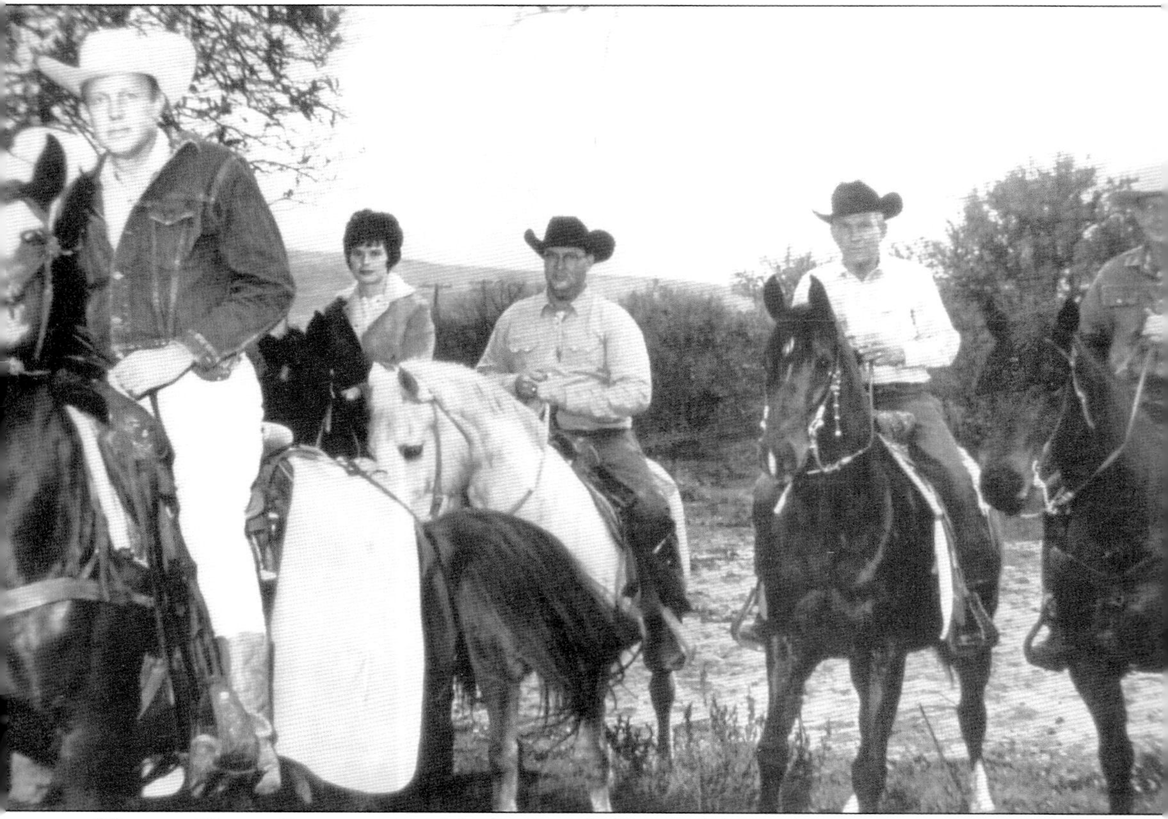

Walnut Valley Riders, 1965. Newly elected officers of the Walnut Valley Riders assemble at the horse ring at Fuerte Drive and La Puente Avenue in Walnut. With about 30 members, the equestrian group held a monthly ride and offered riding classes at the horse ring. From left to right are Pres. Maurice Cofer, secretary Nancy Bennet, board chairman Dale King, Vice Pres. Ralph Peabody, and trail boss Leonard Westhoff. (Courtesy of the authors.)

Carrey General Store, 1911. Ernest Carrey stands on the steps, Frank Thornberry and Jim Crawford are seated, and standing by the buggy out of the picture is Joaquin Monroy, foreman on the Sentous Ranch at the time. Ernest Carrey, son of Peter and Mary Carrey, established a post office and general store on the northeast corner of Valley Boulevard and Lemon Avenue in 1911. He was the postmaster and sold stamps, money orders, and general merchandise. Ernest and his family grew hay and grain and raised cattle on his father's ranch. Later they grew oranges and lemons. To the north of the site is the Bank of America next to the post office. This corner was the site of a Union Oil station, and the lot now sits vacant adjacent to the Walnut Tech Business Center. (Courtesy of the authors.)

IMAGES
of America

WALNUT

City of Walnut and the Walnut Historical Society

ARCADIA
PUBLISHING

ISBN 978-0-7385-9547-4

Published by Arcadia Publishing
Charleston, South Carolina

Printed in the United States of America

Library of Congress Control Number: 2011945067

For all general information, please contact Arcadia Publishing:
Telephone 843-853-2070
Fax 843-853-0044
E-mail sales@arcadiapublishing.com
For customer service and orders:
Toll-Free 1-888-313-2665

Visit us on the Internet at www.arcadiapublishing.com

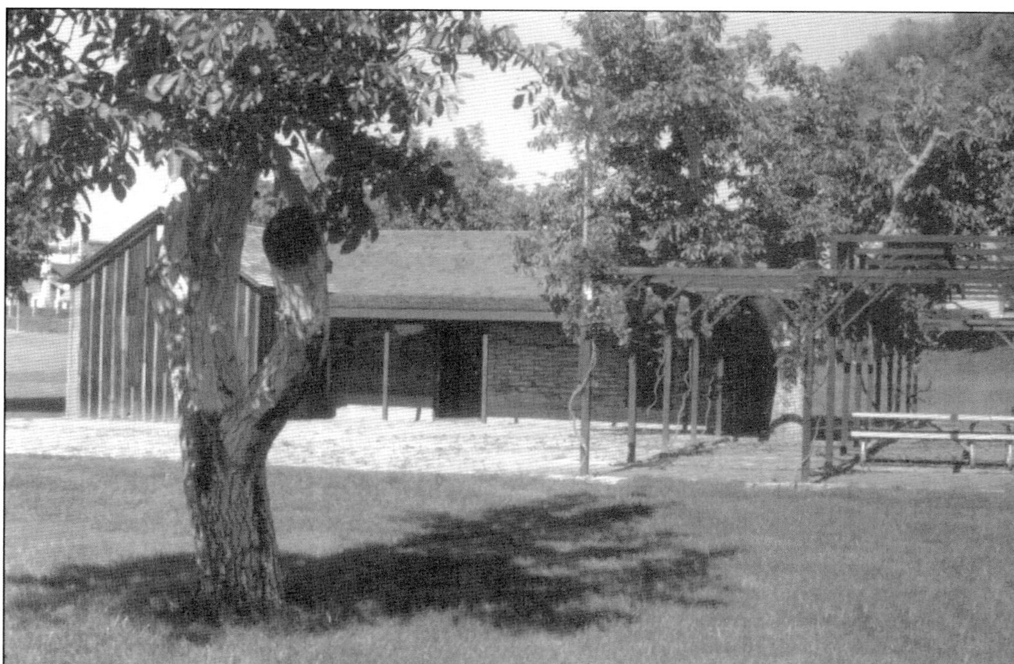

ROWLAND ADOBE RANCH HOUSE, 1883. The redwood component of the ranch house was added in 1883 for Rowland's cattle-ranch foreman, Mr. Meredith. The two-room structure included a kitchen area and a bedroom. He lived in it with his family for one year. (Courtesy of the authors.)

Contents

ACKNOWLEDGMENTS

In 2010, Mayor Tony Cartagena's goals for the city of Walnut included having a history of Walnut written and published to tell the true story of the city from the early 1840s to the present. Mayor Nancy Tragarz chose to continue this effort of the city's history publication. They would like to thank the following authors: former mayor June Wentworth, Debra Martin, Mary Lou Terranova, Carmen Vogel, Mount San Antonio College public affairs director Jill Dolan, photographer Mike Taylor, and Older Adult Program director Mary Lange. They would also like to thank the following who contributed to the telling of the story: Lee Cavanaugh from the Rowland Unified School District; longtime residents Chris Rae, Albert Garcia, and Bella Cristobal; Walnut Water District director Scarlett Kwong; administrative services director Sandra Olson; Pastor Mark Maki; and Mayor Nancy Tragarz.

Photographers who contributed to the story include our official photographer of N2 Graphics, Pasadena, Albert Garcia; June Wentworth; Mount San Antonio College instructor Linda Chang; Salvador Martin De Campo; Millie Deeton; Dee Chambers; Jeff George; and Winnie Ma.

Special thanks to Mount San Antonio College, Walnut Valley Unified School District, Rowland Unified School District, Walnut Valley Water District, Walnut Sheriff Station, Los Angeles County Fire Department community services representative Leticia Pacillas, St. Lorenzo Catholic Church, Walnut City Hall, Walnut Historical Society, Jeanne Burgh, and Randy Bennett for your stories and photographs that have contributed so much to this history.

In addition, we acknowledge the following city staff members: city manager Rob Wishner, deputy city manager Chuck Robinson, public information officer Fabiola Huerta, and city clerk Teresa De Dios. We also thank volunteer interns Jonathan J. Nih, Tiffany Pranajasa, Denise Tran, and Jason Adauto for countless hours of fun work.

All images appear courtesy of the authors.

INTRODUCTION

Walnut is a city which has prospered and grown throughout the years. It has become a city of vast beauty and friendly neighbors. But none of this would have been possible without Walnut's remarkable past.

The history of Walnut dates back to the Indians, who were of Shoshonean stock and had lived in the area for at least a thousand years. These Indians were called Gabrielinos by the Spaniards because they lived in an area controlled by the San Gabriel Mission.

The mission used the land to graze cattle and sheep. The Spaniards then followed in the early 1800s and introduced the concept of ranchos, which led to the start of agricultural development. The area of Walnut was included as part of one of the 24 ranchos belonging to the San Gabriel Mission. The era of the ranchers then swept through Walnut.

In 1841, John Rowland and William Workman arrived in Southern California with visions of new life. Within a year, they received a Spanish land grant, and between both men, they acquired almost 50,000 acres of land. Rowland and Workman's land, including present-day Walnut, was used for raising cattle and growing wheat, grapes, and fruit trees.

Gradually, the flow of Spanish, French, and American settlers rose, and the need to establish a community accelerated. Local ranchers and farmers raised cattle and grew wheat, grain, oranges, lemons, and walnut trees.

Education also became an important part of the growing community, and it is still important today. The original school district was established in 1867 at Spadra, with the original school being a one-story building. In 1869, a second school was built on Water Street, now Fairway Drive, and it accommodated 30 children of local ranchers and farmers. In 1907, the school now on Lemon Avenue was transformed into a two-story building to fulfill the substantial need for more classrooms and officially became Walnut School.

Walnut Elementary is now located on Glenwick Avenue and holds an ancient bell that carried the movement and memories of the past elementary school. Several present-day schools are named in honor of people who have made the history of Walnut. Westhoff Elementary is named after Leonard Westhoff, and C.J. Morris Elementary is named after Cyrus J. Morris, a previous superintendent. Other schools in Walnut include Walnut High School, Suzanne Middle School, Stanley G. Oswalt Academy, Vejar Elementary, and Collegewood Elementary. The advancement of the schools from the original Walnut schoolhouse has developed into one of the finest districts in California.

Soon residents found an urge to not only establish their own community but to form a city. They feared that the two powerful cities surrounding them, Industry Hills and West Covina, would annex their town if they did not soon establish a city of their own. On the memorable day of December 16, 1958, the cityhood of Walnut was placed in the hands of its citizens. The final count was 241 to 22 votes, and Walnut was declared a city on January 19, 1959, by the secretary of state and a city council was installed.

The council was made up of five members. A planning commission of seven members was appointed to give advice and recommendations to the city council. The city council hired a city manager who served as city clerk; it also hired a treasurer and a deputy city clerk. Only the mayor was left to be elected, and Pete Bourdet, Robert Carrey, Roy Coats, Leonard Westhoff, and Max Feigles, the members of Walnut's first city council, had that significant job. Filled with excitement, Walnut's residents cheered when they heard Pete Bourdet was to become their first mayor.

Walnut as a city continued to grow as more and more residents moved into the area for a more comfortable environment. Soon, the old city hall on Carrey Road became too small to fit the demanding needs of the growing city. The new city hall was completed in March 1982 with a total of 14,700 square feet. The city hall would have all the needed space and include a 76-seat council chamber. On August 15, 1981, the happy citizens of Walnut gathered at the site for the ground-breaking ceremony, which was to be done by the council members: Jim Zamary, Harvey Holden, Bert Ashley, Bill Daley, and Joe Hahn. As the council members struck the shovel into the soil, a happy cheer rose from the crowd, for it was to be a new and exciting beginning for Walnut.

Walnut's modern structure is what erupted from its history. The city provides approximately 29,400 residents housing, while only 934 dwelled in Walnut in 1959.

Presently, one library, one community college, and 11 parks are in Walnut's boundaries. Approximately 27 miles of equestrian and hiking trails show the country style of Walnut. The California weather contributes to the pleasantness of living in this community. Stimulating business activity, increasing local revenues, encouraging additional investment in the community, and strengthening the local economy are several goals of Walnut that reveal the constant strive to prosper, growing farther away from its infancy.

Walnut's great achievements throughout the years earned a place among "The 100 Best Places to live in the United States of America with a population 50,000 and under," according to *CNN Money Magazine* in 2011. From yesterday's Native Americans to today's technology-savvy citizens, years of significant events have assisted in Walnut's progression and growth. Today, the city of Walnut is still growing as people, as individuals, and as a community.

One

Walnut Founding Families

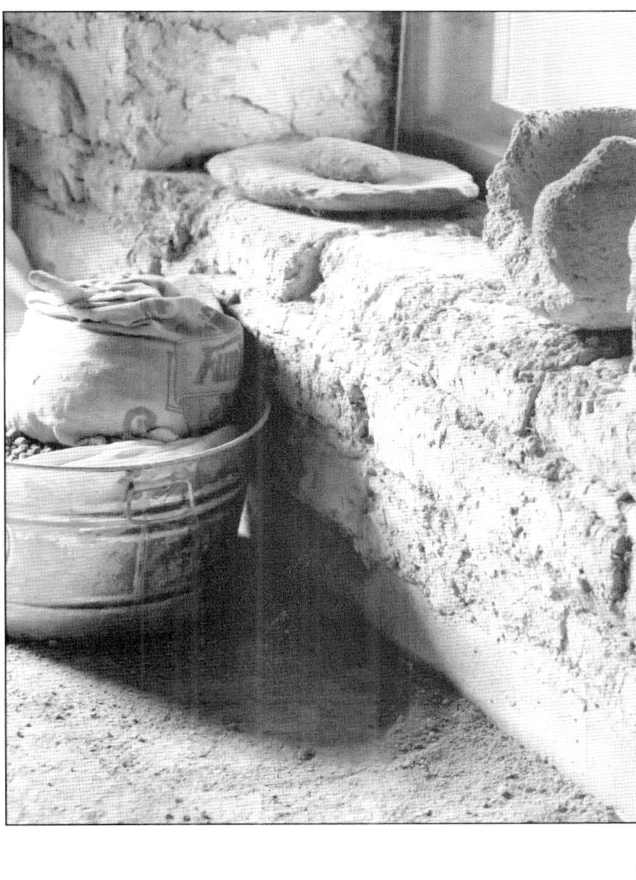

Native American Grinding Stones. Estimated to be 3,000–4,000 years old, these Native American grinding stones were found on the corner of Valley Boulevard and La Puente Road. Randy Bennett, who farmed the area for many years, found the stones. Early Native American tribes in the area included the Tongva, dating back almost 8,000 years. When the San Gabriel Mission was founded in 1771, the Tongva became the Gabrielinos. The Indians settled in the area because of the proximity of San Jose Creek. The fathers used the Native Americans as slaves until 1834, when the mission was seized by the Mexican government during secularization. The land remained barren until ranches were granted to Mexican settlers in the late 1830s and 1840s.

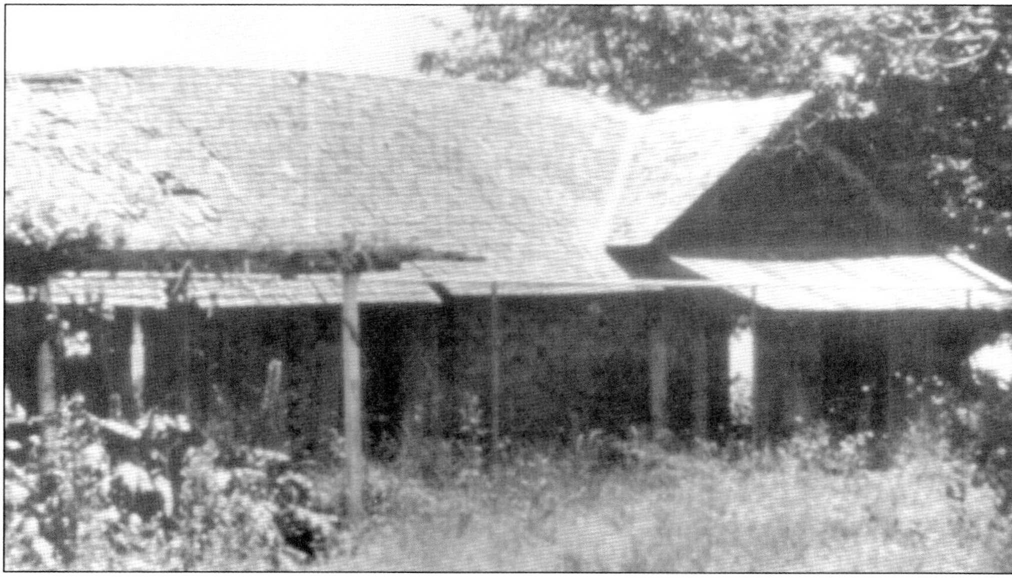

W.R. Rowland Adobe Redwood Ranch House, 1845. John Rowland and William Workman migrated from New Mexico in 1842 and were granted 49,790.55 acres of land. Rowland's 29,000-acre share included the area of the city of Walnut today. The grant for Rancho La Puente, which includes the W.R. Rowland Adobe Redwood Ranch House, was finalized in 1845. The structure was designated as Historical Interest Landmark No. 21 by the State of California Park Commission on October 1, 1975.

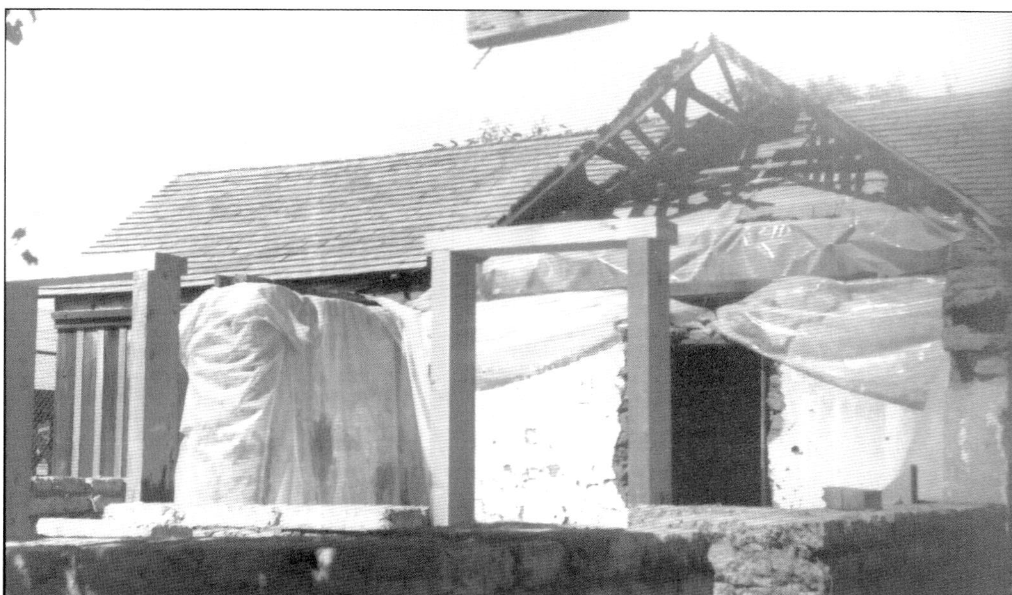

Ranch House Adobe, 1850. The history of the city of Walnut dates back to the Gabrielino Native Americans. The name "Gabrielino" was given to the area natives because they belonged to the San Gabriel Mission. The Native Americans built the adobe component of the W.R. Rowland Adobe Redwood Ranch House in 1850 on the north bank of Lemon Creek. The adobe is typical of 1840s Spanish architecture.

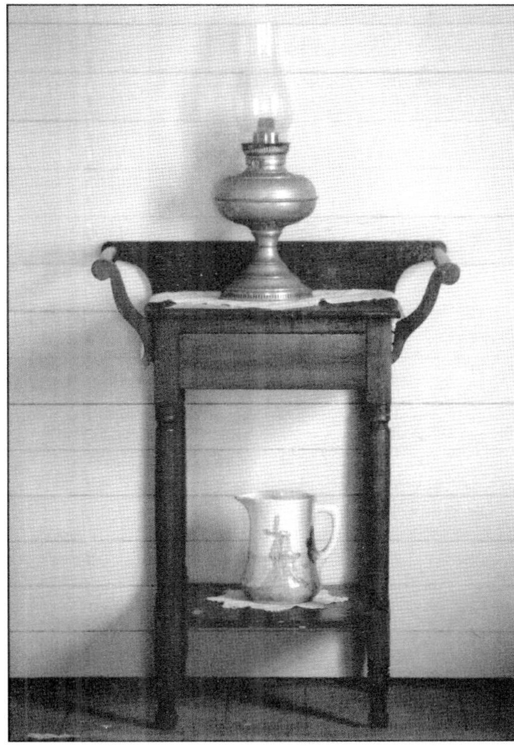

RANCH HOUSE REDWOOD, 1883. The redwood component of the W.R. Rowland Adobe Redwood Ranch House was added to the adobe in 1883 by Los Angeles County sheriff William Rowland for Mr. Meredith, his cattle-ranch foreman. This photograph of the redwood house demonstrates farm life in the early 1880s. The kitchen area was used for cooking with the other room utilized for a bedroom. The redwood house depicts farm life of the 1883 era. The adobe depicts the Spanish era of the 1840s.

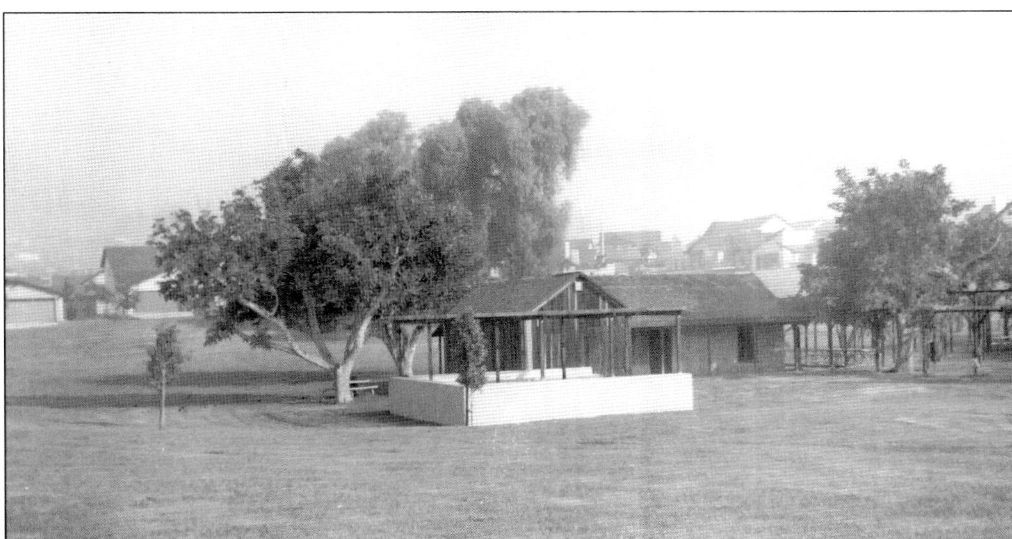

AUTHENTICALLY RESTORED, 1976. The William R. Rowland Adobe Redwood Ranch House harkens back to the lifestyle of frontier men and women who labored long and hard for their livelihood. To complete the authenticity of the William R. Rowland Adobe Redwood Ranch House, citizens of Walnut donated many pieces of c. 1850 and c. 1883 period furniture. Lemon Creek Park, with its grape arbor, wisteria vine, fire pit, barbecue, and running creek, was designed to exemplify the characteristics of the people and times of the past and to provide a historical view into Walnut's ancestry.

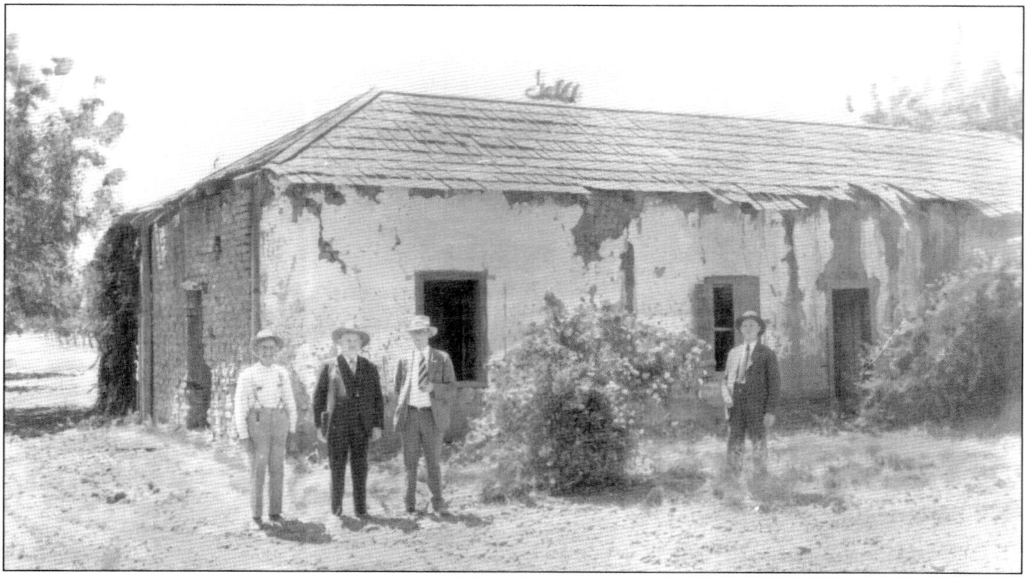

The Martinez Adobe, 1860s. Francisco and Teresa V. Martinez owned and farmed 22.4 acres of land north of San Bernardino Road and east of Lemon Avenue. San Bernardino Road later became Valley Boulevard. The Martinez adobe is typical of farmhouses built by the Spanish. The house was demolished in the 1960s, and the Walnut Elementary School District built Vejar Elementary School on an area of the site. From left to right are road master Jeff Faqua from Chino, foreman of the Rowland Ranch Tom Green, Randall Slack, and Marion St. Clair.

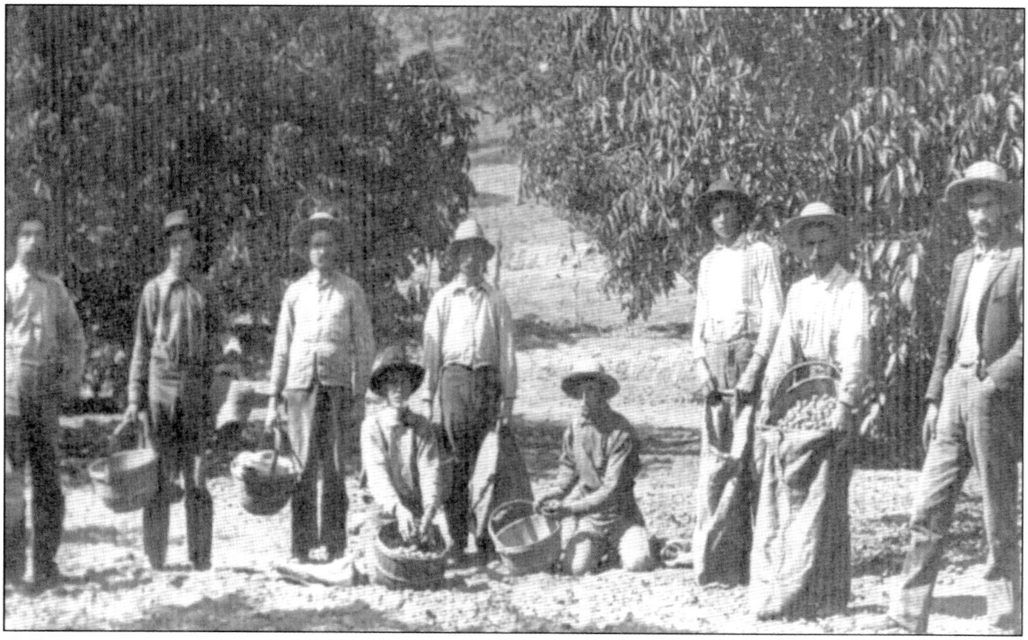

A Peak Year for Citrus, 1945. In the early 1900s, orange, lemon, and walnut groves dotted the landscape. Many of the ranchers made a living by growing citrus fruit. The ranchers also used the Walnut Fruit Growers Association packinghouse to store the citrus, and the nearby railroad made it convenient to ship the produce.

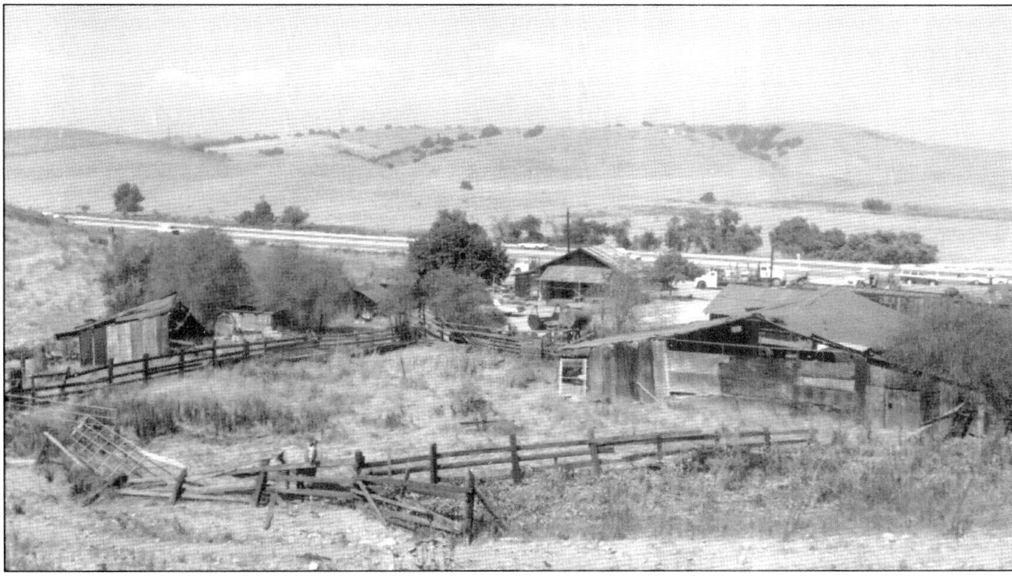

Farm House, 1960s. Around 1913, Poblo Itcea bought a piece of land on Ranch Road north of Valley Boulevard in the San Jose Township. The Lariayas, including two sons, one daughter, and a son's family, farmed the land. The land was worth $400 in 1930. The family, including Clemen Lariaya and his wife, Francis, farmed Itcea land, as well as a parcel of land owned by C.M. Wright and Lynch. In the 1970s, Shea Homes bought the land within the city's border, which they developed into the Snow Creek housing tract. Ranch Road later became Grand Avenue.

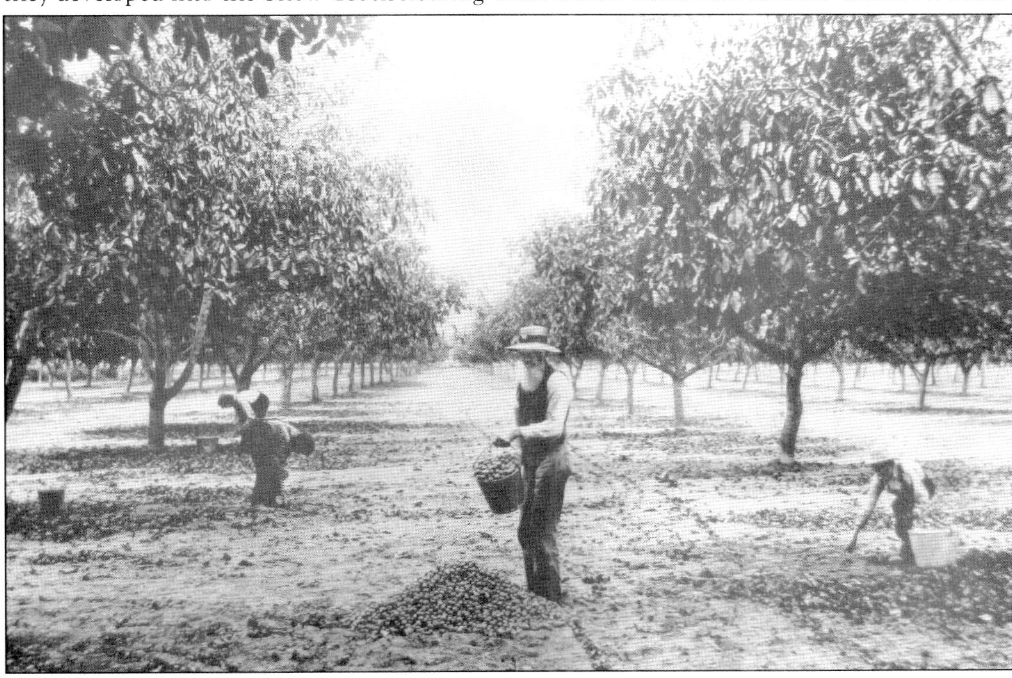

Walnut Groves, Early 1900s. Farming families included the Bourdets and the Woods, both of whom had large walnut groves. In the 1940s, the walnut groves were destroyed due to disease, and farmers went back to oranges or grain.

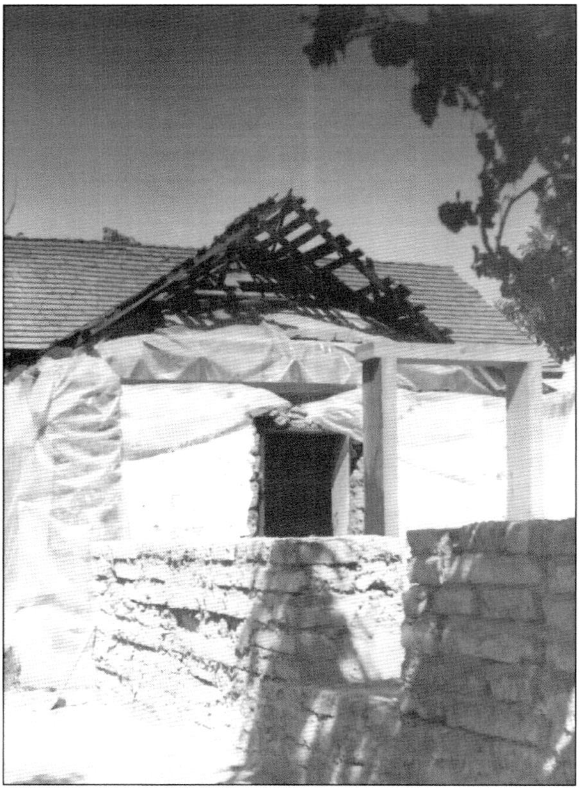

W.R. Rowland Adobe. The W.R. Rowland Ranch Adobe is typical of the many structures that were built on the rancho for ranch hands. It was built in 1850 by friendly Indians who were employed by John Rowland to make great quantities of adobe bricks of mud mixed with straw and dried for months in the sun. The walls were a massive two to three feet thick, capable of resisting the heat in the summer and cold in the winter. The doors of the adobe were heavy and wide. The windows were deep with few curtains or blinds, ceilings were made of cloth, floors were dirt, and roofs were made of wooden shingles. This was the typical Spanish style of the missions. Three of the original adobe walls were still standing with the rest being restored in 1975.
The Rowlands did not live here.

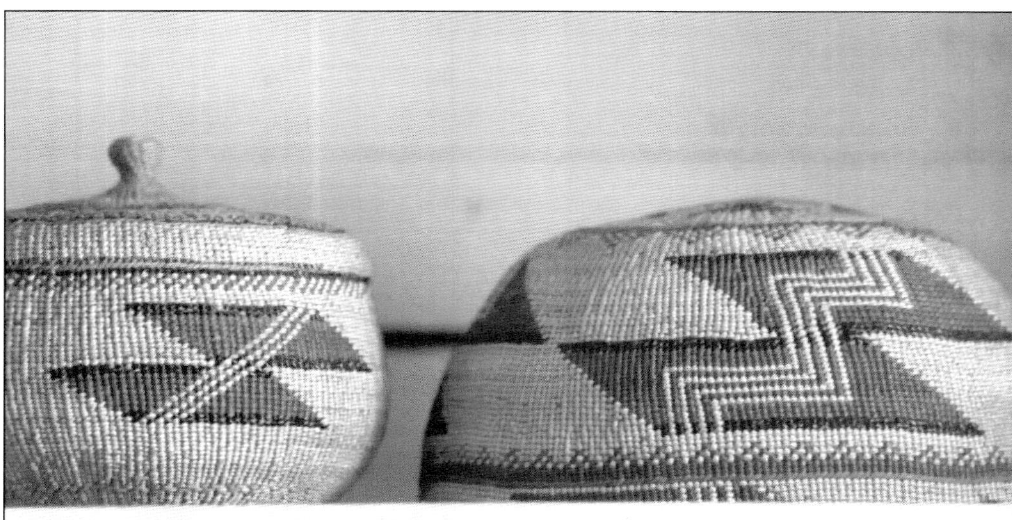

Rancho La Puente, 1840s. Native American baskets are part of a collection of artifacts in the W.R. Rowland Adobe Redwood Ranch House at Lemon Creek Park. The baskets were a gift to the City of Walnut when the adobe was restored in 1976. The Hupa (Karok) Yurok Native American hat and bowl with lid are made out of willow, pine root, bear grass, maidenhair, and woodwardia. In the 1840s, Walnut was dotted with adobes that were built by the Native Americans on Rancho La Puente.

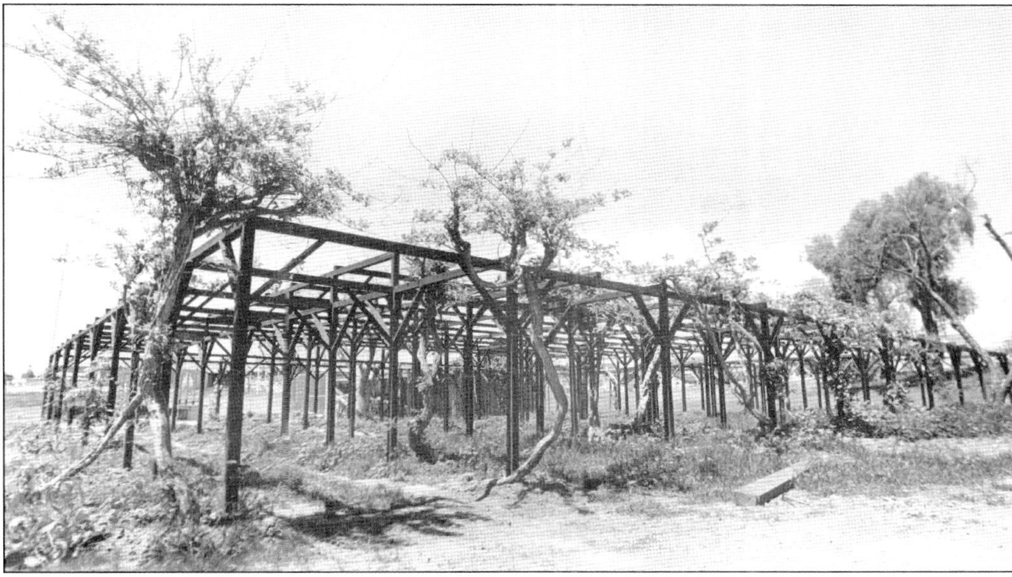

BICENTENNIAL COMMISSION, 1976. In order to preserve part of the community's history, the City of Walnut's 1976 Bicentennial Commission selected the reconstruction of the William Rowland Adobe Redwood Ranch House and development of Lemon Creek Park as Walnut's Bicentennial project. Sheriff William Rowland inherited the property in 1882 from the estate of the 29,000-acre ranch called Rancho La Puente the belonged to his father John Rowland. This 1974 photograph shows the park prior to construction.

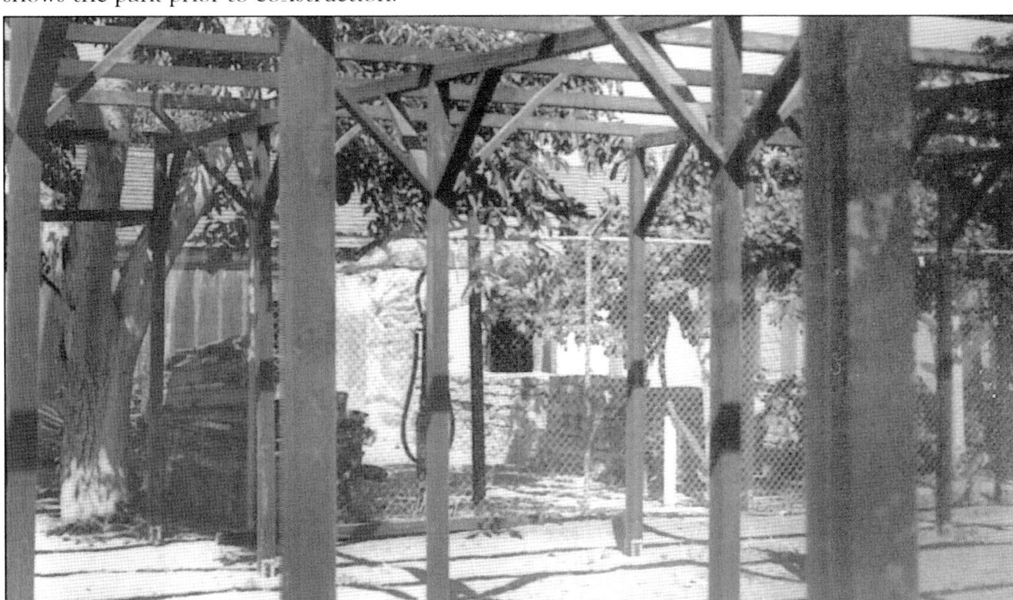

GRAPE ARBOR, 1970s. The W.R. Rowland Adobe Redwood Ranch House was further enhanced by a grape arbor. Ranchers in the 1850s grew fruit and vegetables. Patios were common and cooking was done outside. The creek nearby supplied the inhabitants with water. During the 1840s and 1850s, the Rowlands and the Workmans raised cattle and grew grapes, which they later turned into wine.

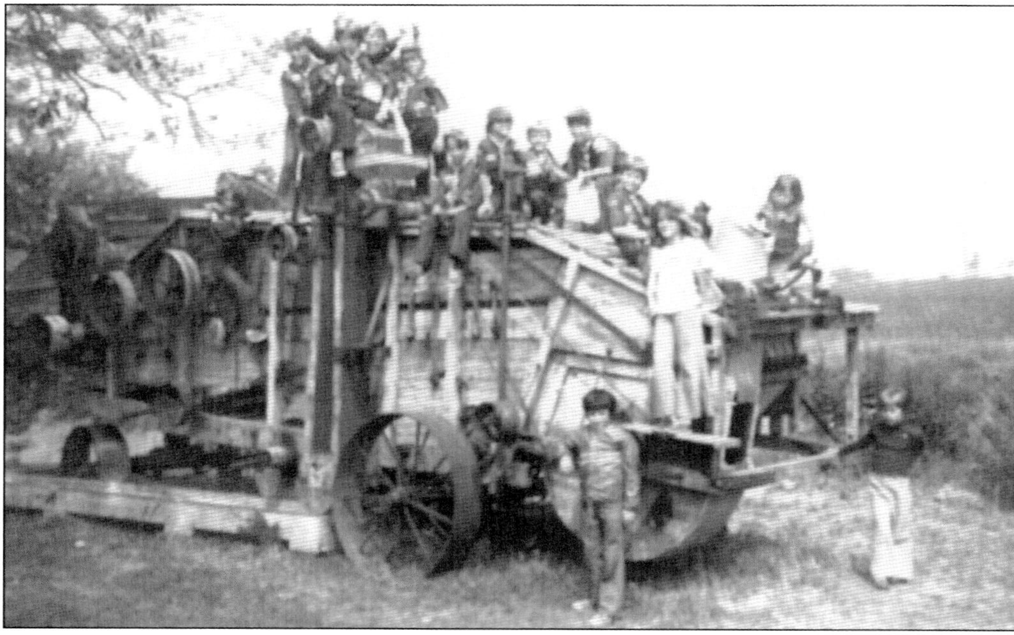

Harvester Combine, 1900s. This harvester combine was found on the Woods property off Lemon Avenue. The machine was used for separating wheat, grain, peas, soybeans, and other small grains and seeds. It was patented in 1837 by Himan and John Pitts. Earlier threshers were pulled by horses.

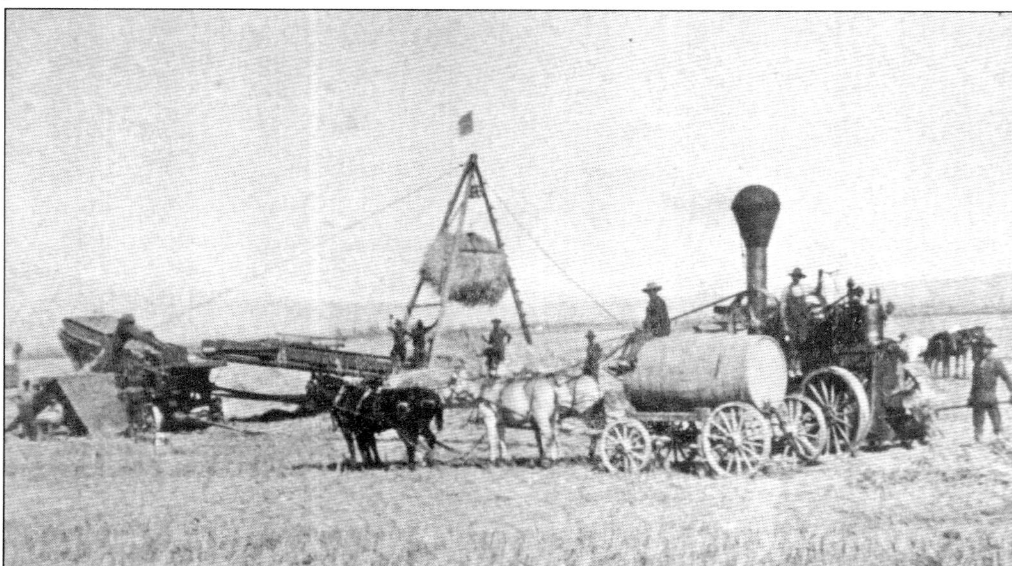

Sentous Ranch, 1800s. The 5,200-acre ranch was once part of Rancho La Puente and Rancho San Jose. Exupere, Louis, and Vincente Sentous ran a successful meat business in Los Angeles. In the late 1880s, they bought the ranch, which took in the western part of Walnut, to raise livestock. When the ranch was divided, 1,800 acres were owned and farmed by Exupere. In 1903, Exupere moved to his ranch, where he used 900 acres to grow grain and 900 acres to raise sheep, horses, and cattle. Exupere died in 1906 at the age of 47.

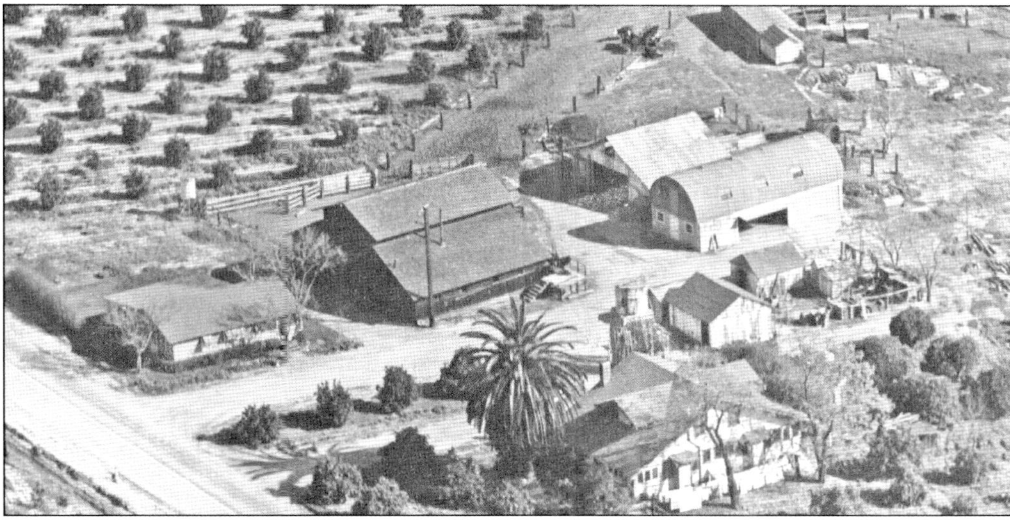

CARREY FAMILY, 1883. In 1883, Pierre (Peter) and Mary Carrey immigrated to the United States from France. Peter worked at the Puente Ranch, owned by the late John Rowland. In 1884, the Carreys bought 50 acres of property from the Rowland estate on La Puente Road. Carrey and his family, including Justin, Ernest, Mary, and Gaetan, farmed the land until 1965, when the house was demolished to make way for Walnut High School. His son Justin built a home on Carrey Road; the home is still inhabited in the 21st century. His son Robert became an attorney and was counsel to the Mexican Consulate in Los Angeles. Robert Carrey died in 1931 at his parents' home in Walnut.

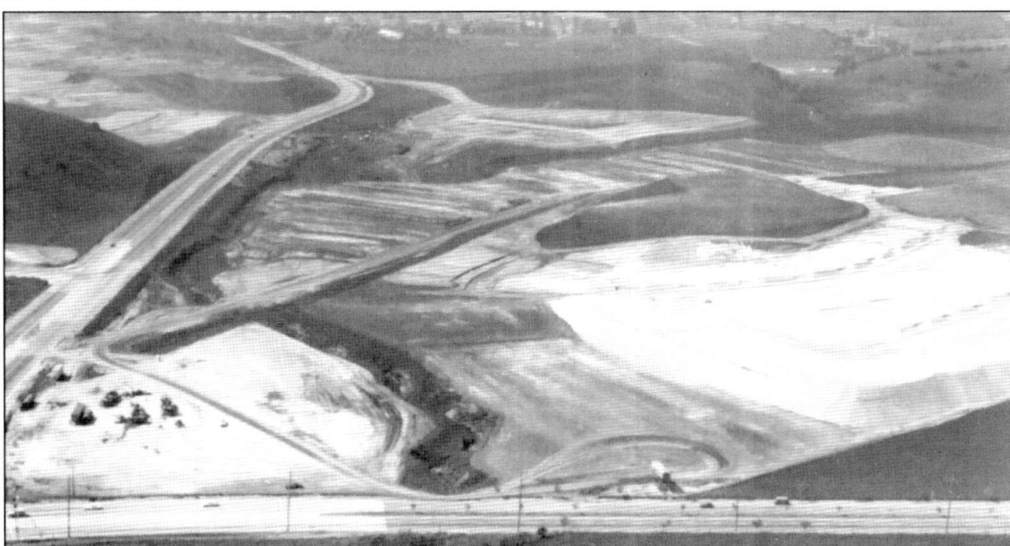

CHARLES M. WRIGHT AND LYNCH, 1888. Charles Wright owned the eastern portion of Walnut, which was originally part of Rancho La Puente. According to the San Jose Township Spadra voter list, Wright was one of the country's electors and was listed as a farmer in 1888. The land remained a farming area until the 1970s, when Shea Development Co. purchased the land in an effort to build homes. The grading began in 1979 on the eastern side of the property, and the development opened in the early 1980s as Snow Creek.

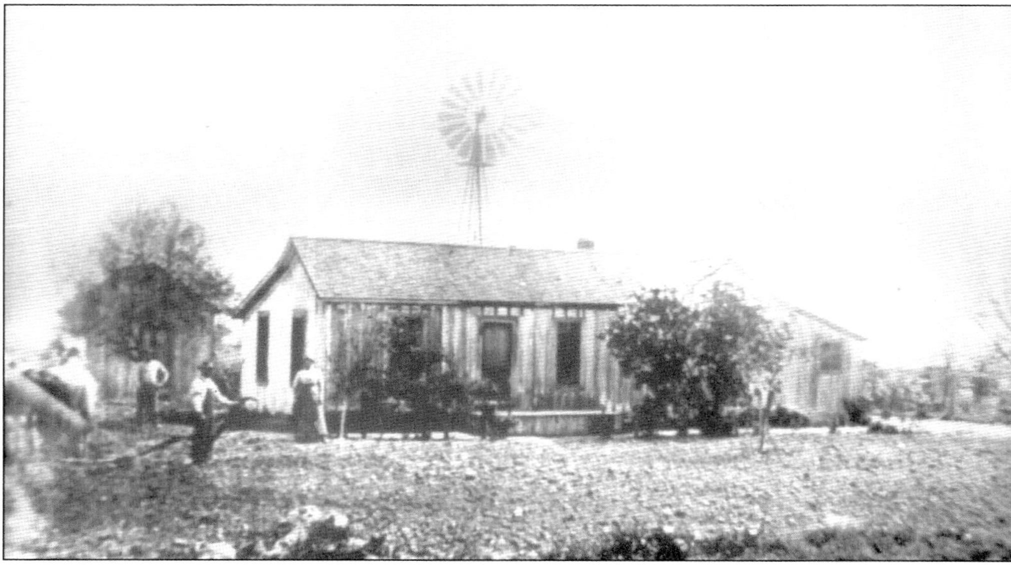

Bourdet Family, Early 1900s. When they came to Walnut in the early 1900s, Jean and Marie Bourdet farmed for the Sentous family. The Bourdets lived on the Sentous Ranch, where their first son, Peter, was born in 1907. In 1909, they purchased property two blocks south of the ranch on Lemon Avenue where they constructed a house. The Bourdets moved into their farmhouse several years later and had two more children, Veronica and Louis. The home and its iconic windmill were still standing as of late 2011.

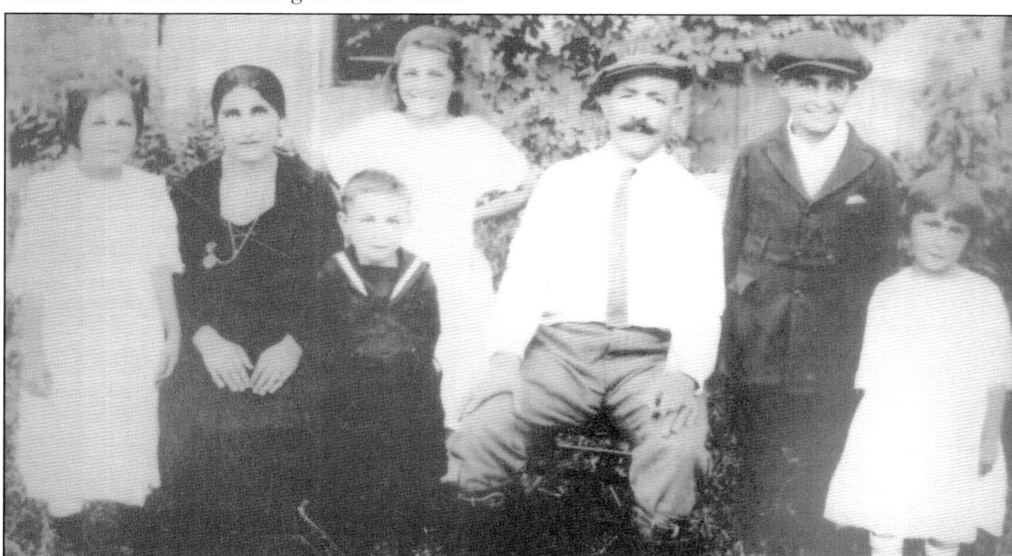

Griegorian Family, Early 1900s. Arden and Mary Griegorian migrated to California from Armenia in the early 1900s. They started a hog ranch in San Bernardino, and their farm expanded to over 2,000 hogs. They moved to higher ground in Walnut during the 1930s due to area floods. Their ranch was located on Pierre Road and included horses, chickens, rabbits, and peacocks. At this time, everyone living in the area resided in the San Jose Township of Spadra in the County of Los Angeles. Pictured here from left to right are Rose, Mary, Dick, Mary, Arden, Arden, and Polly.

JUSTIN CARREY, 1910. Justin Carrey built a home on Carrey Ranch Road for his family in the early 1910s. Justin Carrey owned and farmed the land around his home. He and his wife, Appollonie Carrey, had four children: Henry, Edward, Albert, and Robert. Upon Walnut's incorporation in 1959, Robert Carrey was elected to city council. Robert Carrey's garage was the first Walnut City Hall. Carrey Ranch Road is now known as Carrey Road.

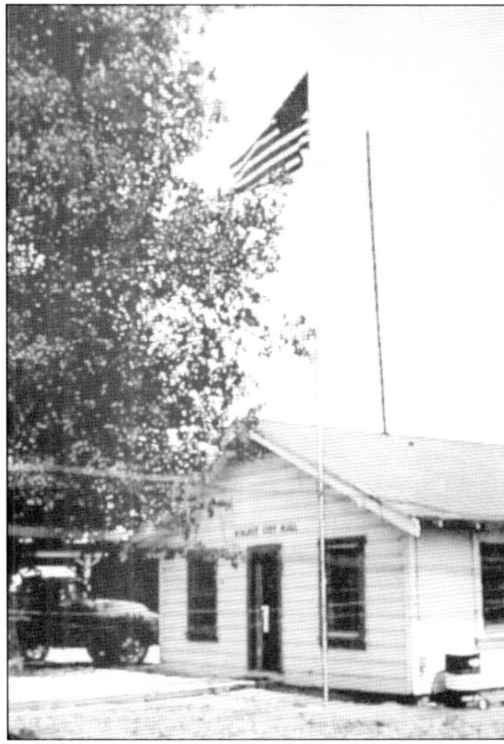

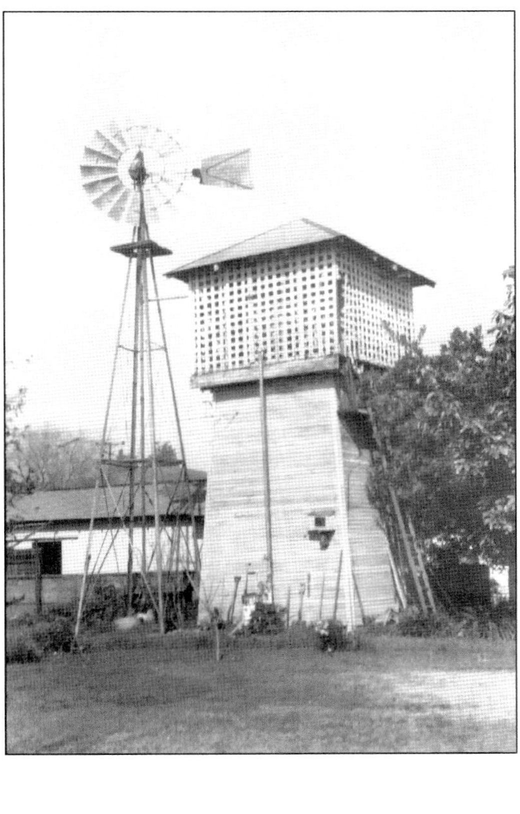

BOURDET WINDMILL, 1911. The Bourdet family constructed a windmill and well when they moved into their home. Jean Bourdet began as a dry grain farmer and moved to planting walnut trees in 1914. Unfortunately, the trees were removed in 1940 as a result of disease. The family resumed dry farming, and eventually the land surrounding the house was sold. Walnut's first housing development was constructed on Bourdet land; the farmhouse was spared.

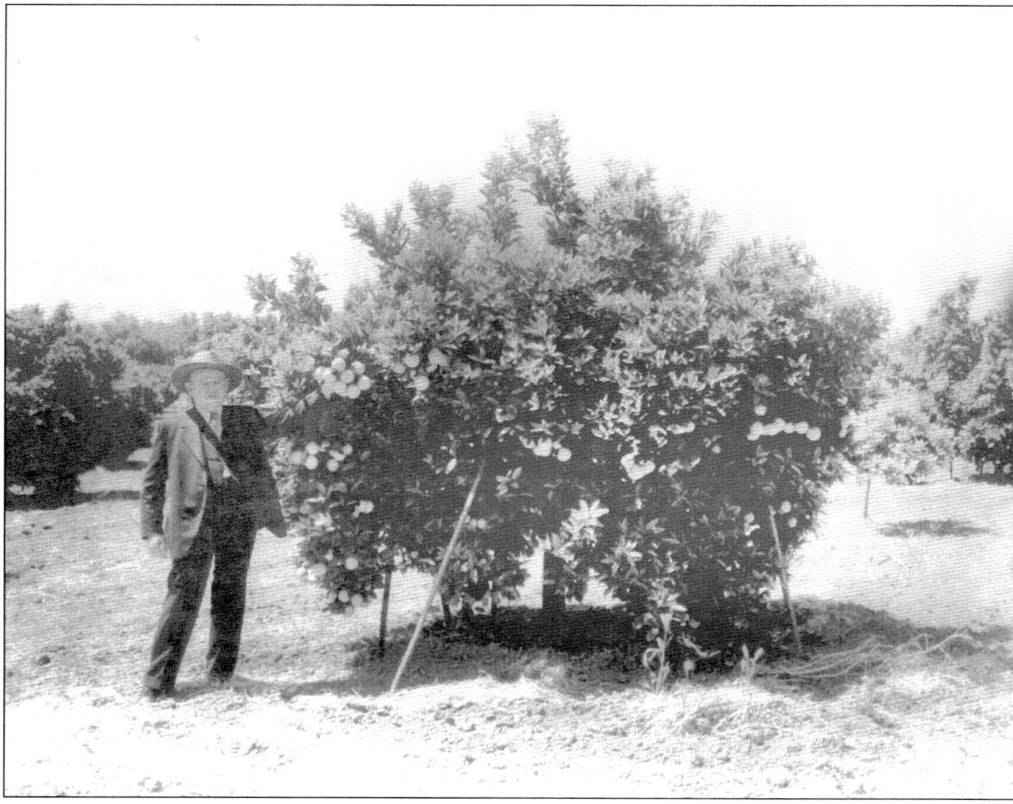

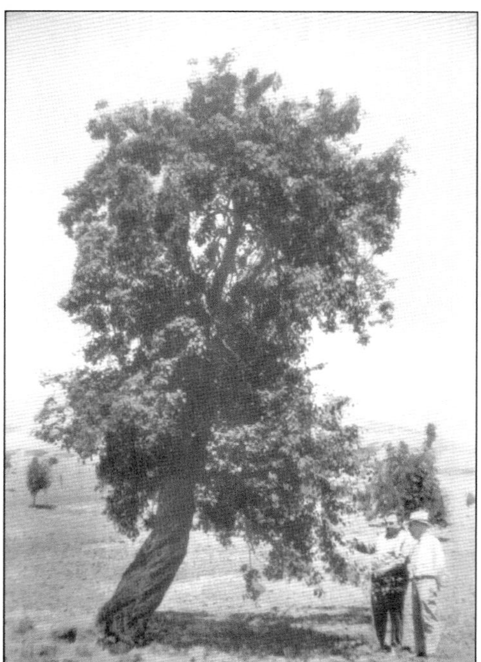

Isenberg Family, 1920. In 1930, Tom Green was a foreman for the Rowland cattle ranch; he is pictured here on the Isenberg property. Beginning in 1920, the Isenbergs rented this property on Valley Boulevard and Lemon Avenue. Born in 1919, the Isenbergs' son Joseph later lived on a ranch on La Puente Road with his wife, Sadie.

Forster Family, 1920s. John Forster and his wife, Lorraine, moved to Walnut in the late 1920s. They lived on Carrey Ranch Road with their three children. Carrey farmed the property for many years. A 150-year-old pepper tree, which was removed in the late 1970s to make room for a housing development off Carrey Road, was located on his property. During the 1930s, pepper trees lined Valley Boulevard; the pepper tree on Carrey Road was the last of its kind in this area.

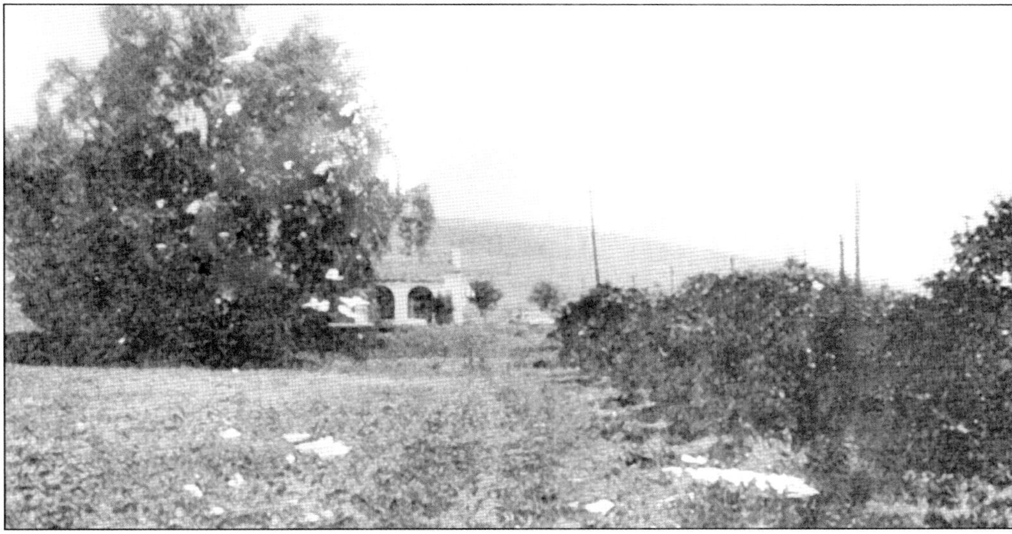

Forster Family, 1920s. John Forster and his wife Lorriane moved to Walnut in the late 1920s. They lived on Carrey Ranch Road with three children. John farmed the property for many years. On his property was 100-year-old pepper tree. The tree was removed in the late 1970s to make room for a housing development off Carrey Road. During the 1930s, pepper trees lined Valley Blvd. The pepper tree on Carrey Road was the last of the pepper trees in this area..

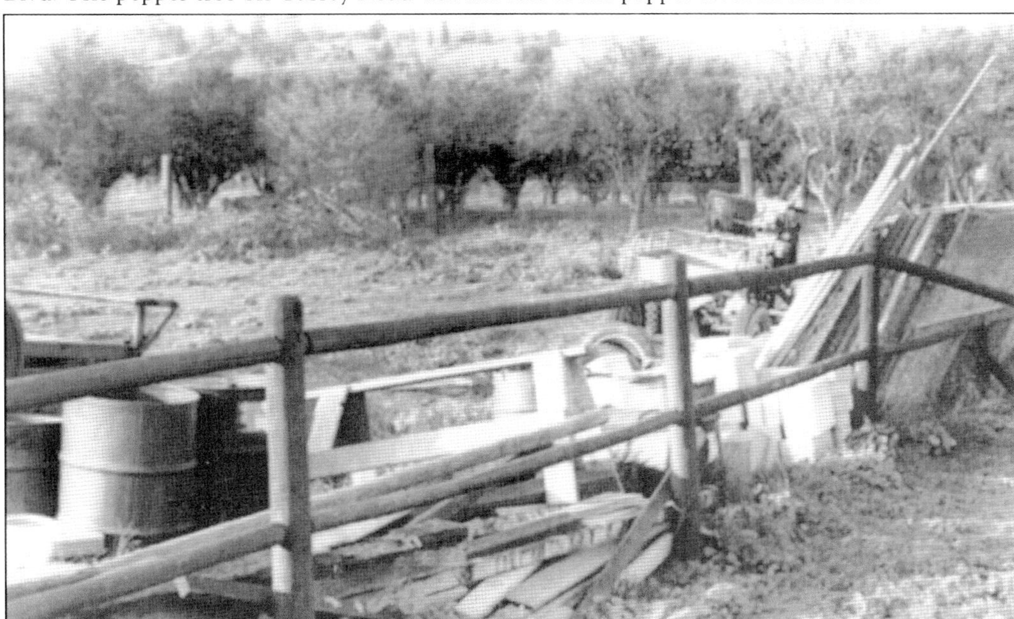

Types of Farming, 1900s. Dry farming was conducted on farms in Walnut during the 1920s and 1930s. Grain and hay were grown with only rainwater, due to the lack of irrigation. In the 1960s and 1970s, the area in and around La Puente Road was utilized to dry farm primarily hay and barley. Alfalfa was grown by the Dotta family on land owned by the Lutheran and Mormon churches off Marcon Drive. Orange trees occupied the land beyond Suzanne Middle School into Gartel area. When recycled water was no longer available, the orange trees died.

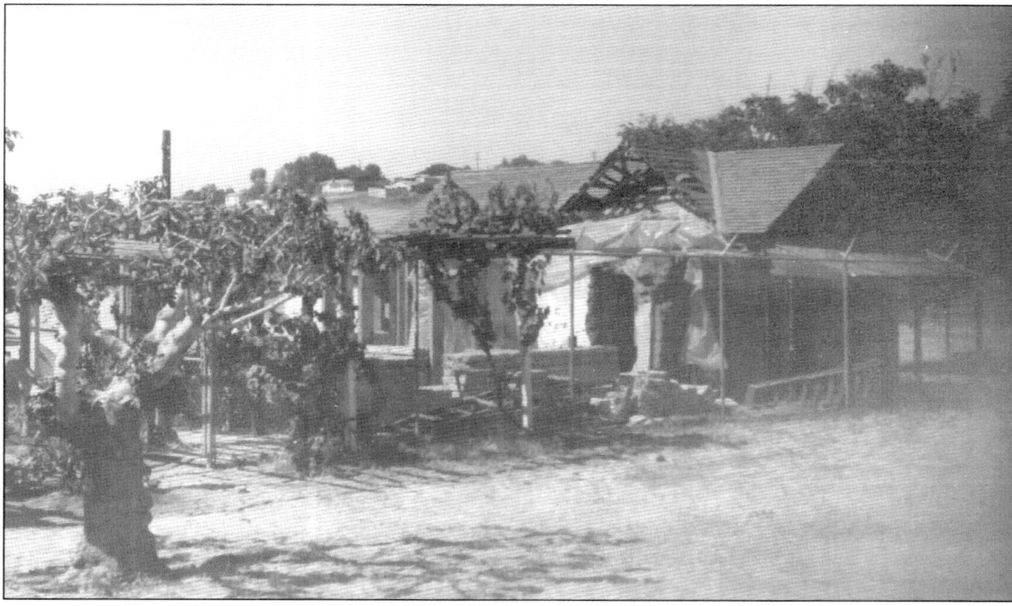

W.R. ROWLAND, EARLY 1900s. Rowland rented some of his properties. He sold 90 acres of land in approximately 1916. John A. Wood, his wife, Edith, and their sons, John and Alvin, farmed this land bordering La Puente Road and Lemon Avenue. They hired Ray Wheeler to help. He used the adobe-and-redwood structure and a wine cellar for many years. The home was then abandoned and left barren. In the 1970s, the Woods sold the land, and Larwin homes were built, with three acres of the land becoming Lemon Creek Park.

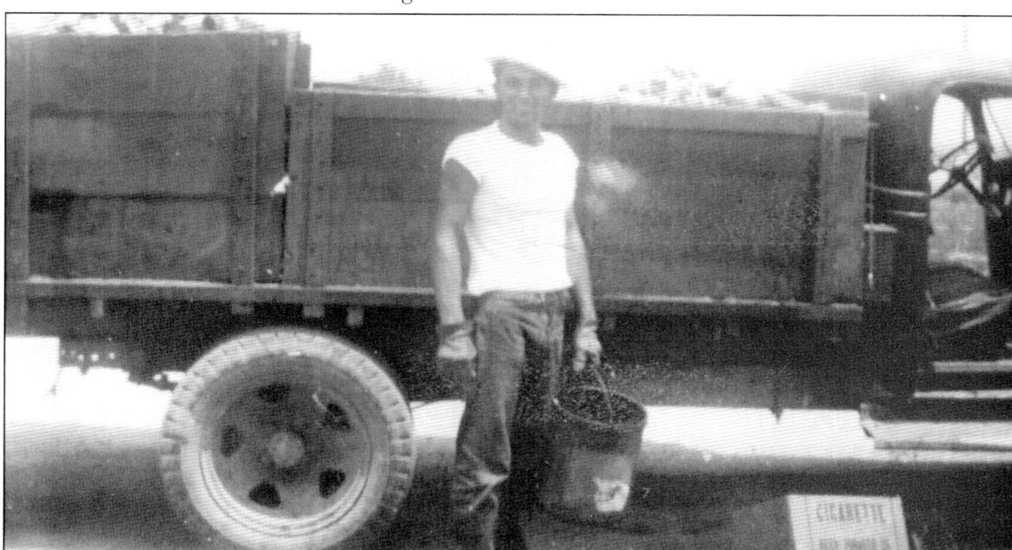

GRIEGORIAN DISPOSAL, 1930s. Due to the Great Depression of the 1930s, the Griegorians had difficulty feeding their hogs. Their youngest son, Dick, took his father's truck and traveled on Valley Boulevard to East Los Angeles, asking markets and cafés to separate their trash. He would then pick up the separated trash for free, feeding the hogs with the food items and disposing the rest. This first "recycler" started Griegorian Disposal; he sold it in 2000.

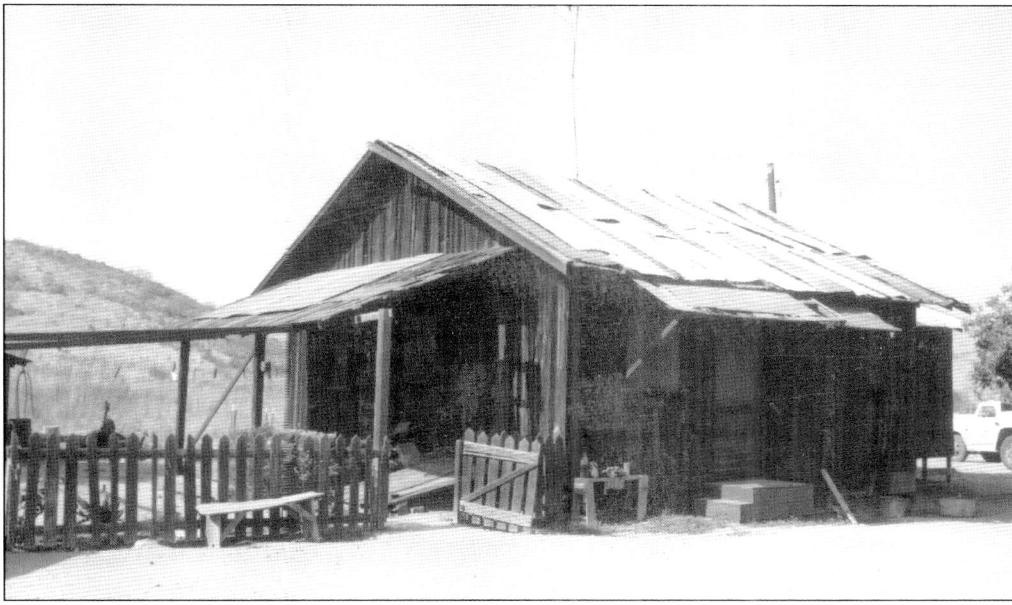

Holmes Family, 1930s. Eugene and Marie Holmes lived on Ranch Road (now Grand Avenue), north of San Bernardino Road (now Valley Boulevard) with their grandson, Frank Fitzgerald. Amongst three farms, the Holmes, Dunns, Lariayas, and the families of Pablo Itcea lived concurrently on Ranch Road. They farmed and raised hundreds of cattle, which roamed across the hills adjacent to Mount San Antonio College.

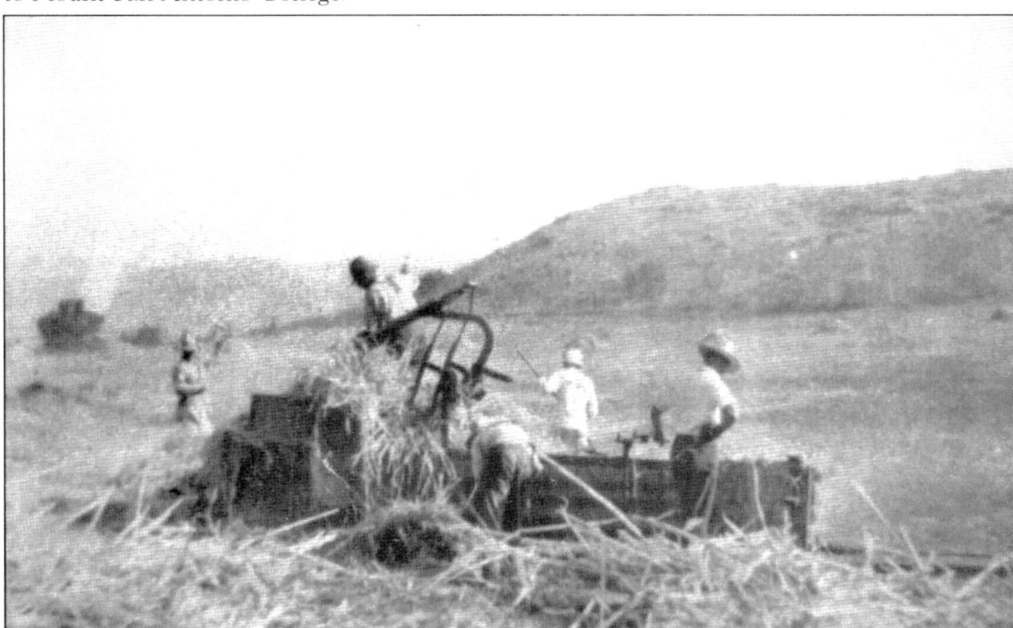

Bennett and Carrey Dry Farming, 1930s. The Bennett and Carrey families dry farmed their lands off Valley Boulevard and La Puente Road. Randy Bennett and Albert Carrey continued farming into the late 1970s. The farming stopped when Shea Homes began to build houses on the property.

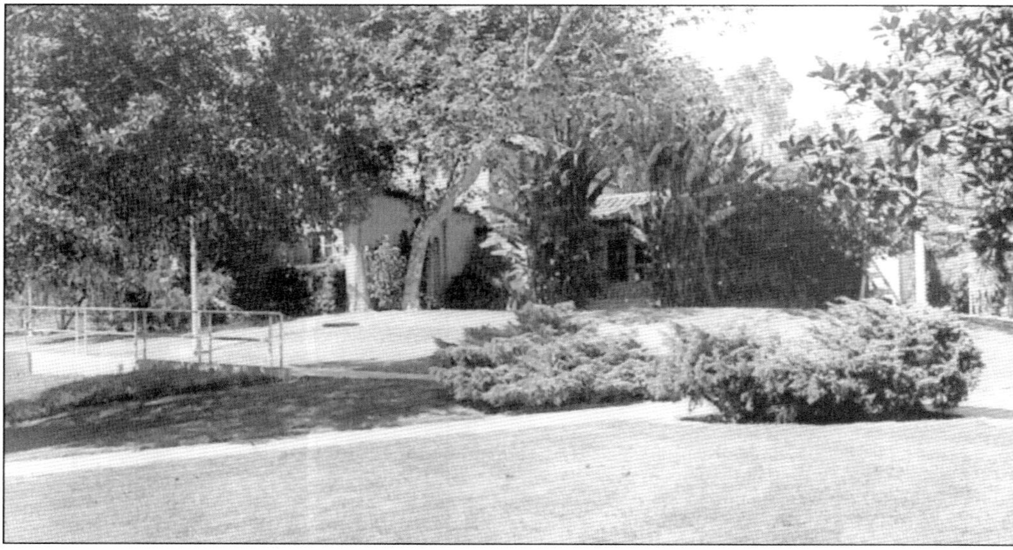

Winnett and Sentous Homes, 1930s. The large home belonged to J.P. Winnett, and the small home in the background could be the Sentous home. When Exupere Sentous died, he left his wife, Anna, and four children his ranch, located off La Puente Road. The 1930 census shows that Anna, Alvin, Frank, Zoe, and Antonette occupied the home. Zoe's husband, Adrien Casartbon, also lived there. The Sentous family continued farming the land, and when Winnett bought the property in 1935, he left the house intact. It was not until a housing development was built in the 1980s that the house was torn down.

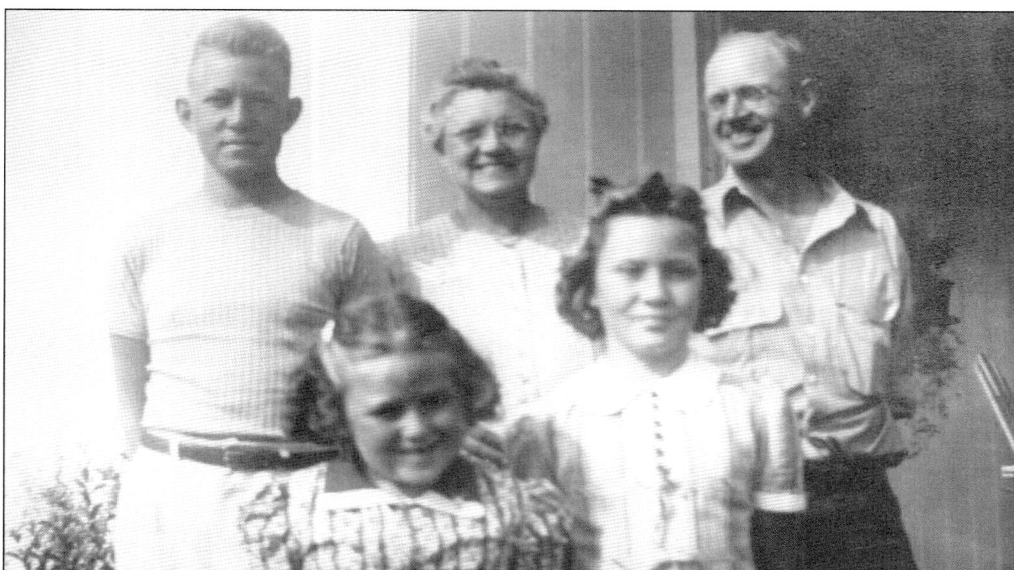

Jerry Westhoff and Randy Bennett, 1940s. When Leonard and Madoline Westhoff moved to Walnut with their three children, Marilyn, Jeanne, and Anthony "Jerry," there was not much in the area. As Leonard said, "They were raising alfalfa; there were walnut and orange groves and very few people." Leonard worked for Standard Oil Company; Madoline taught fifth and sixth grades at Walnut School.

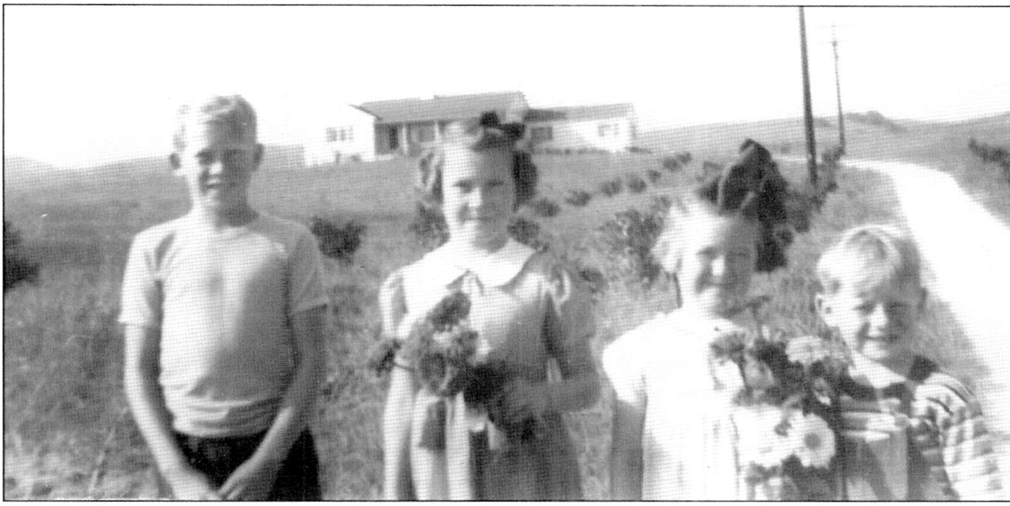

FIRST DAY OF SCHOOL, 1940. Randy (left) and Dennis Bennett (right) and Marilyn (second from left) and Jeanne Westhoff (second from right) stand in front of the Westhoffs' new home on La Puente Road. Leonard turned the home into a ranch with horses and a barn. Leonard enjoyed riding horses. He rode with the De Anza Trail Riders, he was a member of Los Caballeros Riding Club, and he was a founder of the Walnut Valley Riders. Many times he helped with cattle drives to Chino through Diamond Bar Ranch. He also served on the Los Angeles County Sheriff's Posse for 24 years.

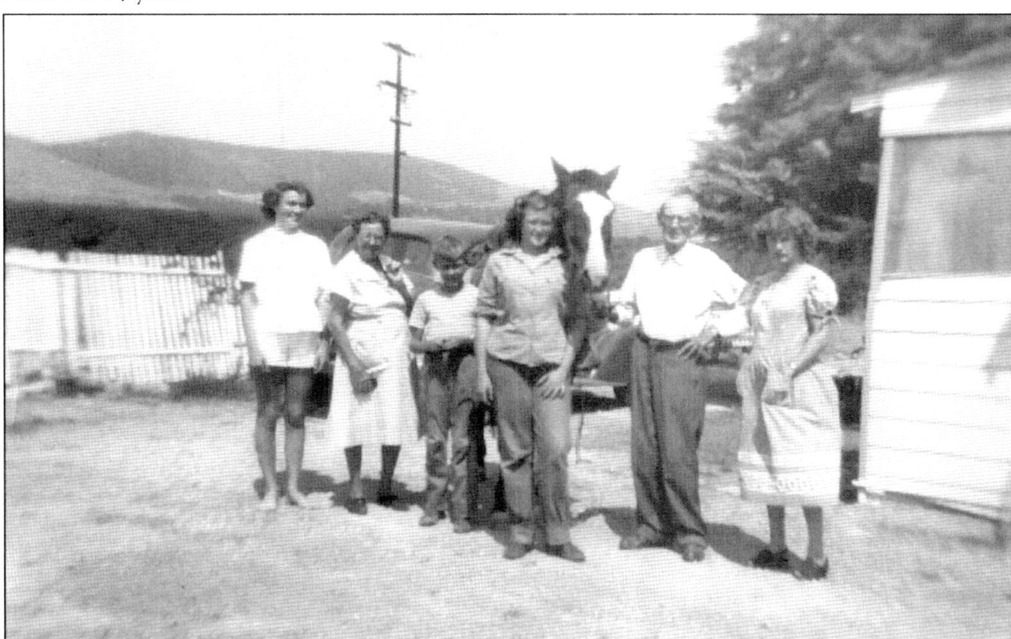

EMMA AND ANTHONY WESTHOFF, 1950S. Leonard Westhoff's mother and father moved to the Walnut area in the 1940s. They lived on Pierre and La Puente Roads. They enjoyed many days on their farm with their grandchildren. From left to right are Jeanne Westhoff, Emma Westhoff, Jean Carrey (Albert Carrey's son), Marilyn Westhoff, Anthony Westhoff, and Leonard's sister Gertrude Carrey, who was married to Albert Carrey.

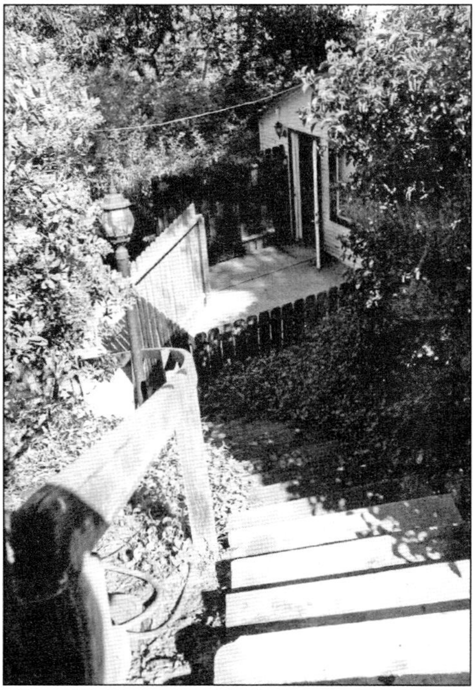

The Prentiss Family, 1940s. William and Karla moved into their Walnut home in the early 1940s. William was in the construction business, and their property was over an acre of land. The entrance of the lot was off Gartel Drive with the mailbox leading to a steep staircase, and the back of the lot was located off Fuerte Drive. Large lots were common at that time.

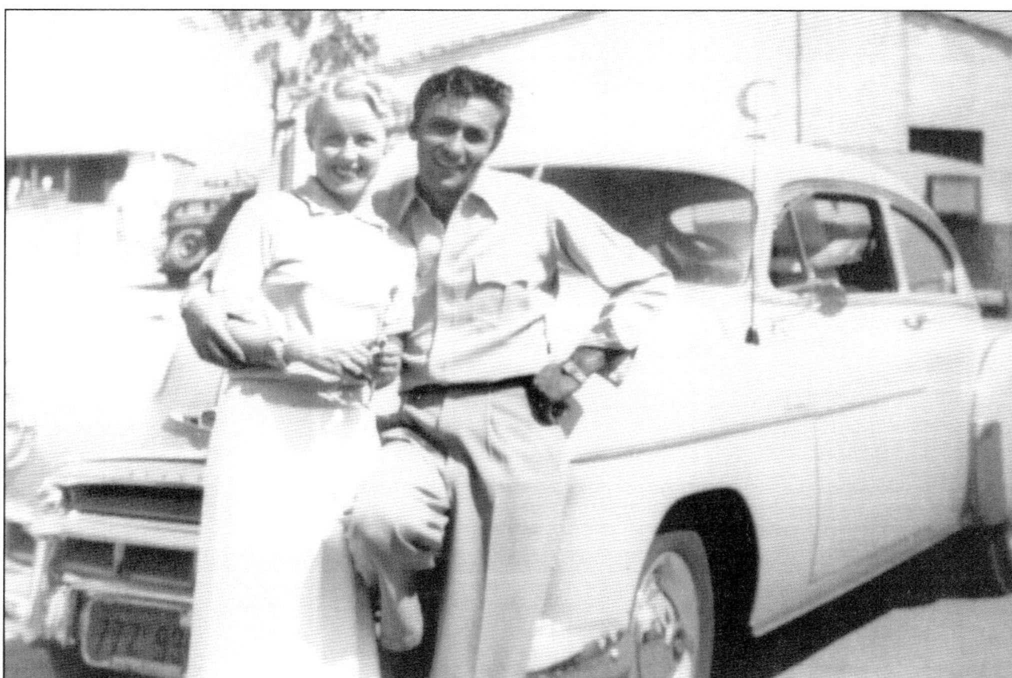

Dick Griegorian and Grayce Morrison, 1941. When Dick and Grayce Morrison married, they ran Griegorian Disposal. Grayce helped with new business and drove the trash truck, while Dick dumped the trash. In the late 1960s, they changed the name to Modern Disposal—the first trash hauler to operate in the San Gabriel Valley.

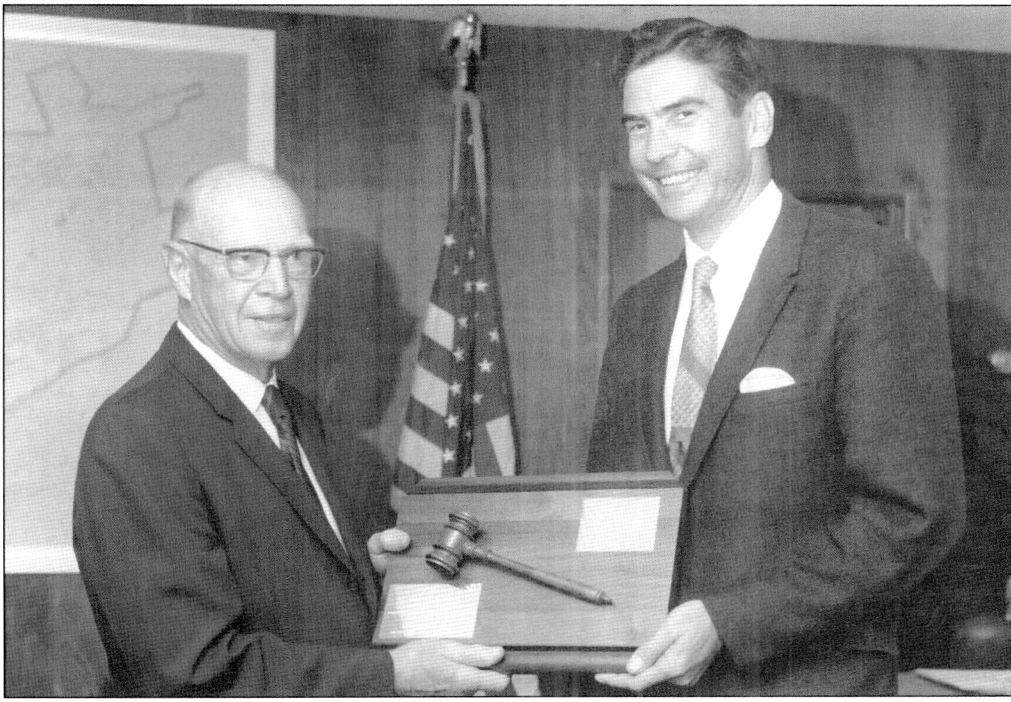

Leonard Westhoff Receives Plaque, 1970. Leonard Westhoff was active in Walnut's growth, and he was instrumental in Walnut's 1959 incorporation. He served on the first Walnut City Council and served as Walnut's mayor from 1962 to 1966, succeeding Bourdet. Westhoff first served on the Walnut Elementary School Board of Trustees during the 1940s. Later he served on the La Puente Union High School District Board of Trustees and the personnel commission for the merit system for classified employees in the same district. He then went on to the personnel commission for the Walnut Valley Unified School District (WVUSD) in 1970. Born in Ohio in 1899, he came to live in the Walnut area in 1940 when he and his wife Madoline bought 15 acres off La Puente Road. Leonard has a WVUSD elementary school named after him on Country Hollow Road in Walnut. In this 1970 photograph, Mayor Bill Daley (right) presents Leonard Westhoff with a plaque.

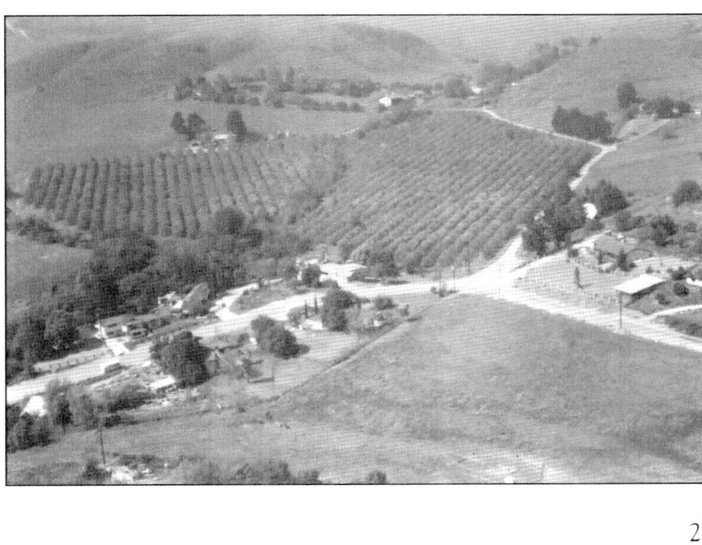

Bourdet Orange Grove, 1960s. Pete Bourdet and his mother, Marie, brother, Louis, and sister, Veronique, owned this 18-acre orange grove north of Pierre Road. The photograph of Amar Road, with Kelso Road on the left and Fuerte Drive on the right, shows Walnut Hills prior to residential development. Pete Bourdet farmed his land until he died in 1987.

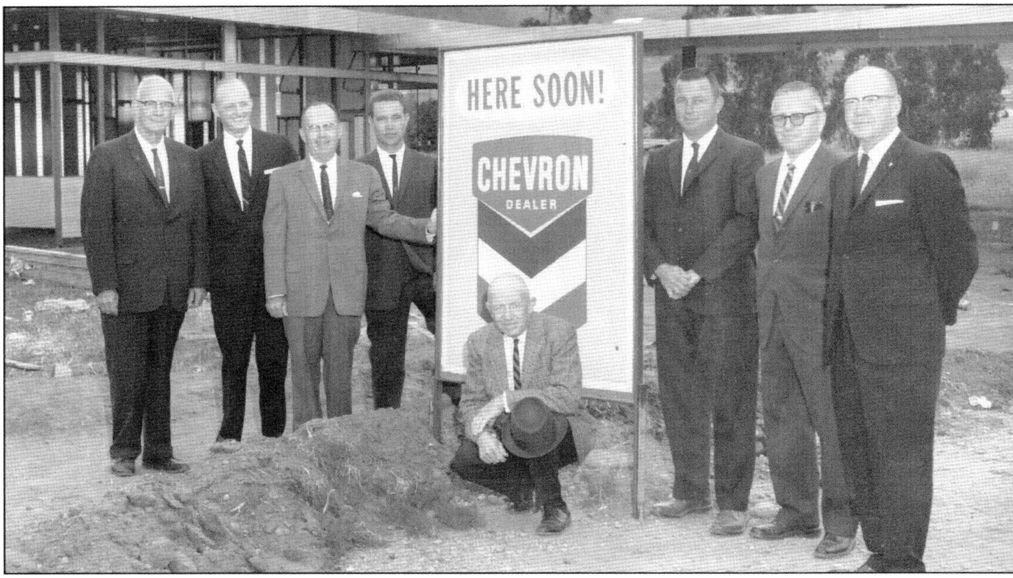

CHEVRON GAS STATION ANNOUNCEMENT, 1960S. Walnut mayor Leonard Westhoff (right) and Standard Oil executives announce the building of a Chevron gas station on Grand Avenue and what would become Amar Road. Behind the station are several farms, rolling hills, and canyons; to the west is Mount San Antonio College. The station is still at the same location in 2011.

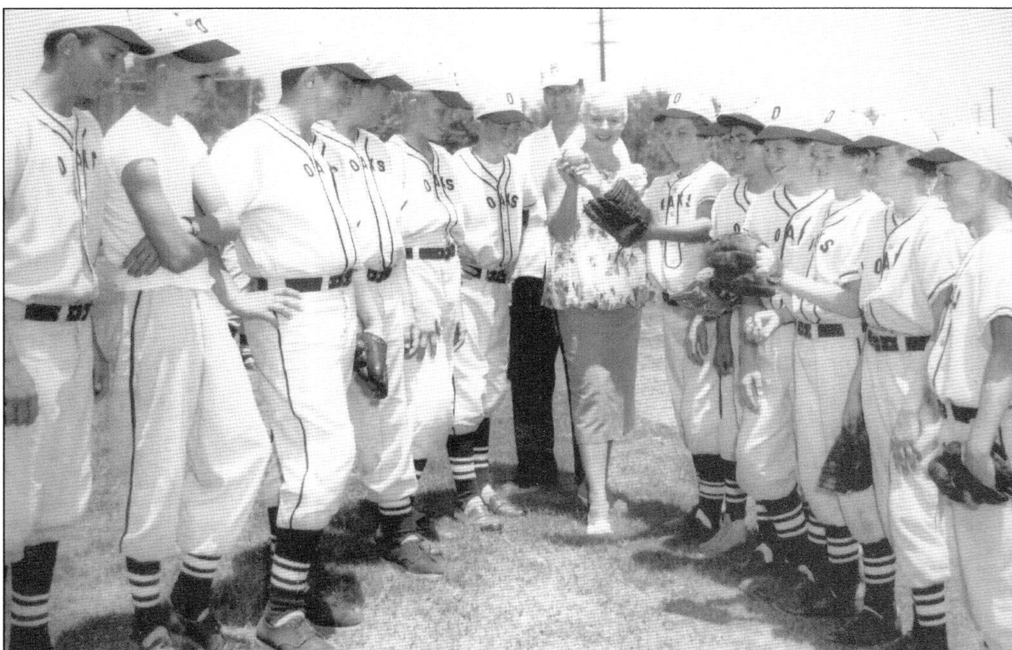

GRIEGORIAN PROPERTY, 1960S. Dick and Grayce Griegorian were involved in community activities such as Pony Baseball and daughters Debra and Danielle's Brownie Troop. An orange grove and creek surrounded the property. The family loved the beautiful rolling hills, the fragrance of orange blossoms, and the large fields of wildflowers that dotted the landscape of Walnut in the early years. The main street in front of the Griegorian home in 2011 is called Meadowpass Road.

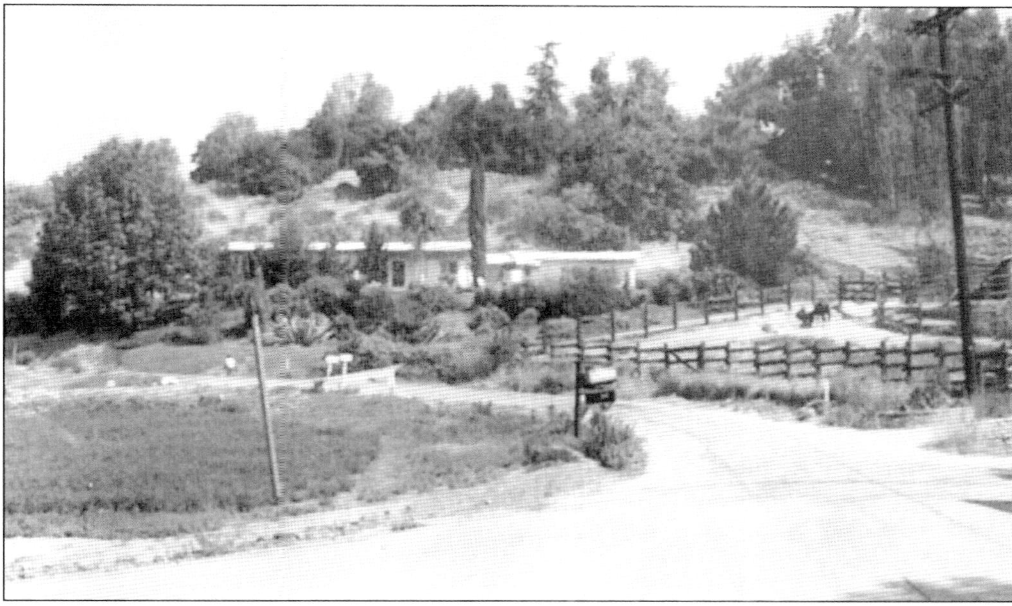

HUDSON HOME, 1960s. George Hudson and his wife, Kathleen, built a home on Gartel Drive in 1964. George served as a parks and recreation commissioner from 1974 to 1995. Their home was typical of the homes in the Gartel area in the 1960s.

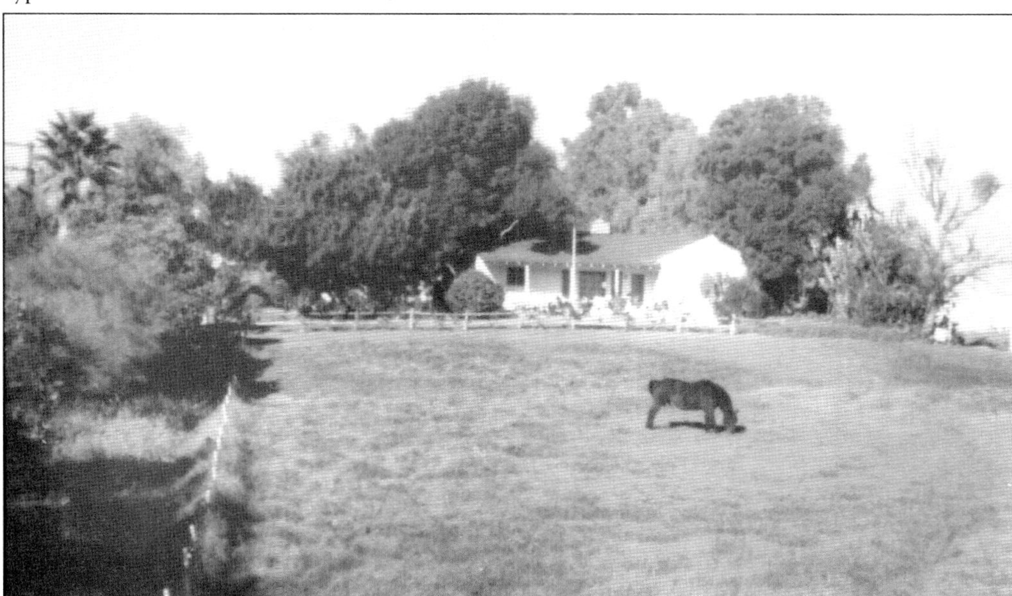

WESTHOFF HOME, 1965. The home sat at the end of a long driveway off La Puente Road. Trees lined both sides of the driveway, and the family's dry farming turned the front area into a pasture for horses. The house is typical of the farm homes in the area in the 1940s. The Westhoffs bought the 15-acre property at 20505 La Puente Road from William Rowland. "I still have the original deed to the house that says the Rowlands have the right for ingress and egress on my property," Westhoff said in 1989. When the property was bought, there was a lease for an oil well, but only sand oil was found; there was no productive oil.

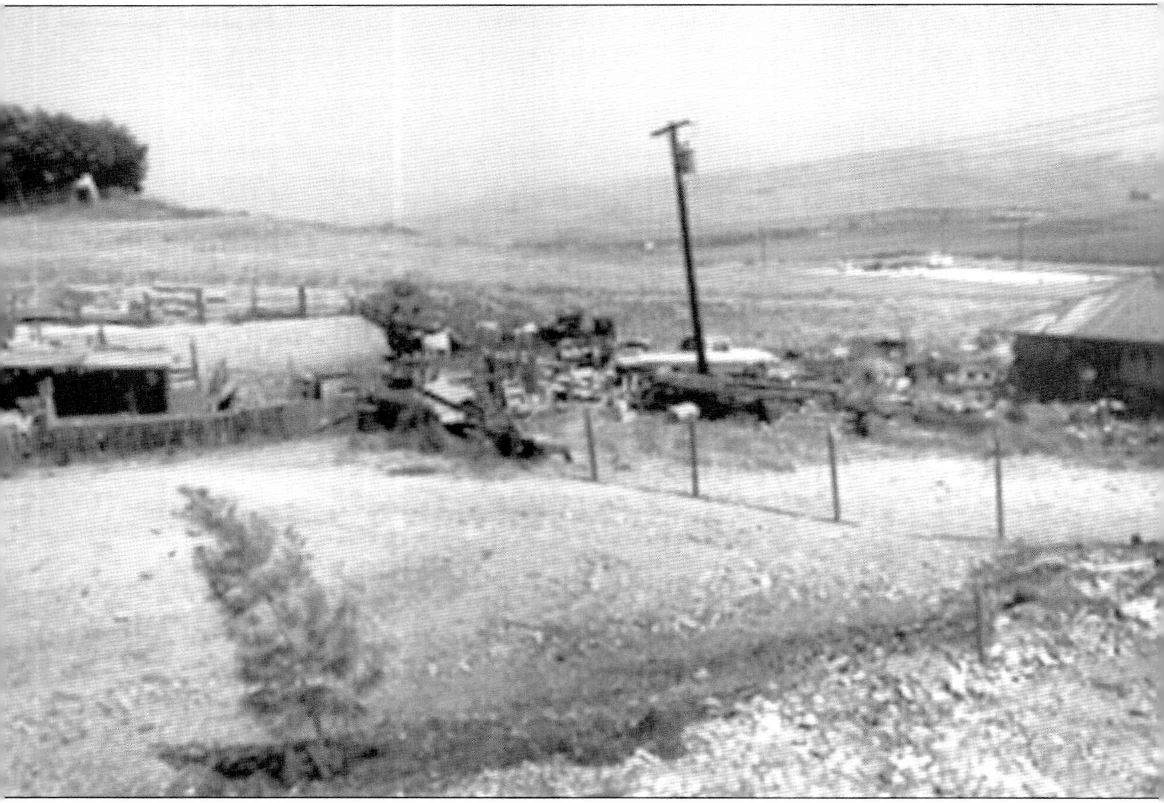

Dotta Family, 1960s. Giacomo and Mary Dotta and their daughters, Marguerita and Mary Lou, moved to Walnut in 1965. Giacomo farmed alfalfa until 1987 in the area south of La Puente Road. He also raised rabbits, chickens, cows, and, in the early days, pigs. The Shelton family lived on the hill; the rest of the hills provided pasture for cows and sheep. As development began on La Puente Road and Marcon Avenue, Giacomo had less and less land to farm. Walnut City Hall was built in 1982 in front of the farm on La Puente Road.

Two

EDUCATION

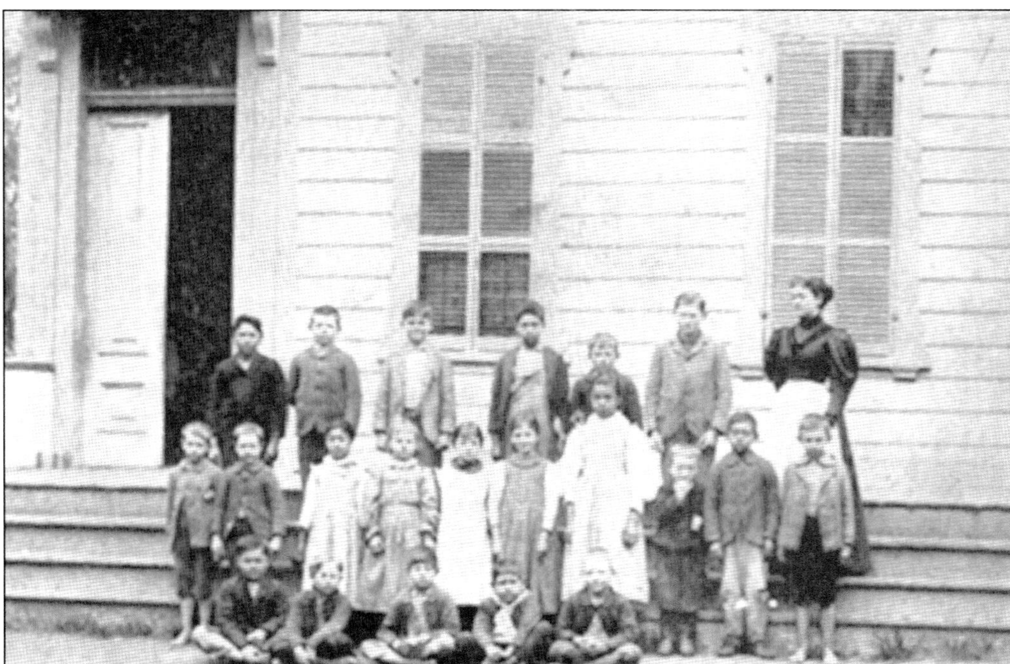

THE SPADRA SCHOOL DISTRICT, 1860s. Originally called the San Jose School District, the Spadra School District was established in 1867. In 1869, the school district built a second school, a two-story frame building on Water Street in the City of Industry. Approximately 30 students attended until it burned near the end of the 1891 school year. For more than a decade, it was the only school located between Spadra and La Puente. The only teacher would travel from El Monte by train each day.

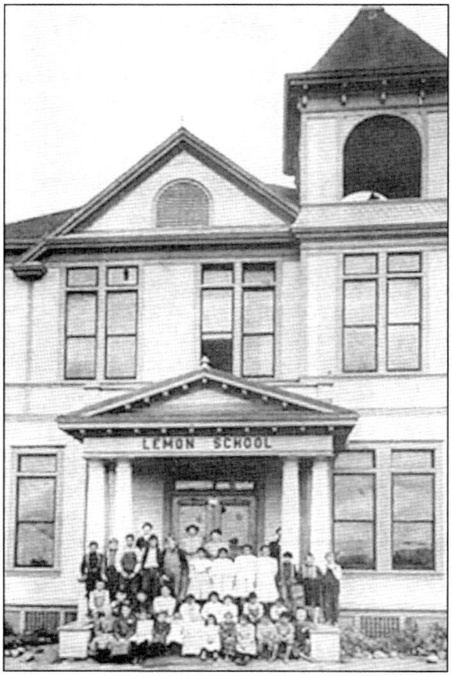

LEMON SCHOOL, 1893. After the fire of 1891, the school district built the Lemon School in the Lemon School District on Lemon Avenue in 1893. By 1898, the school grew to 50 students in eight grades. Between 1898 to 1906, five teachers were hired. Because of the need for more classrooms, the school was moved to the south. The one-room school was lifted up and another room was built underneath to make a two-story building. In 1907, the school officially became Walnut School. Upon eighth-grade graduation, students traveled by train to attend high school in Pomona and El Monte.

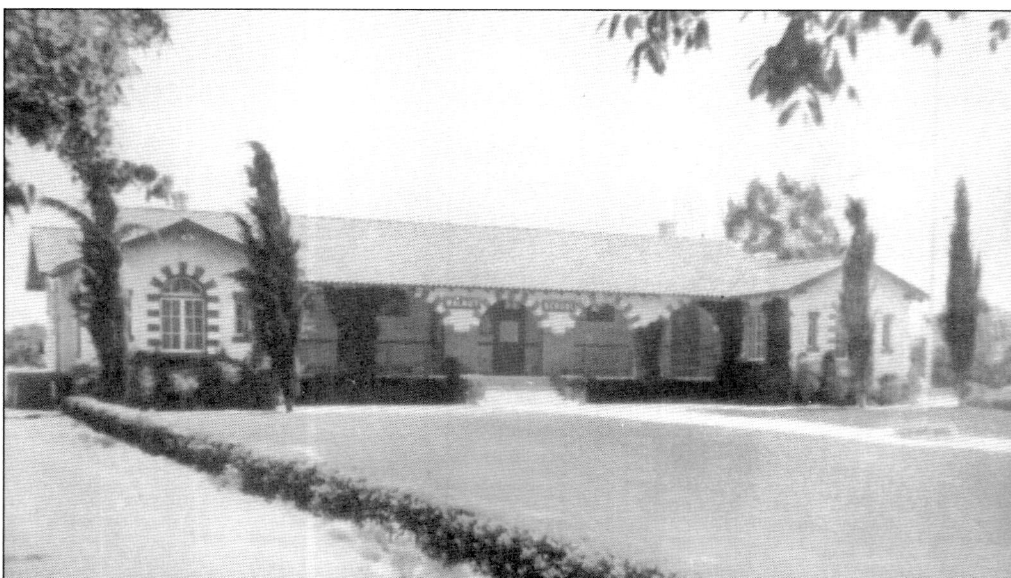

WALNUT SCHOOL, 1920. The two-story frame schoolhouse was replaced with a brick building with a tile roof. After the Long Beach earthquake in 1933, the trustees were required to replace the tile roof of the school with a shingle roof. The Walnut Elementary School District was formed in 1946. By 1952, the school had 147 students. The old brick building was torn down in 1954 to make room for additional classrooms, and by 1960, approximately 250 students attended the school. The high school students in Walnut attended La Puente Union High School District until the Walnut Elementary School District unified in 1970 and became the Walnut Valley Unified School District (WVUSD), offering kindergarten through 12th grade.

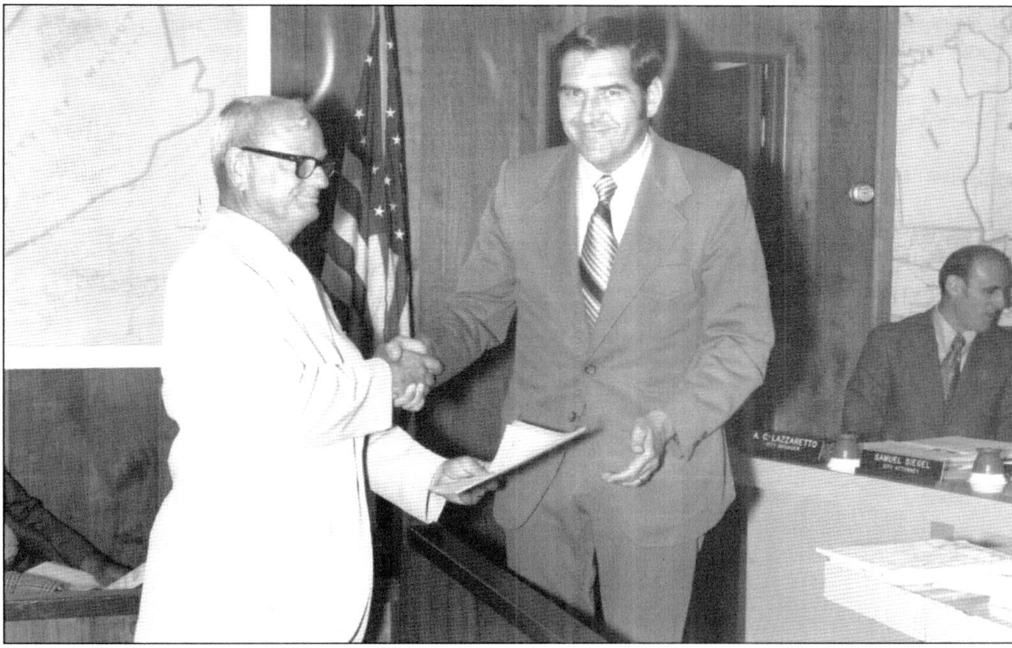

CYRUS MORRIS CONGRATULATED, 1972. Cyrus Morris began his career with WVUSD in 1952 as a principal, superintendent, and eighth-grade teacher. During this time, the school had 149 students with a graduating class of 14 students. Later he became the district's full-time superintendent. For 20 years, Morris was at the helm of Walnut's educational structure. He was responsible for building Suzanne Middle School, Vejar Elementary, and Collegewood Elementary. Then, in 1970, when the district unified and took responsibility for Walnut High School, he was there to guide the students and staff through the transition. When he retired, the school district had grown to seven schools with almost 5,000 students. In this 1972 photograph, Mayor Bill Wentworth (right) congratulates Cyrus Morris on his retirement.

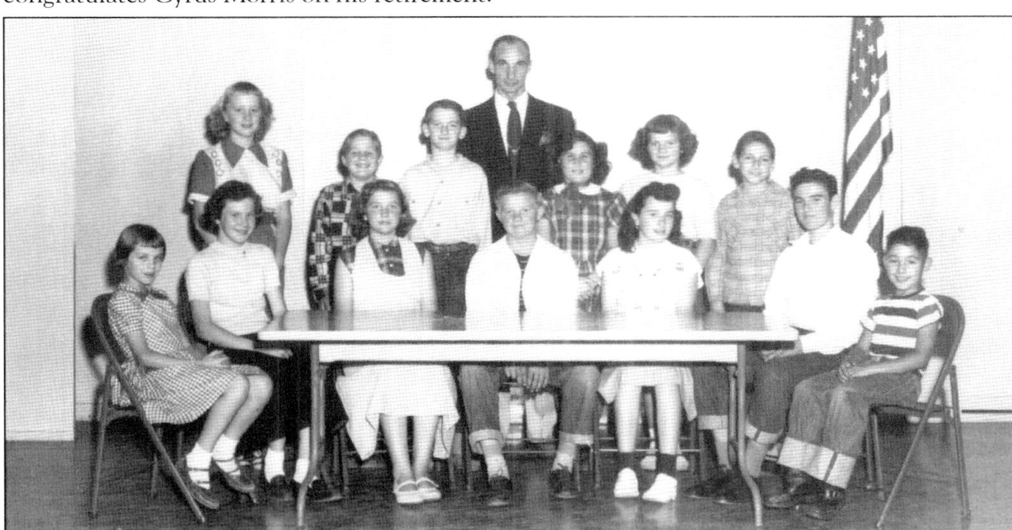

WALNUT SCHOOL STUDENT COUNCIL, 1951. Approximately 135 students attended Walnut School on Lemon Avenue and Valley Boulevard.

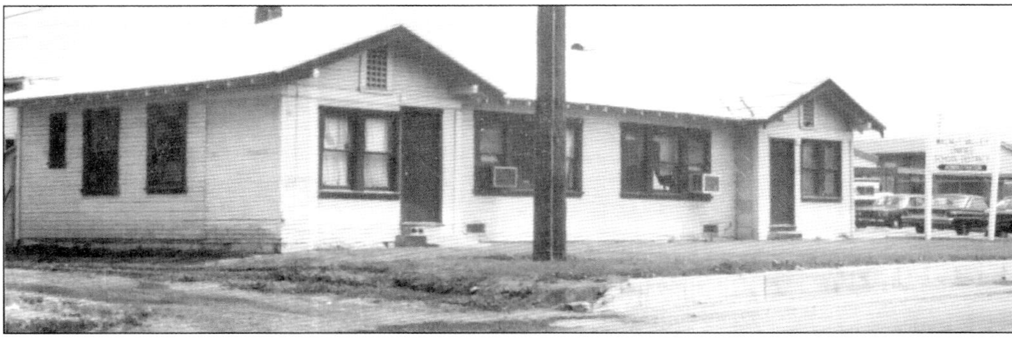

WVUSD ADMINISTRATION OFFICE, 1950s. Cyrus Morris and his wife, Harriet, were listed as registered voters living at the district's administration office address in 1952. In the 1970s, trailers were installed behind the office when the district unified. Cy Morris ran the school district and taught eighth grade. The small building served as the district office until 1983, when the district office moved south on Lemon Avenue toward Golden Springs Drive. In 2011, the building still served as the district's administration office.

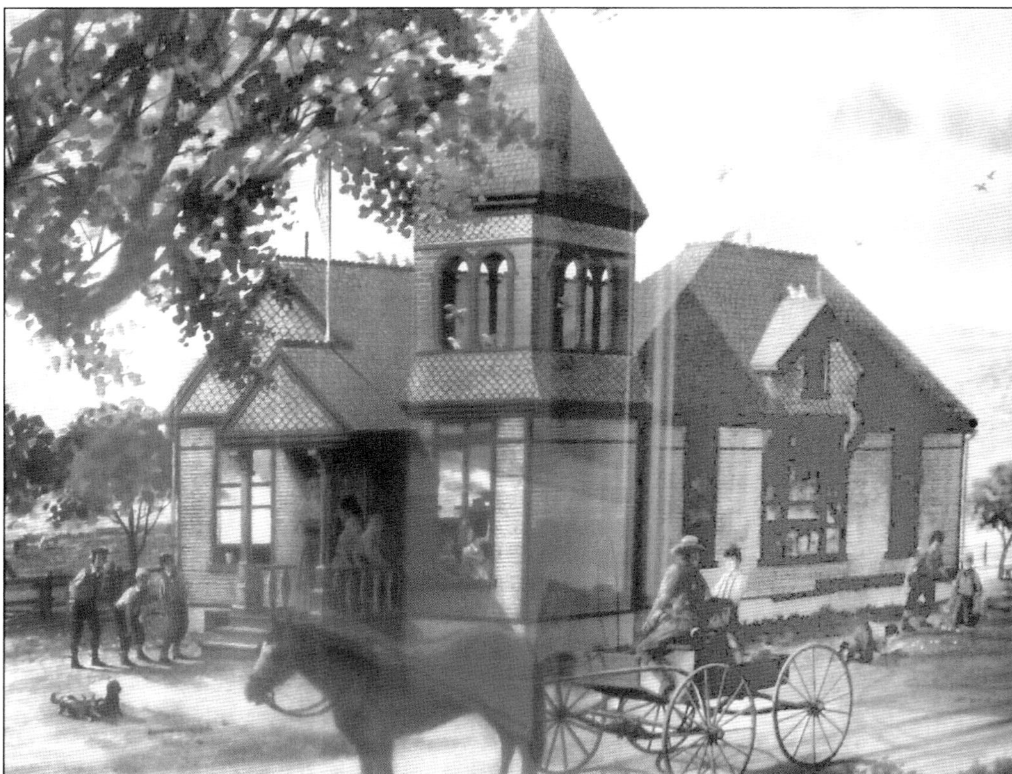

ROWLAND UNIFIED SCHOOL DISTRICT, 1870s. Upon the petition of William Workman, Rowland School District was formed on February 9, 1871. It began with a one-room school at the corner of Anaheim-Puente Road and Chestnut Street. By 1910, the district had 48 pupils. The first official Rowland School was built on Fullerton Road in 1929 amid walnut trees and strawberry patches. The present Rowland Elementary School was built in 1955 in Rowland Heights. District unification took place in June 1970, and the district currently serves over 15,000 kindergarten through 12th-grade students and 5,000 adult learners at 20 sites.

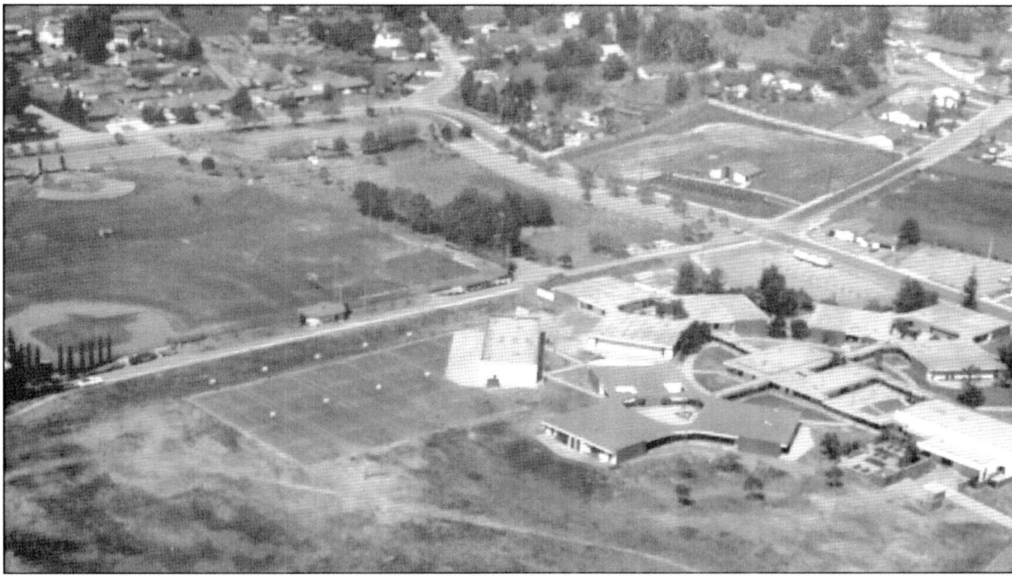

SUZANNE MIDDLE SCHOOL, 1960S. In 1962, Suzanne Middle School opened its doors, offering kindergarten as well as fourth through eighth grade for Diamond Bar, Rowland Heights, and Walnut students. It was built on La Puente Road and Suzanne Road. Barney Davis was the first principal, and when Collegewood Elementary opened in 1965, it then became a junior high school for seventh- and eighth-graders. Suzanne Park, Walnut's only park at the time, was behind the school. It had new baseball and softball diamonds that opened in 1970.

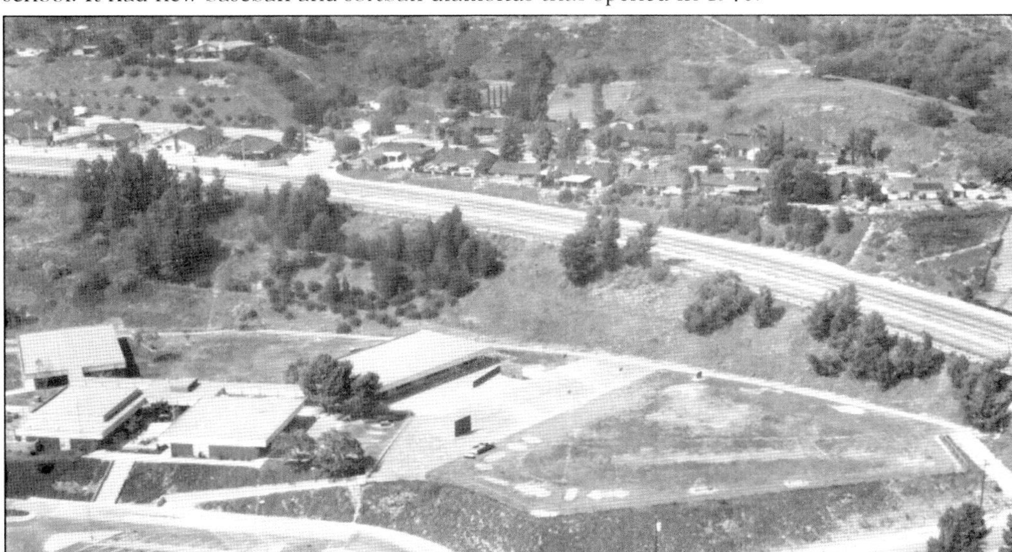

COLLEGEWOOD ELEMENTARY, 1960S. Collegewood was the first elementary school built in Walnut in 1965, with Albert "Al" Ross as the first principal. Students previously attended Suzanne School on La Puente Road. In 1963, the superintendent of Walnut Elementary School District, Cyrus Morris, reported "that the districts master plan called for the eventual construction of 55 schools." The expected growth of the area did not occur, and in 2011, WVUSD had 15 schools serving approximately 14,700 students.

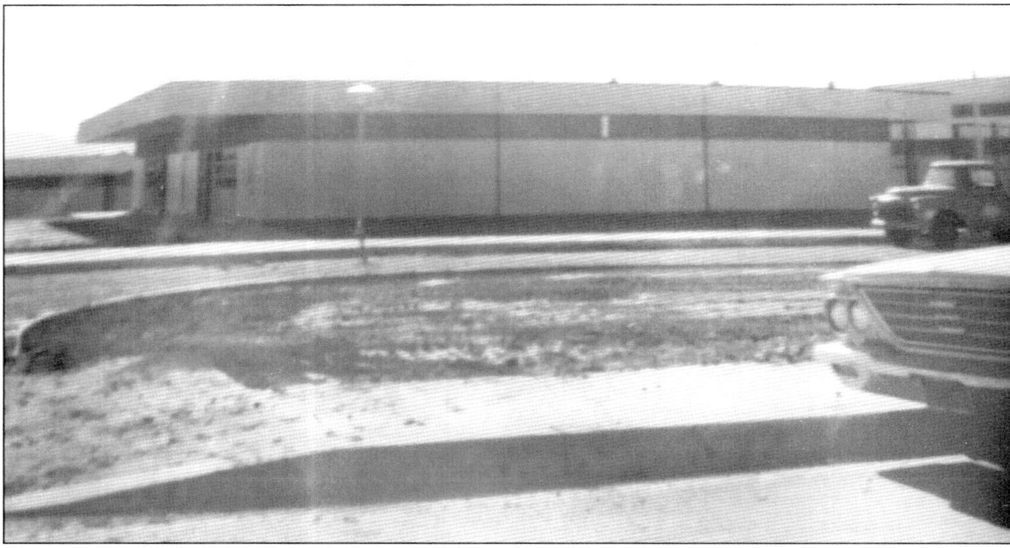

VEJAR ELEMENTARY SCHOOL, 1966. The district finished construction of Vejar Elementary School in 1966. Douglas Rosenow served as the first principal, and Bill Gage was the first custodian. Earlier, in 1964, the Walnut Elementary School District acquired the property from Fullerton Mortgage Company through condemnation proceedings. Entry to Vejar was off Lemon Avenue. Shortly after the school opened, a dirt path was constructed to give access to students on the east side of town. In earlier years, the Martinez family lived in an adobe that was constructed on the property around the 1850s.

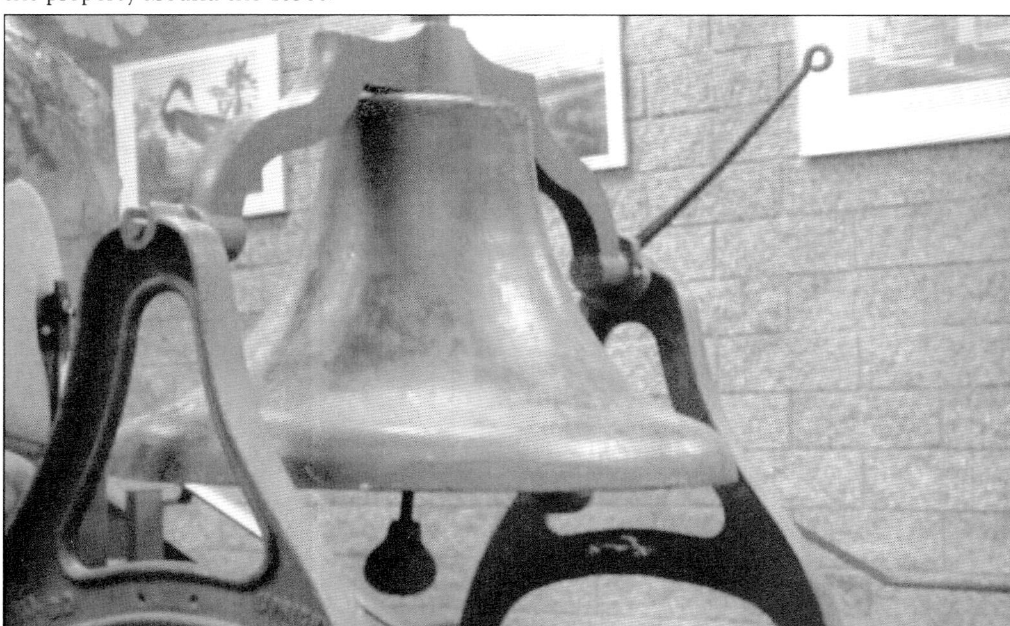

SPADRA SCHOOL BELL, 1860S. The 150-year-old brass bell hung first in the belfry of the Spadra School, then in the Lemon School, followed by the Walnut Elementary School, and is presently housed in the lobby of the current Walnut Elementary School on Glenwick Avenue. The pioneer children from the Walnut area heard the bell calling them to school.

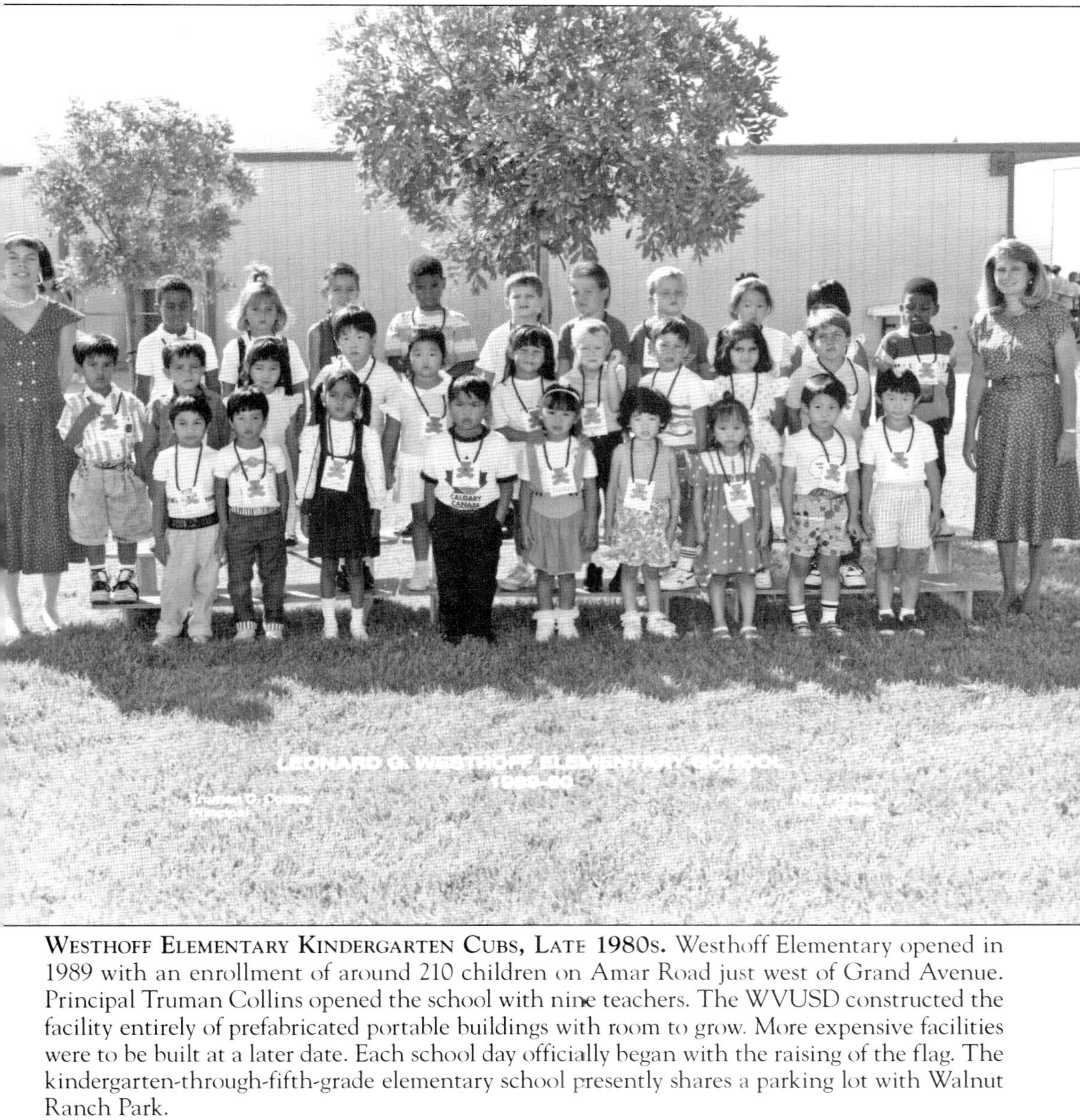

WESTHOFF ELEMENTARY KINDERGARTEN CUBS, LATE 1980s. Westhoff Elementary opened in 1989 with an enrollment of around 210 children on Amar Road just west of Grand Avenue. Principal Truman Collins opened the school with nine teachers. The WVUSD constructed the facility entirely of prefabricated portable buildings with room to grow. More expensive facilities were to be built at a later date. Each school day officially began with the raising of the flag. The kindergarten-through-fifth-grade elementary school presently shares a parking lot with Walnut Ranch Park.

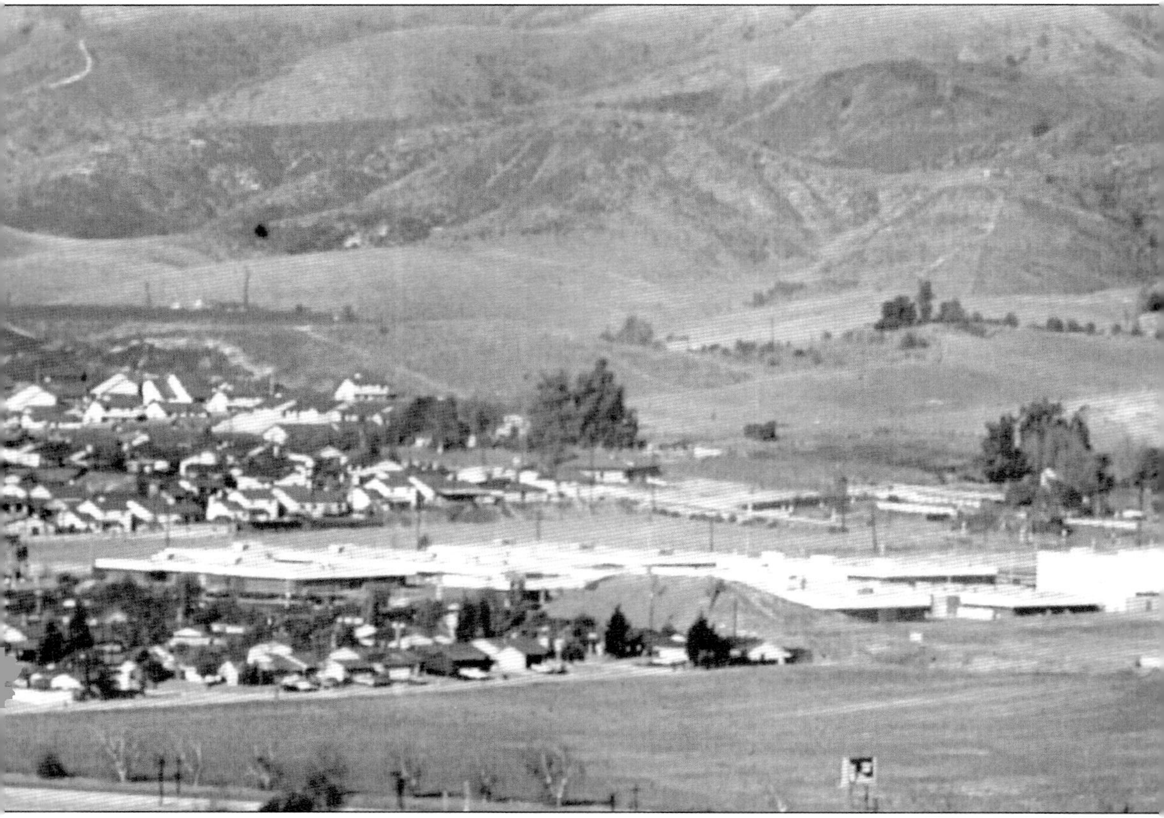

Walnut High School, Late 1960s. The district's high school opened in 1968. The Carrey farmhouse was torn down to make room for the new high school. Located on Pierre Road, it was first part of the La Puente Union High School District. In 1970, Walnut High School became part of the WVUSD when it unified to become a kindergarten-through-12th-grade district. Jack Ingram served as the first principal.

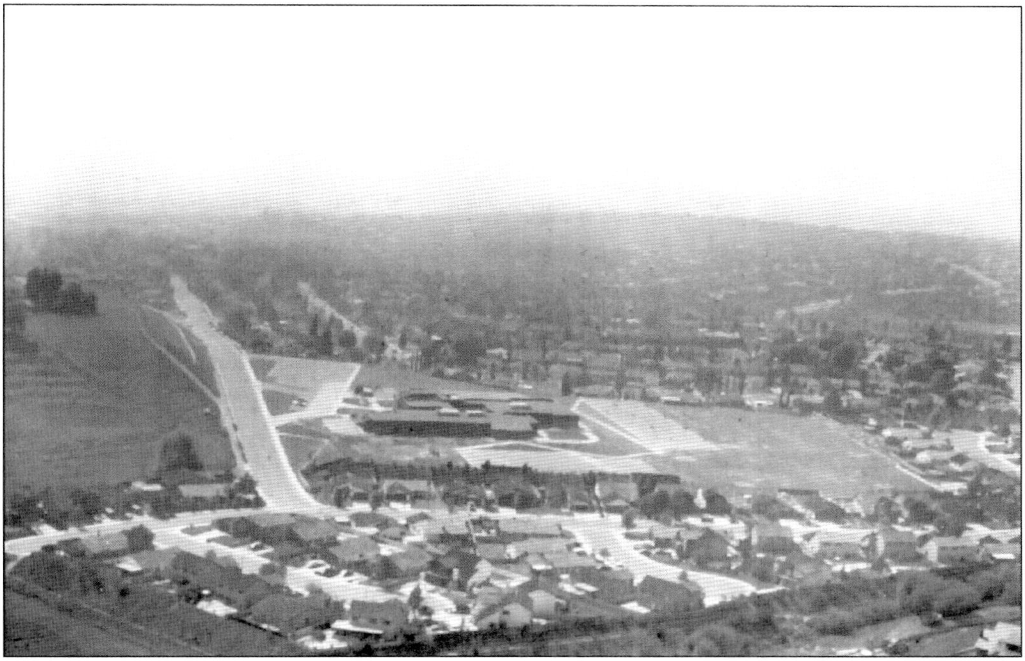

C.J. Morris Elementary School, Late 1970s. The school, named after Cyrus Morris, who served as superintendent for the district from 1952 to 1972, opened its doors in 1976. His vision was to create not only an adequate school district but also a superior school system at a cost within sensible bounds for its sponsors. Cy Morris and his wife, Nancy, settled in the city of Walnut in the early 1960s and lived there until he retired in 1972.

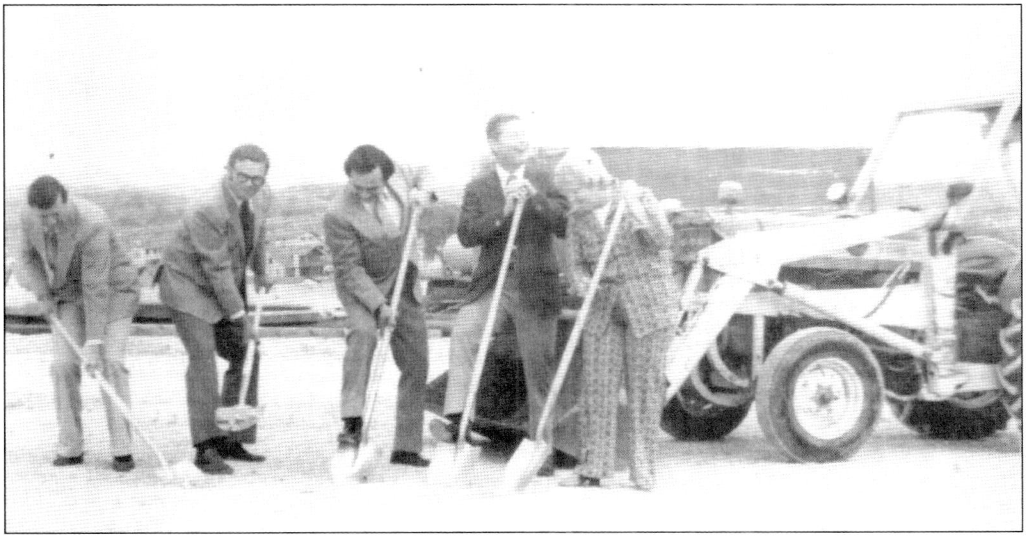

School Ground-Breaking, 1975. C.J. Morris Elementary is located on Calle Baja. It was the WVUSD's first round school; all classrooms along with the library were open to each other. Attending the ground-breaking ceremony are, from left to right, Walnut city council member Dick Laughter, WVUSD board of trustees member Jim Hannan, Frank Morales, Principal Cliff Wellington, and an unidentified woman.

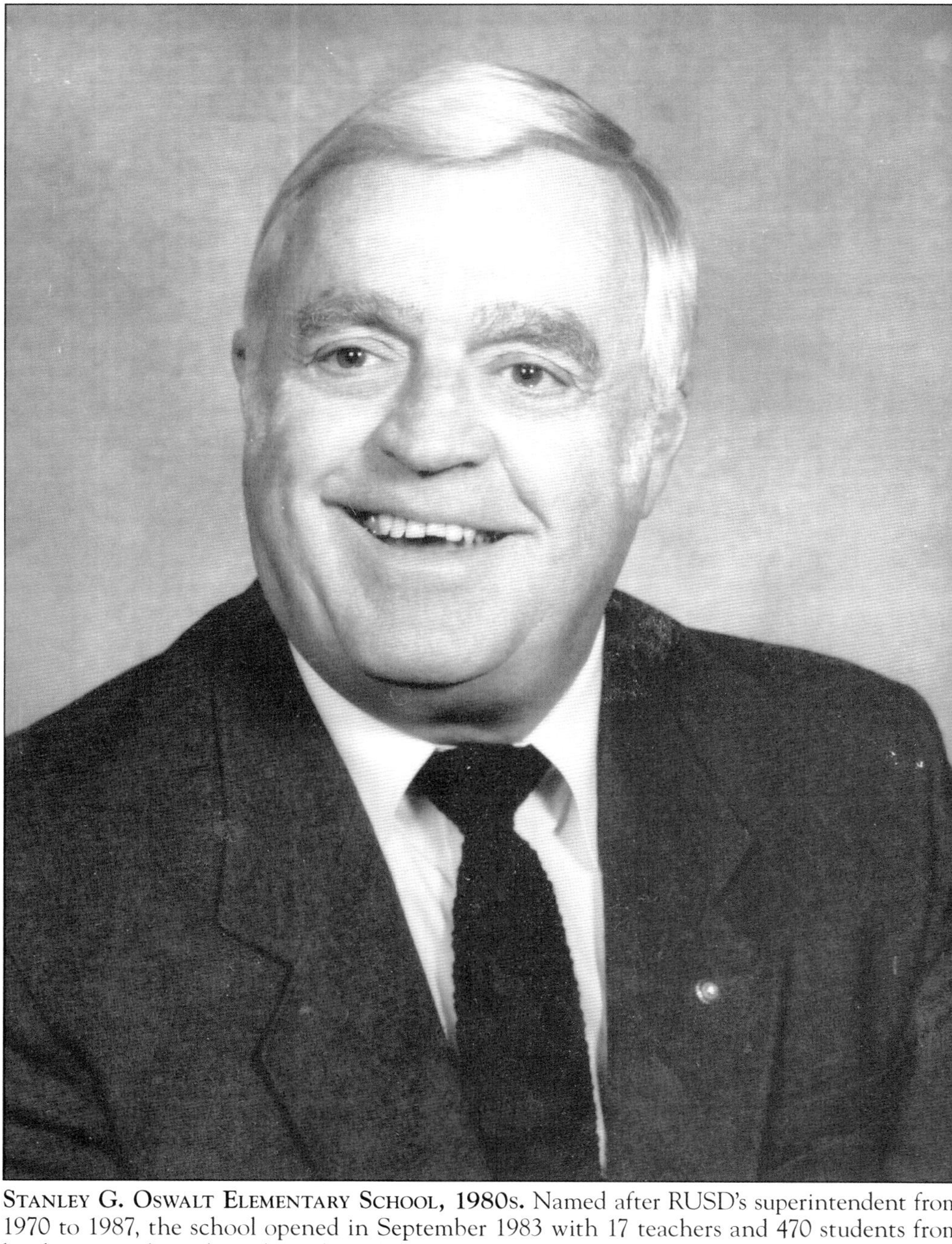

Stanley G. Oswalt Elementary School, 1980s. Named after RUSD's superintendent from 1970 to 1987, the school opened in September 1983 with 17 teachers and 470 students from kindergarten through sixth grade under the leadership of Principal Harold L. Moe. The school, off Creekside and Shadow Oak Drives in the city of Walnut, expanded to kindergarten through eighth grade in August 2008 and was renamed Stanley G. Oswalt Academy. This school serves students in the northwest of the city.

Three

Municipal Services

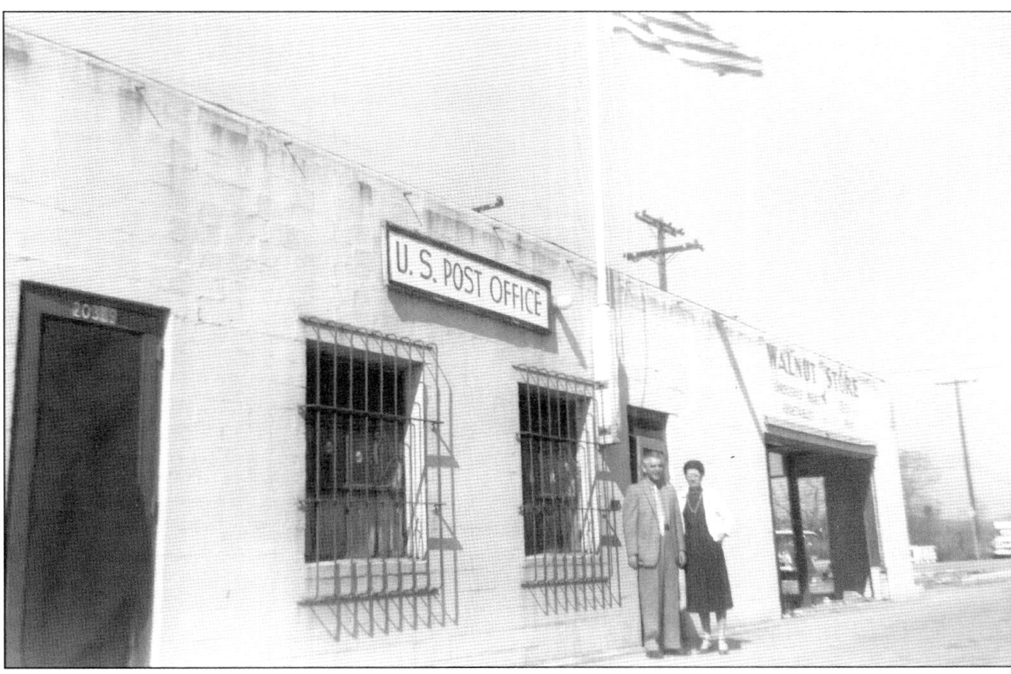

Post Office and General Store, 1920s. Located on Valley Boulevard, the post office and general store were located side-by-side. Christina Buck was the postmaster in 1924, and her husband, Ellsworth, was the weight master. Bacil Best ran the general store, which sold groceries. Bacil lived on Gartel Drive with his wife, Fern, who was a schoolteacher.

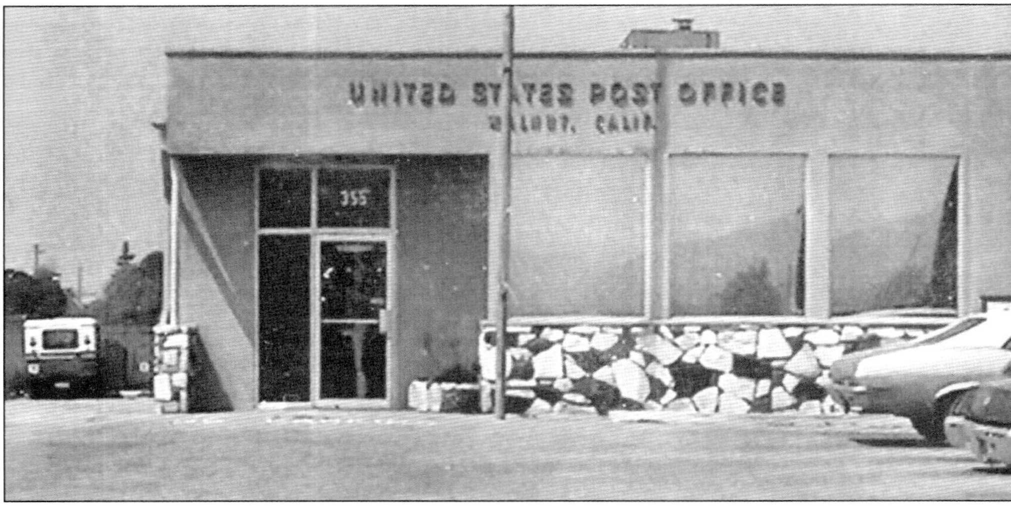

Walnut's Second Post Office. Walnut's second post office opened up in 1961 on the corner of Lemon Avenue and Valley Boulevard. Henry Davis, who had been the postmaster for the area since 1958, operated the $35,000 building. Then Stella David Wood took over the duties until a new post office was built in the late 1970s.

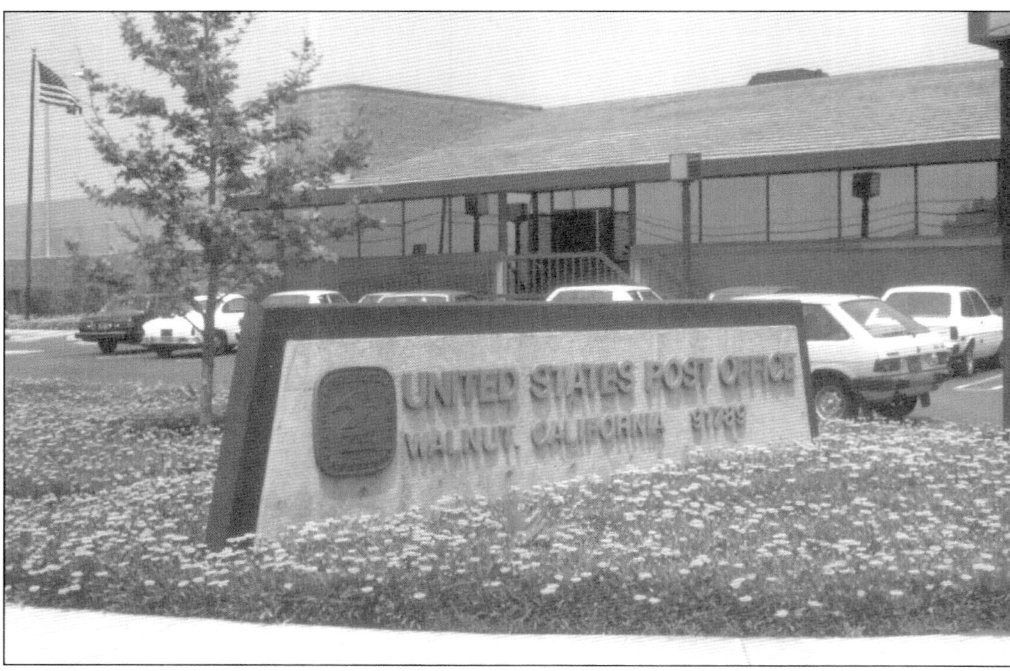

Walnut Post Office, 1970s to Present. The present post office was built in the late 1970s by Corwin and Way. Ron Way, a Walnut resident, was the architect. The post office is located on Lemon Avenue, and Bruce Dennis serves as postmaster.

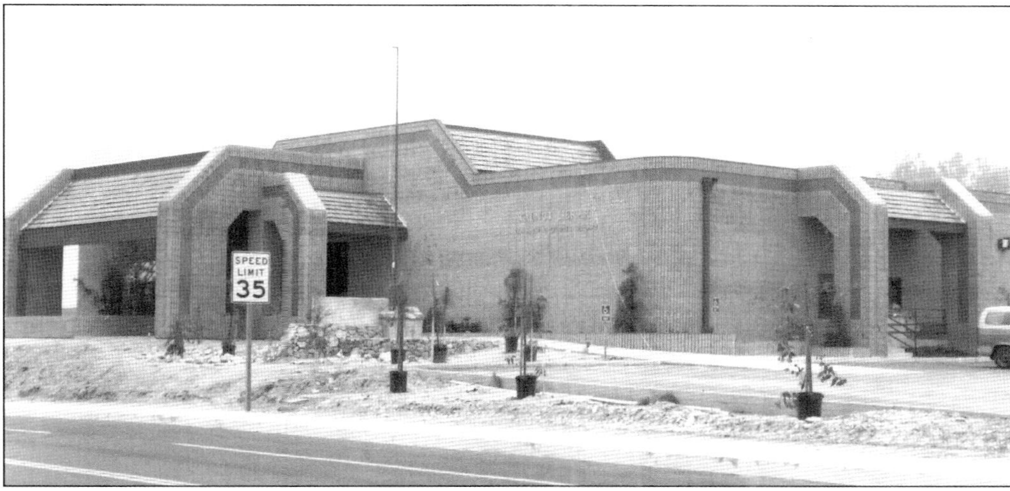

Walnut Public Library, 1910s. Founded in 1916, the Walnut Public Library was operated in the Walnut School on Lemon Avenue south of Valley Boulevard by Los Angeles County. In 1964, the library room was replaced by a county bookmobile to bring books to schools and residents within the immediate area. To serve the increasing population, the library leased a 3,260-square-foot storefront at 134 Pierre Road in 1970. The library moved to its La Puente Road location in 1985. This new facility, built by Los Angeles County and the City of Walnut, featured a meeting room, three study rooms, and a Friends of the Library bookstore. In 2011, the La Puente Road library features the Walnut community gymnasium to the west and the Walnut City Hall to the east.

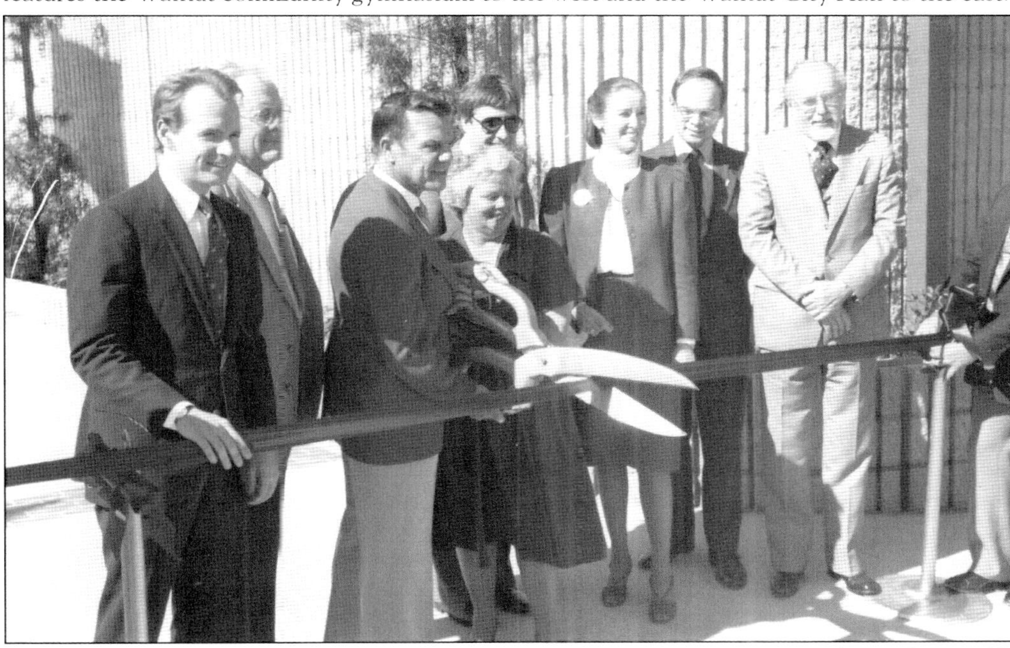

Public Library Dedication, 1985. On February 13, 1985, the dedication of the Walnut Public Library was attended by the following, from left to right: Congressman David Drier, Walnut city council member Harvey Holden, supervisor Pete Schabarum, Mayor Bert Ashley, Walnut city council member Drexel Smith, Los Angeles County librarian Linda Crismond, Mayor Pro Tem Chuck Richardson, and council member Joe Hahn.

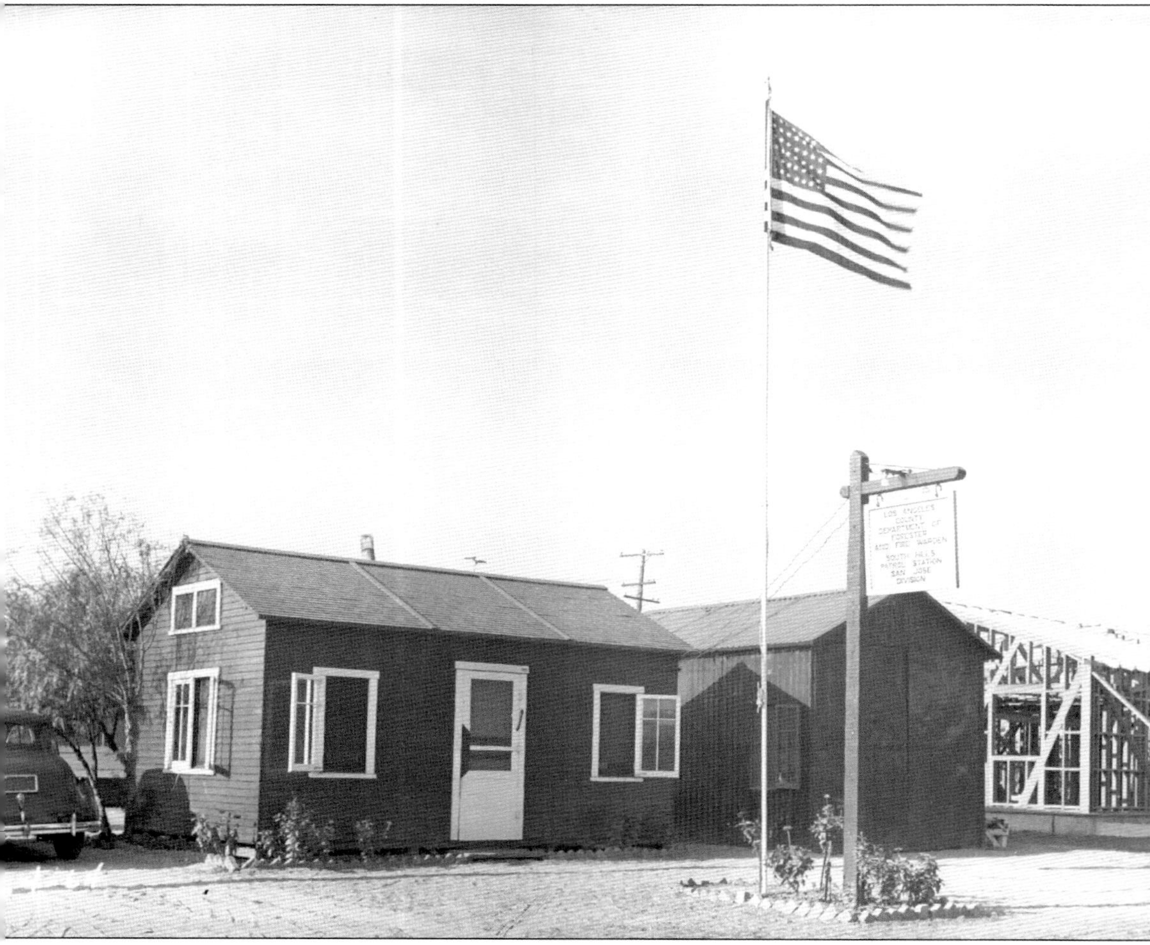

SOUTH HILLS PATROL STATION ENGINE 89. Before the City of Walnut incorporated, Forester and Fire Warden Land provided fire services—the name used at the time when services were provided to an unincorporated area. At first, the station's name was South Hills Patrol Station Engine 89, and then later it became Engine 61. The station on Valley Boulevard was used to cover the area in general and was not considered a Walnut fire station. The City of Walnut joined the Fire Protection District of Los Angeles County on January 19, 1959, upon the city's incorporation.

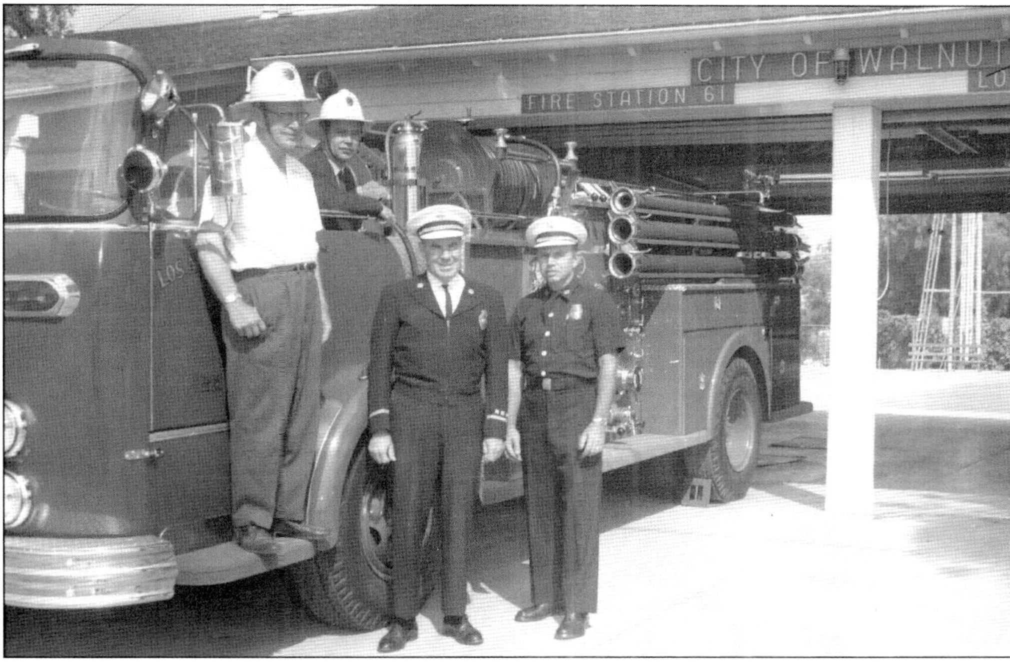

FIRE TRUCK DEDICATION, 1960s. No. 61, the City of Walnut's first fire station, was located on the corner of Valley Boulevard and Camino De Teodoro in 1963. From left to right are Mayor Leonard Westhoff, city clerk John Tapp, division assistant chief Robert M. Parsons, and branch chief Guy Goodwin.

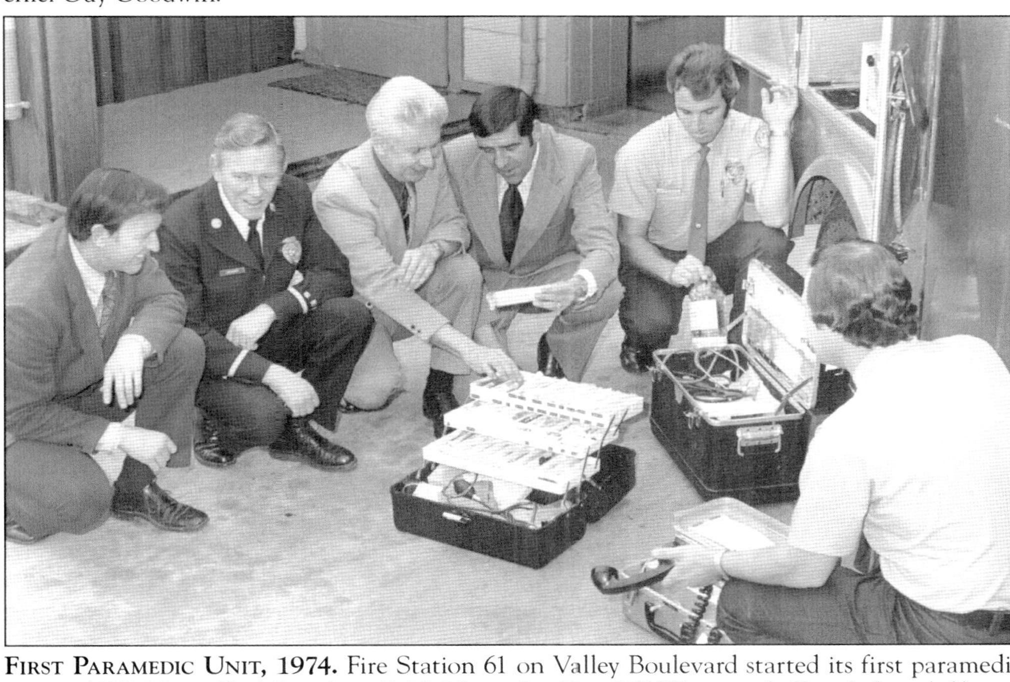

FIRST PARAMEDIC UNIT, 1974. Fire Station 61 on Valley Boulevard started its first paramedic unit in 1974. Mayor Dick Laughter (left), Mayor Pro Tem Bill Wentworth (fourth from left), and the paramedic unit look at the new equipment.

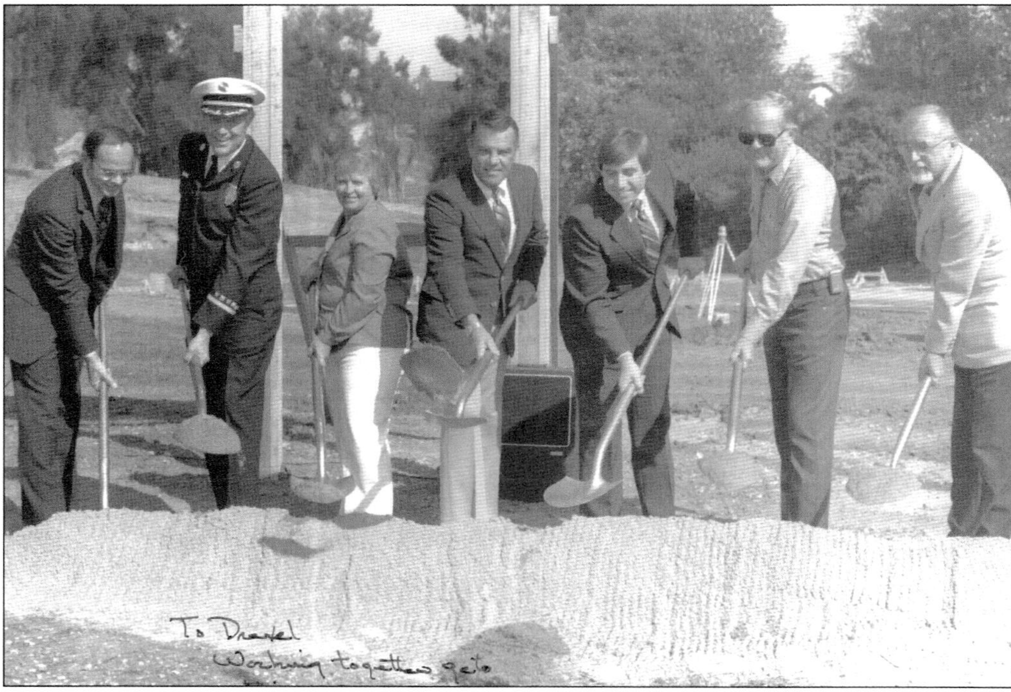

FIRE STATION 61 BREAKS GROUND, 1984. The new fire station was located on the corner of Lemon Avenue and La Puente Road. From left to right are council member Chuck Richardson, fire chief Clyde Bragoon, Mayor Pro Tem Bert Ashley, supervisor Pete Schabarum, Mayor Drexel Smith, and council members Harvey Holden and Joe Hahn.

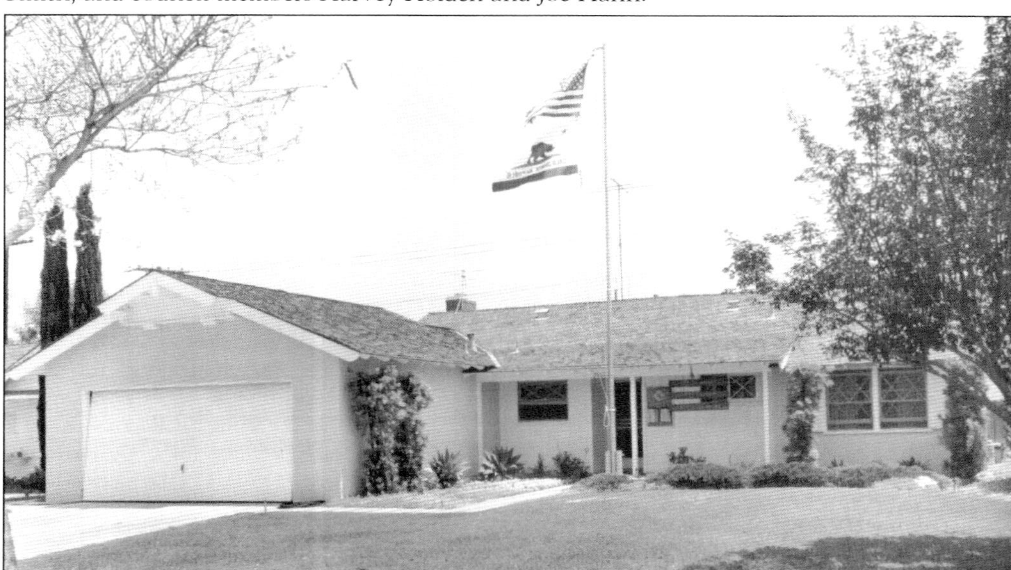

FIRE STATION 146 OPENS, 1969. In the Collegewood area at San Jose Hills Road and Loyalton Drive, Fire Station 146 opened in 1969. A Walnut home was converted to a fire station, providing Walnut with a second station. Station 146 was opened to meet the needs of Mount San Antonio College and increasing development.

Four

COMMUNITY COLLEGE

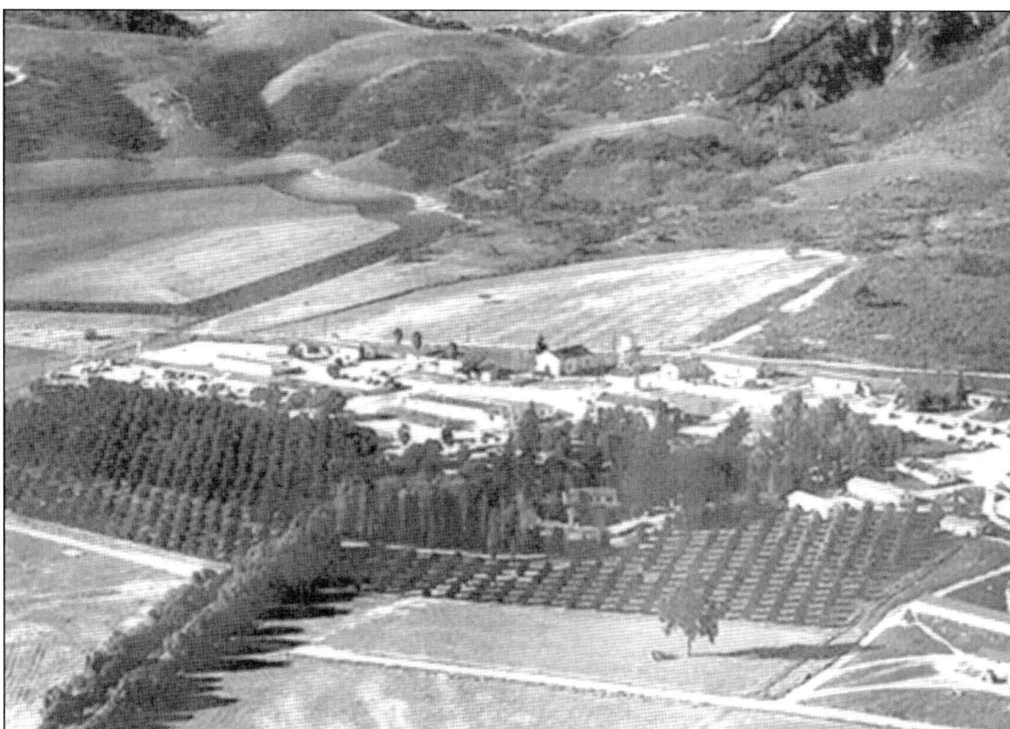

MOUNT SAN ANTONIO COLLEGE, 1840S. The history of the 445 acres where Mount San Antonio College is presently located goes back to January 14, 1842, before California became a state. Gov. Juan Avarado issued a land grant for property belonging to the San Gabriel Mission, John Rowland, and William Workman. They paid $1,000 for the 48,790-acre ranch, dividing the land between them. In 1845, Gov. Manuel Micheltorena confirmed the grant to Workman and Rowland. Rowland's half included the land that in 1959 became the city of Walnut.

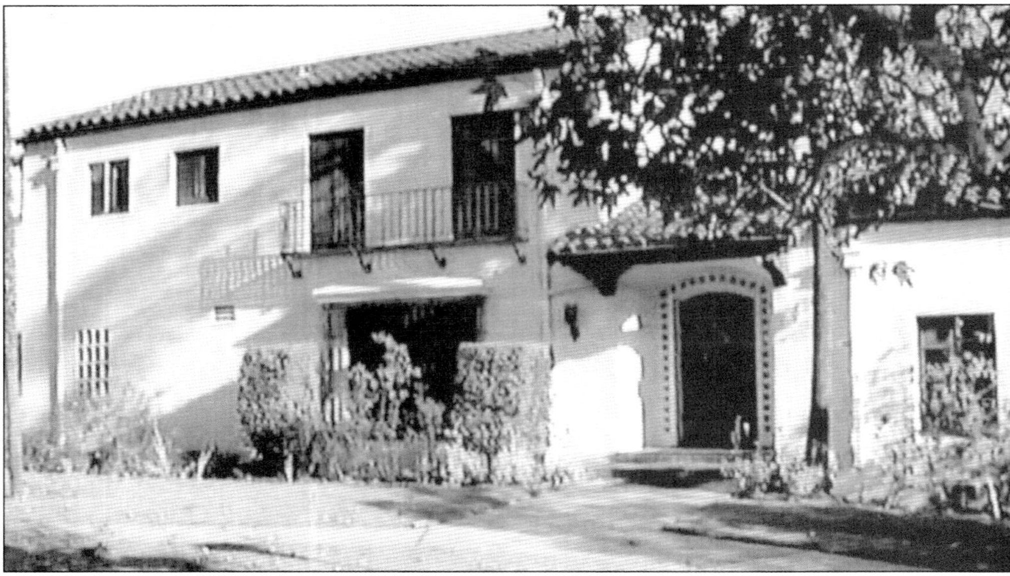

FOUNDERS HALL, 1930s. Located on the grounds of Mount San Antonio College as a home for the director of the state narcotics hospital, Founders Hall housed the president of the college after the college opened in 1946. In 2011, it is used as an office for the president and staff and a location to hold receptions and social affairs.

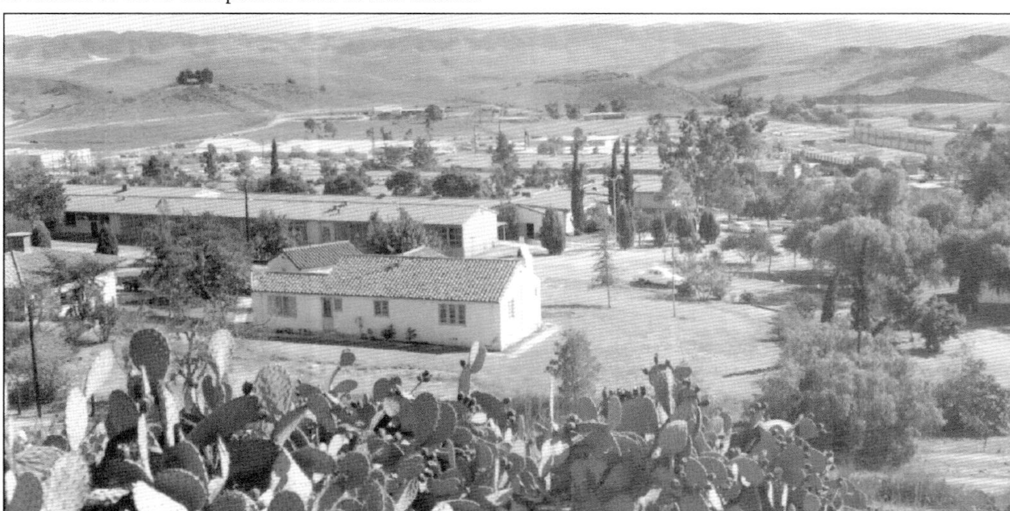

MOUNT SAN ANTONIO COLLEGE LAND, 1921–PRESENT. In 1921, Pacific Colony, a state hospital for the mentally infirm, occupied the area. Pacific Colony then turned into a home for wayward boys, a state narcotics hospital in the 1930s, a US Army hospital, and a US Navy hospital during World War II. In 1945, districts Pomona, Covina, La Puente, and Bonita petitioned the California Board of Education for a junior college to serve the combined areas. The campus was formed off Grand Avenue in 1946 on the site of the former hospitals. Founders Hall, which is still in use today, as well as several other buildings, was part of the hospital buildings. After the property became a junior college, the existing buildings transferred to become part of the newly formed campus. Dr. George Bell, the college's first president, made his residence in Founders Hall, previously lived in by the director of the narcotic hospital.

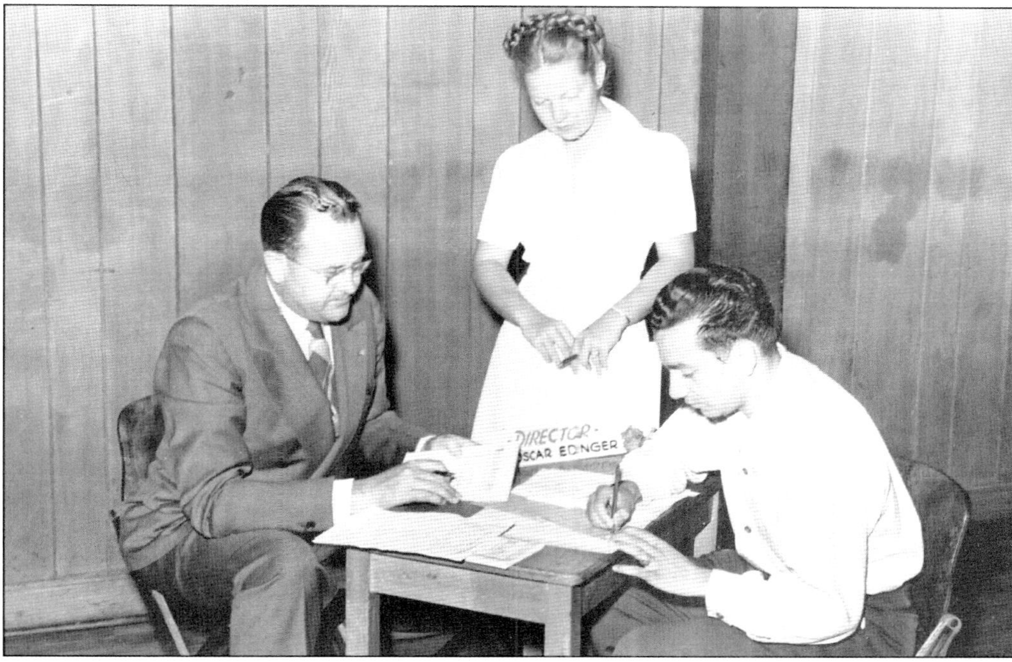

The First Day, 1946. From left to right are dean of men and director of instruction Dr. Oscar H. Edinger Jr., student Darlene Dickson, and Robert Boyajian. Student registration for the fall semester at Mount San Antonio College began on August 15, 1946. The college did not have a name selected at its opening; it was only known as the East Los Angeles County Junior College of Pomona. The board of trustees held a contest, and the name "Mount San Antonio" was chosen in honor of the snowcapped mountains visible behind the college.

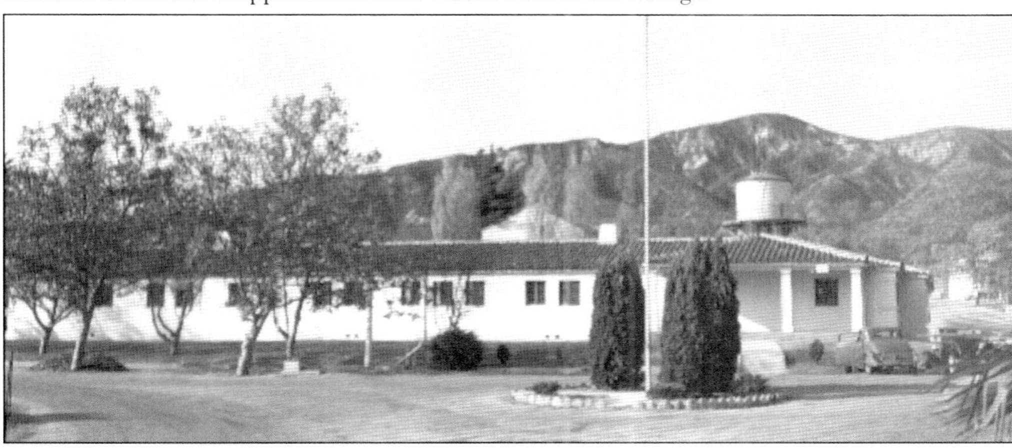

First Administration Building, 1946. Camphor trees lined the driveway to the Mount San Antonio College campus. West of the driveway was a small orange grove, and at the end of the road was the red-tile-roofed, Spanish-style stucco administration building with a flag pole in front. Bars enclosed the windows—a security measure during its time as a narcotics hospital. The building contained treatment rooms, some equipped with Jacuzzi baths. There were 99 temporary buildings spread over the campus. These typical barracks were mere shells composed of siding, a few windows, temporary foundations, and bare interiors with rafters showing. No paths lined the barrack steps—only clay, weeds, and rattlesnakes.

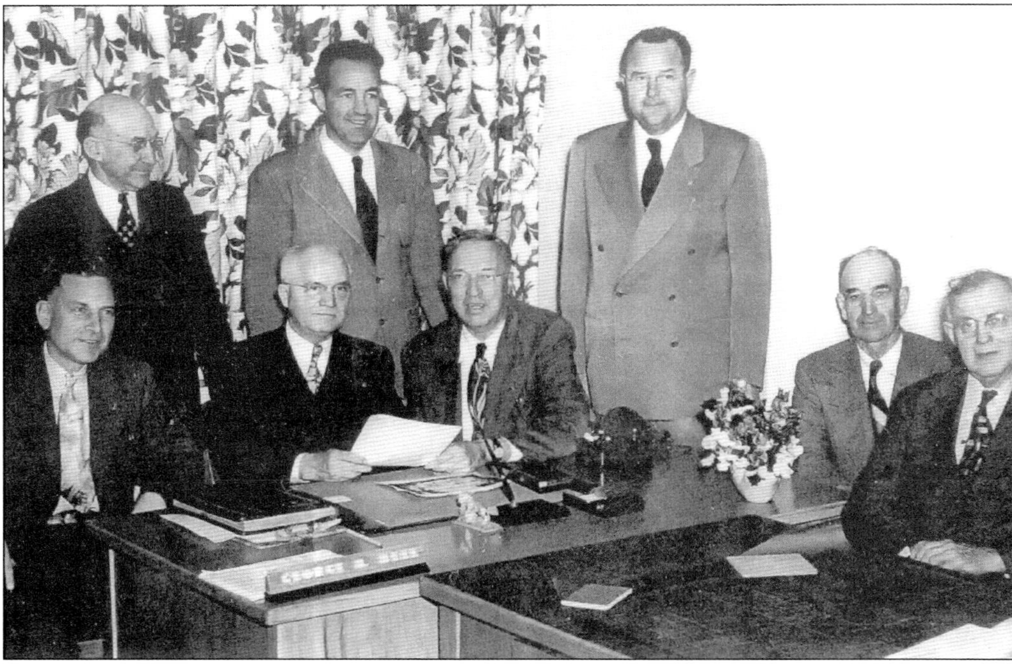

FOUNDING MOUNT SAN ANTONIO COLLEGE BOARD OF TRUSTEES, 1946. From left to right are (first row) Fred H. Harmsen, A.L. Hickson, Dr. George Bell, Pres. Herbert G. Langdon, and Dr. Verne Ross; (second row) A.T. Richardson, business manager Ernest W. Carl, and director of instruction Oscar H. Edinger Jr. The first president was Dr. George Bell. He oversaw passage of the first measure, which enabled construction of the first buildings on campus. In 1946, the college opened its doors to 635 students with a staff of 32.

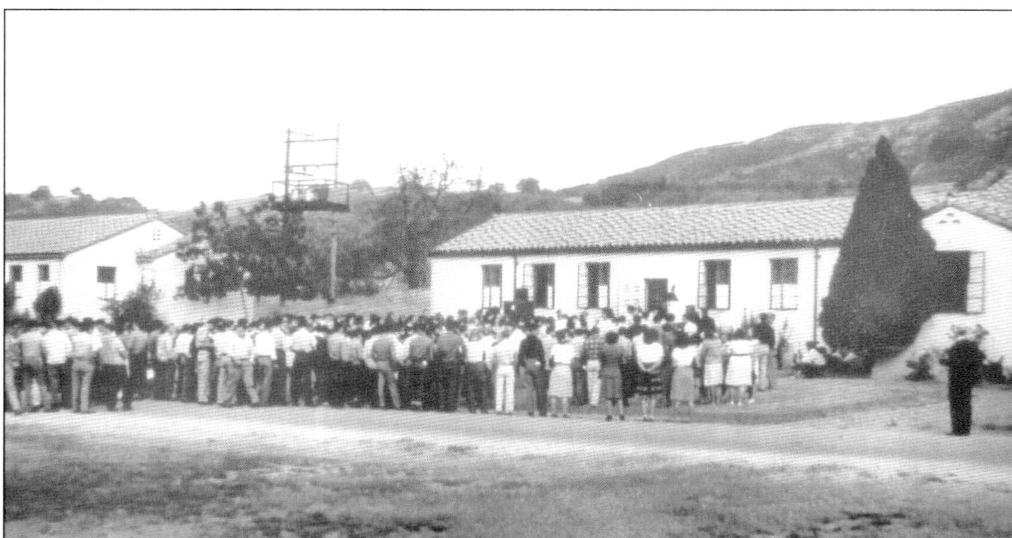

FIRST COMMENCEMENT, JUNE 14, 1947. The outdoor site was chosen for the 73 graduates who formed the first graduating class. Parents, friends, students, and 32 faculty and administrators attended the ceremony. At the same time, Gov. Earl Warren signed Assembly Bill 1904, making it possible for the college to acquire the present site as a permanent home for Mount San Antonio College.

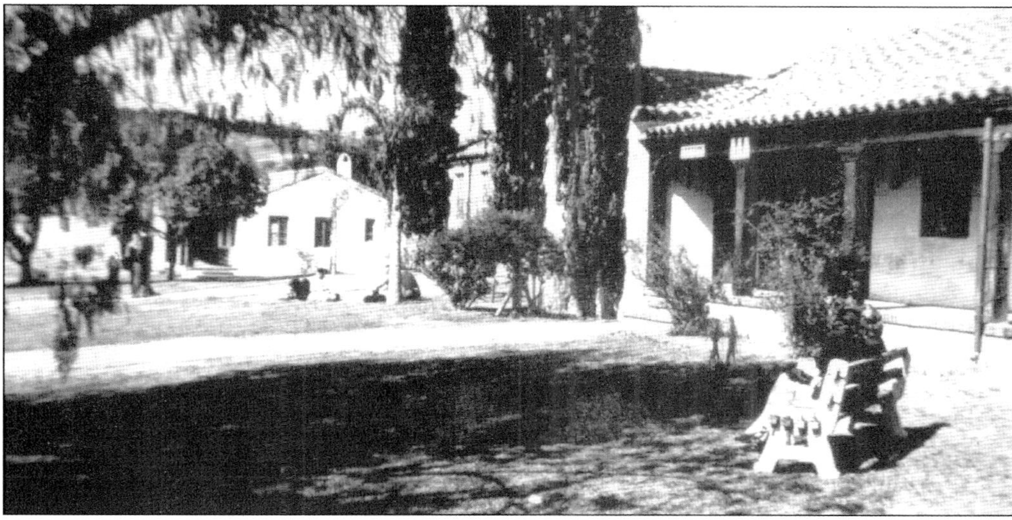

PACIFIC COLONY, 1910S. California state legislators recognized the need for an institution for the mentally infirm in Southern California. Pacific Colony was approved in 1917 and built for $250,000 on a site in Walnut. In 1921, the first patients or "inmates" were admitted with an anticipated capacity of 50. It soon became evident that the site was not appropriate due to lack of water and limited access. The facility closed its doors in 1923. The site and remaining buildings were used by Mount San Antonio College, which obtained the property after World War II.

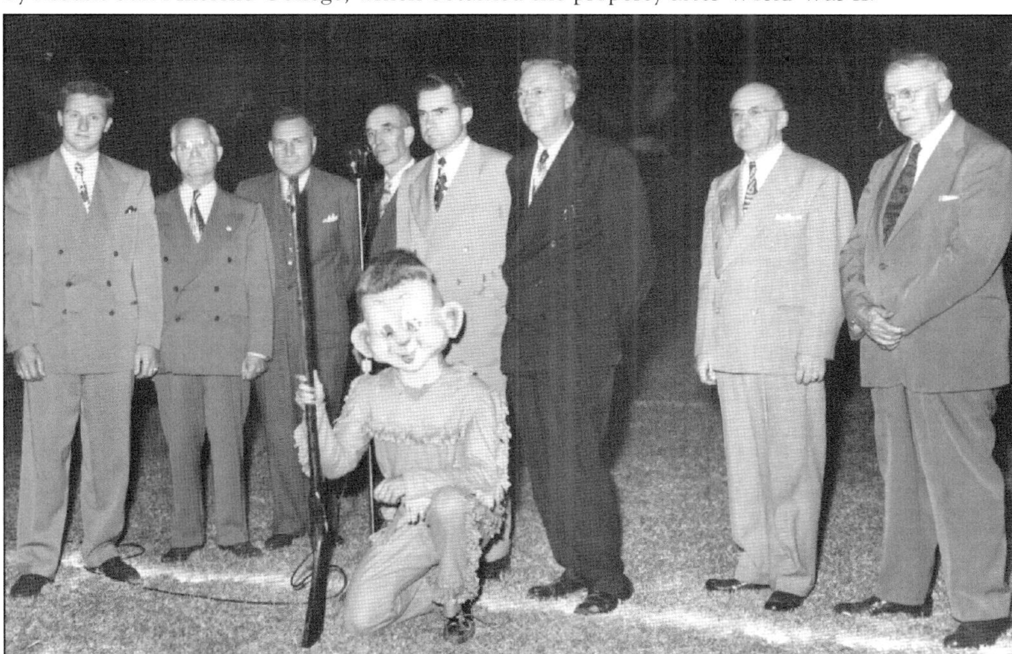

STADIUM DEDICATION, 1948. College development began in 1947, and sketches for a new stadium were approved. A year later, on October 8, 1948, Congressman Richard Nixon dedicated the Mount San Antonio College stadium. From left to right are student body president George Martin; trustees A.L. Hickman, Fred Harnsen and Herbert Langdon; Congressman Richard Nixon; school mascot Little Joe; Pres. George Bell; and trustees A.T. Richardson and Verne Ross.

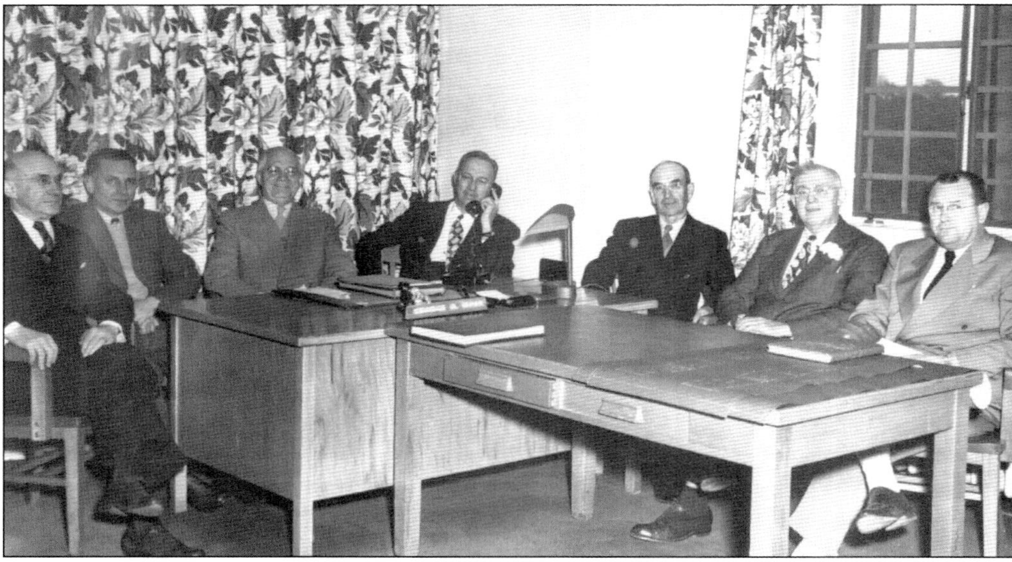

MOUNT SAN ANTONIO COLLEGE BOARD, 1949. From left to right are A.T. Richardson, Fred Harnsen, A.L. Hickson, Dr. George Bell, college president Herbert Langdon, Dr. Verne R. Ross, and director of instruction Oscar Edinger.

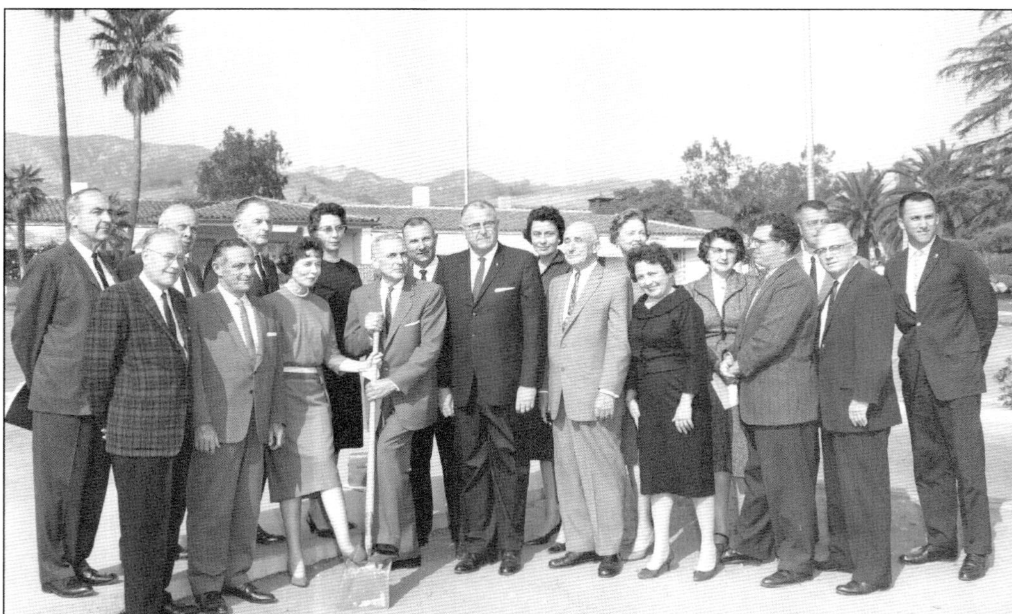

CAMPUS LIBRARY, 1949. The first library on campus was built in 1949. In the 1950s, it proved to be too small for the 1,500-student population. A new library was dedicated in 1961 with a final seating of 1,050. Then–Mount San Antonio College president Oscar Edinger's philosophy was "Large enough to serve you, small enough to know you." The two-level building was to serve a student population of 20,000. The philosophy of Oscar Edinger guided the design of all buildings and services on campus, especially the library, which was completed in 1963. The board of trustees, administrators, and librarians attended the ground-breaking for the new library in 1961.

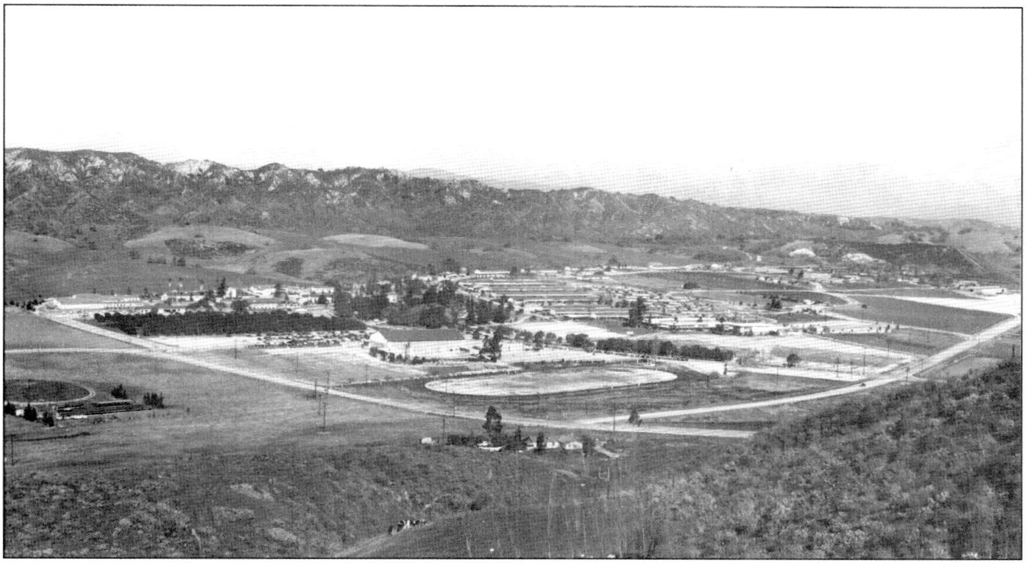

Mount San Antonio College Hills, 1950s. Hay and barley pastures surrounded Mount San Antonio College. Cattle belonging to Marin Itcea grazed from the area around the college to the corner of La Puente Road and Gartel Drive, where the teen center, gym, and senior center presently stand.

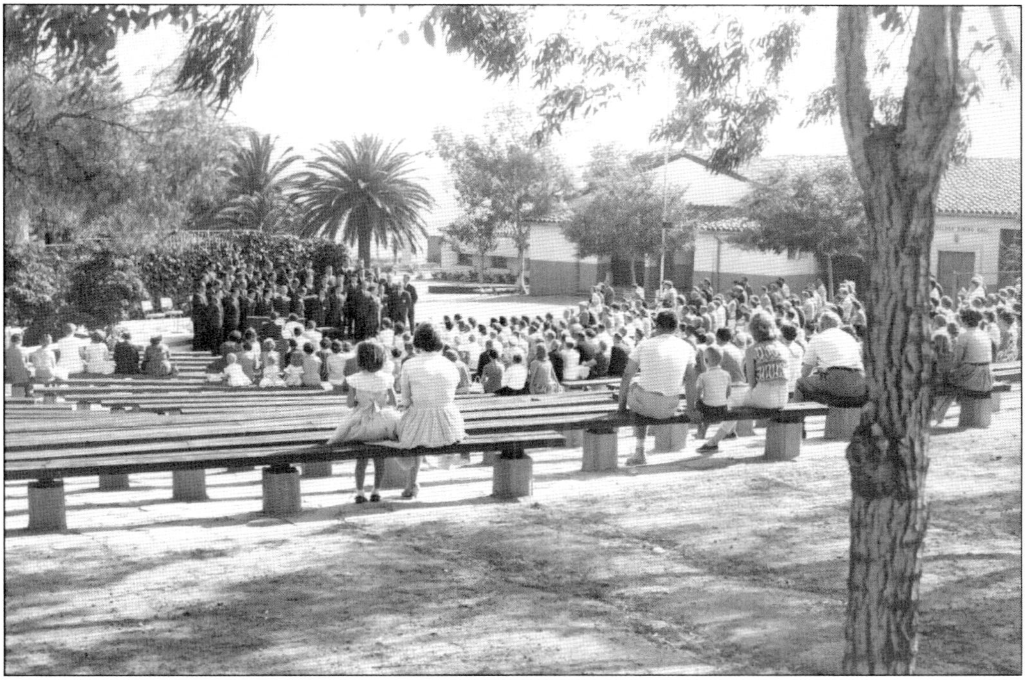

Rally Bowl Concert on Campus, 1950. Tom Oden began his career with the college as a janitor and then moved on to maintenance chief in 1946. Oden lived on campus with his family. During the first years of the college, there was little money available for maintenance and repairs. Oden saved the lumber from a water tank that was torn down and built benches in the rally bowl. The bowl was used for years for outdoor meetings and other functions.

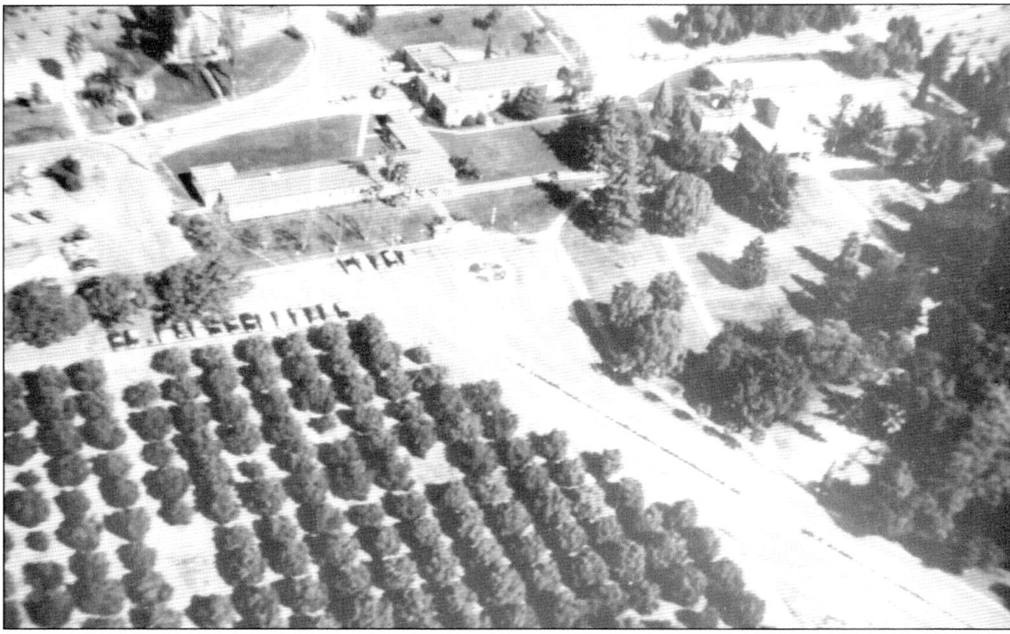

Campus Aerial View, 1953. The campus post office, the old chapel building, the rally bowl, the second library, and the president's office are nestled among the trees. Former Navy barracks were converted into classrooms, laboratories, and faculty offices. A large orange grove borders the college entrance leading to the administration and admission buildings.

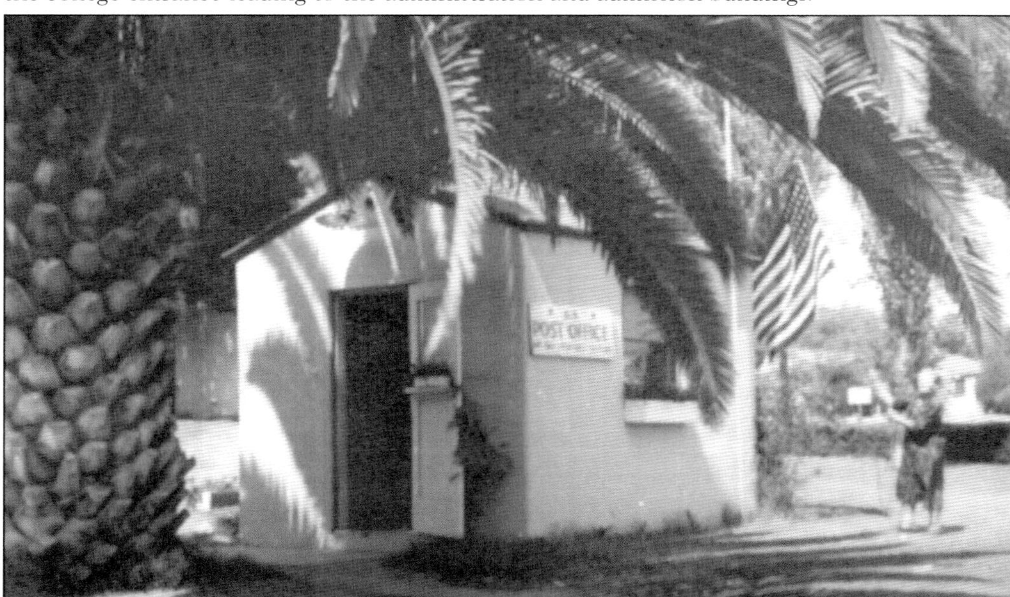

Mail from College Post Office, 1953. The 10-foot-by-12-foot building offered all the services of a big-city post office. It opened in 1949 and served as a college substation post office. Despite its small size, the substation handled more than 50,000 pieces of mail per year and made a substantial business in stamps and money orders. Mount San Antonio graduate manager Don Brooks served as the clerk. The substation closed in 1959.

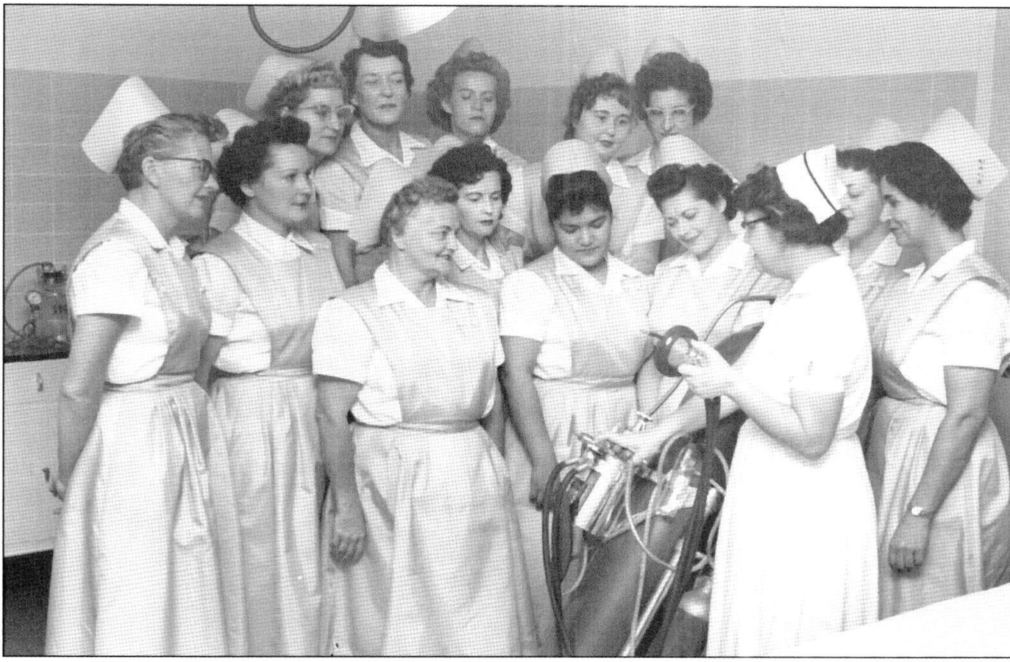

NURSING PROGRAM, 1950s. The first class of vocational nursing was offered in 1955, directed by Evelyn Chamberlin. Nursing courses began in the World War II barracks. The instructor arrived early to light oil stoves to warm the classrooms. Skunks could be heard rambling under the building during class. The students laboratory was a long room with six beds given to the college by a local hospital. In 1958, the associate degree program admitted its first class, and 15 students graduated in that year. In 1995, around 1,500 students graduated from the program.

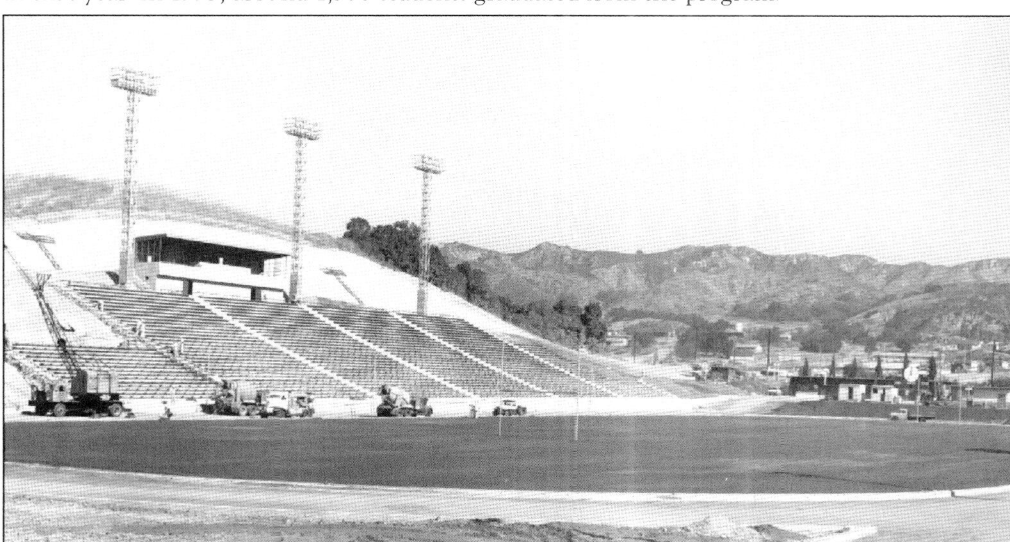

COLLEGE STADIUM, 1958. The Mount San Antonio College track and field stadium underwent a $425,000 remodeling in the late 1950s. The transformation was completed in 1959, just in time for the world-renowned Mount San Antonio College Relays. The stadium was renamed Hilmer Lodge Stadium in the 1960s.

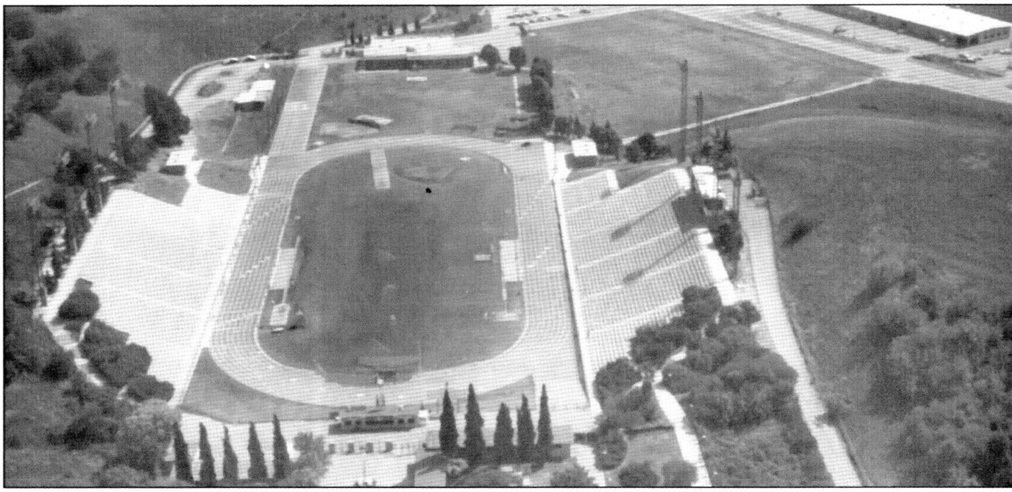

HILMER LODGE, LATE 1950s. As part of the 1959 Mount San Antonio College Relays steering committee, Hilmer Lodge was instrumental in planning the annual track and field event. That year, Hilmer convinced the board of trustees to construct a state-of-the-art track and field facility inside an already beautiful complex. Thus, in 1959, a major track and field event to match the well-established Penn and Drake Relays began. By 1985, the Mount San Antonio College Relays had become the largest meet in the world.

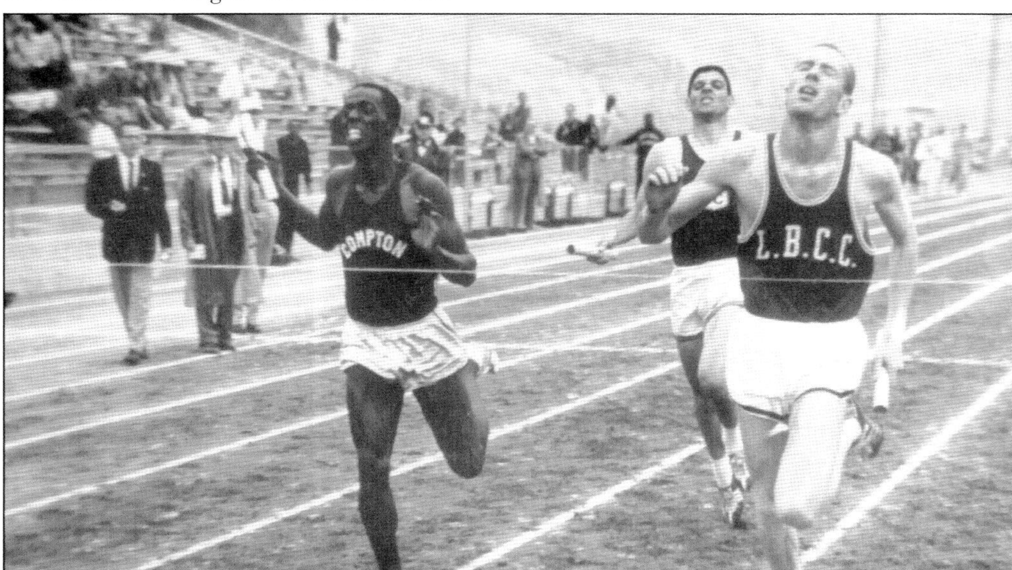

FIRST MOUNT SAN ANTONIO COLLEGE RELAYS, 1959. April 24 and 25 were cold and windy days for the first Mount San Antonio College Relays. The composition of the track was of volcanic ash, clay, and diatomaceous earth. When completed, it was considered one of the fastest all-weather tracks in the world. At the conclusion of the 1959 affair, *Track and Field News* reported, "The first annual Mount San Antonio College Relays got off to a good start with first class performances in every event and excellent standards of achievement in all areas. The West Coast's only two-day affair outclassed the old established meets by a wide margin in a competition of winning performances."

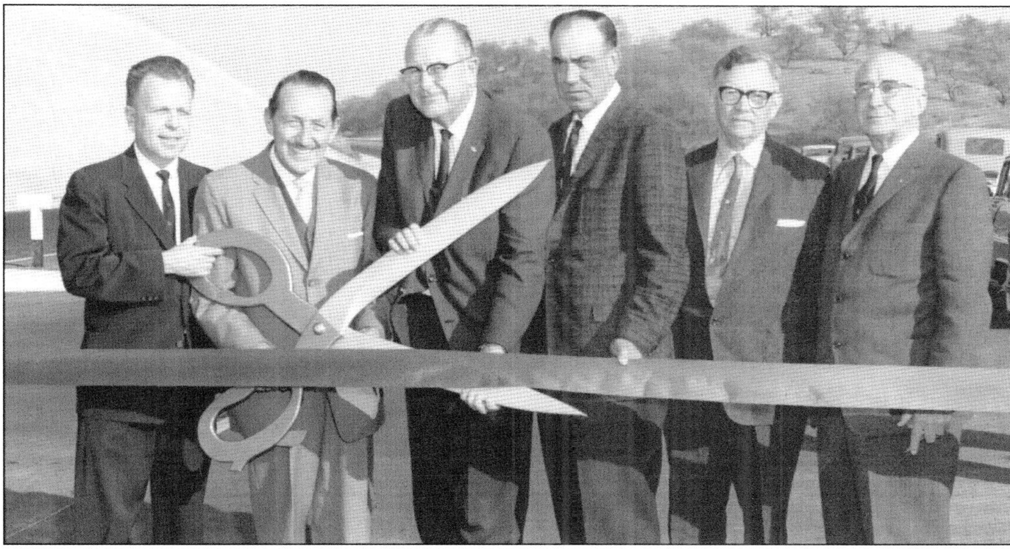

Temple Avenue Grand Opening, 1960s. From left to right are unidentified, supervisor Frank Bonelli, Mount San Antonio College president Dr. Oscar Edinger, mayor of the city of Walnut Pete Bourdet, and two unidentified. The opening of a new road, Temple Avenue, provided a more direct route to the city of Pomona. Temple Avenue also provided easy access to Mount San Antonio College and the college stadium.

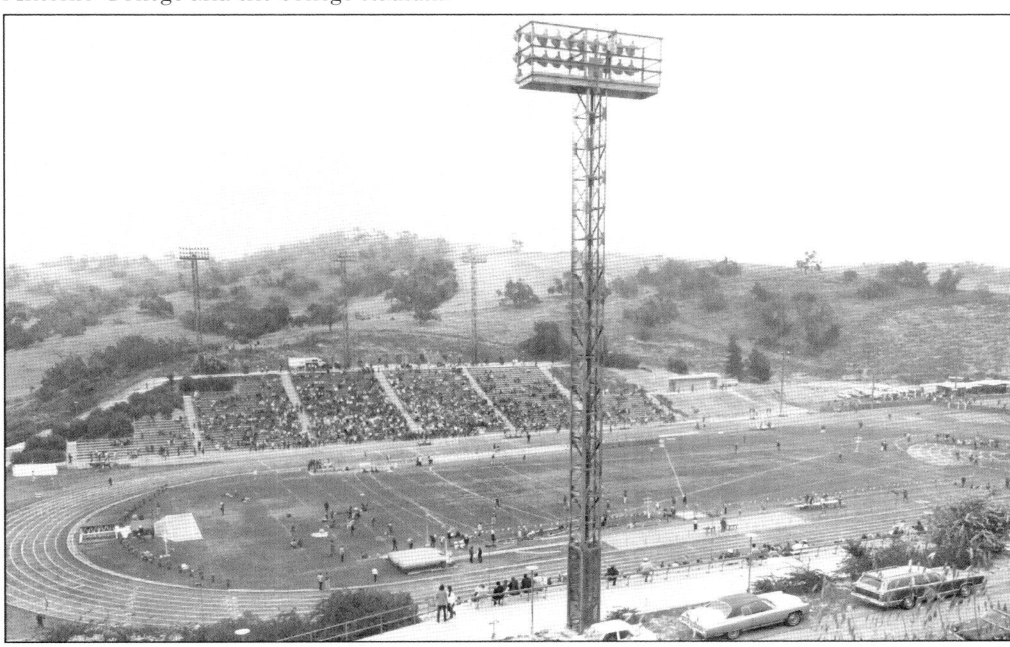

Getting Ready for the Relays, 1973. Mount San Antonio College's stadium served as the site for the 1960 and 1964 Olympic Track and Field Trials as well as the site for 20 world records. Held in April of each year, a short time before the Olympic Games, the Mount San Antonio College Relays has become a season opener for many Olympians from the United States and the world. By the 1980s, the stadium became an international affair as athletes from around the world attended, looking for quality competition in near ideal conditions.

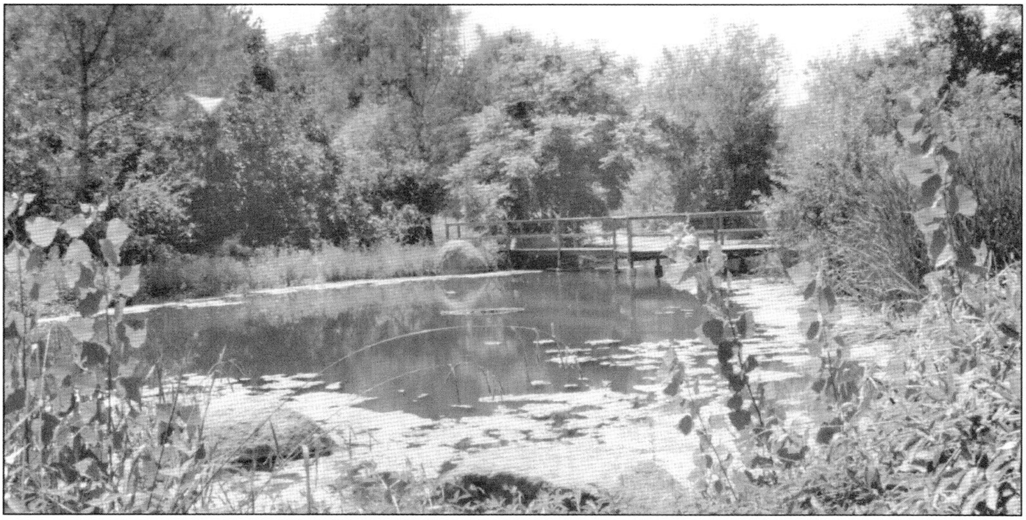

Wildlife Sanctuary, 1940s. Surrounded by foothills, the college was home to an abundance of wildlife. Many native birds, roadrunners, skunks, and coyotes lived in the swamp at the south edge of the property. Several deer could also be seen to the east, and large tarantulas, as well as rattlesnakes, roamed the campus. During the 1940s and 1950s, the campus posted warnings saying, "Rattlesnakes may be found in this area. They are important members of the natural community. They will not attack, but if disturbed or cornered, they defend themselves. Give them distance and respect." Another warning read, "No hunting on campus." The swamp became the wildlife sanctuary in 1964.

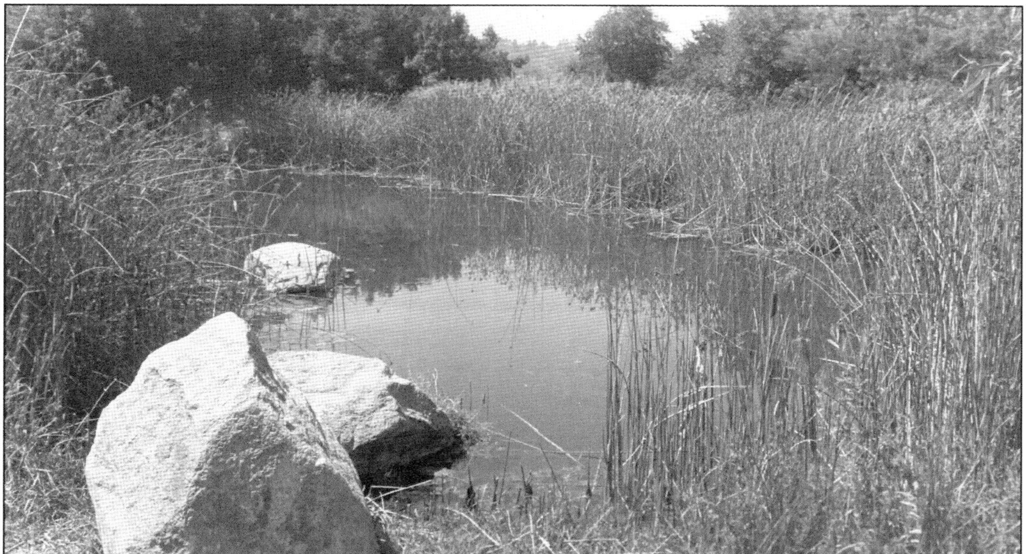

Wildlife Sanctuary, 1964. The Mount San Antonio Wildlife Sanctuary is a 10-acre protected and cultivated preserve. The sanctuary protects trees, shrubs, and flowers that once grew in abundance here, as well as birds and other animals that use it as a migratory refuge and breeding ground. It also supports a natural stream and pond, which has become a home and visitation spot for many bird species. The wildlife sanctuary was constructed in 1964 as a way to preserve the natural habitat of the Walnut Valley.

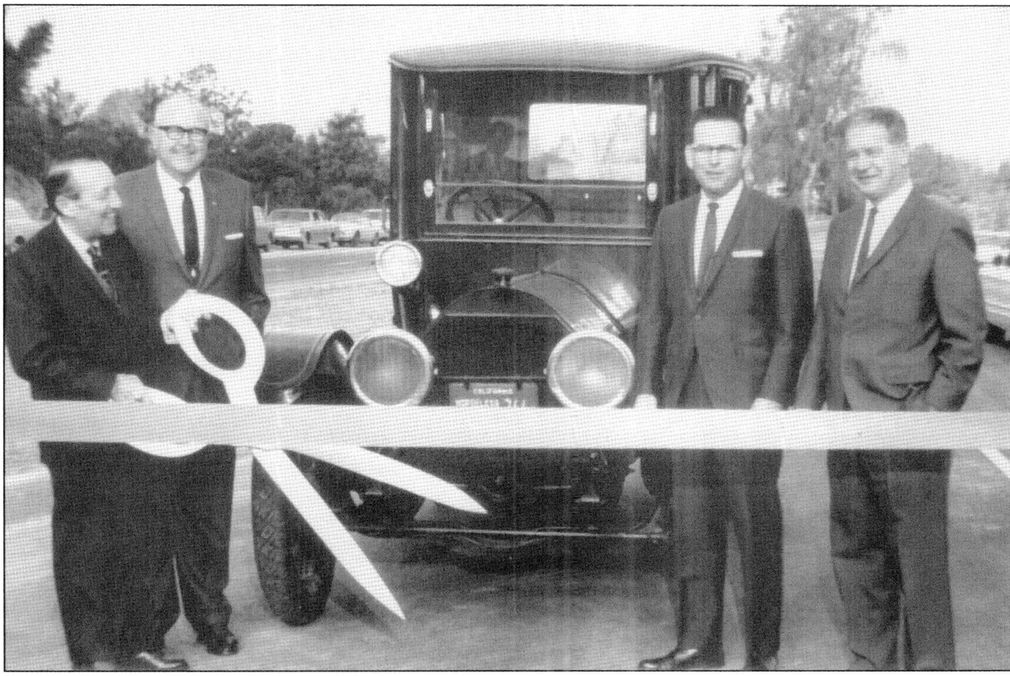

GRAND AVENUE DEDICATION, JANUARY 29, 1968. The ceremony took place in front of Mount San Antonio College. The following officials attend the ribbon cutting, from left to right: supervisor Frank Bonelli, Dr. Oscar H. Edinger Jr., city of Walnut mayor Lee Hale, and unidentified.

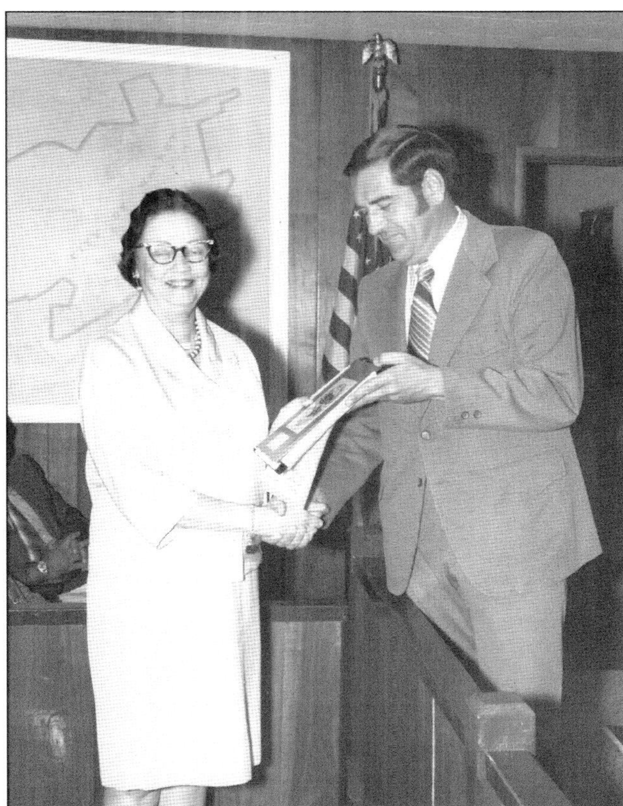

MARIE T. MILLS, 1969. Mayor Bill Wentworth presents a City of Walnut plaque to Marie T. Mills. As the only woman president to lead Mount San Antonio College, Mills was one of the earlier advocates for equal opportunity and diversity in higher education. She enhanced opportunities for women and students of color, hiring the college's first diversity coordinator to recruit and nurture African Americans, Latinos, and Asian–Pacific Islanders. Marie Mills joined the Mount San Antonio College staff in 1946 and retired in 1972.

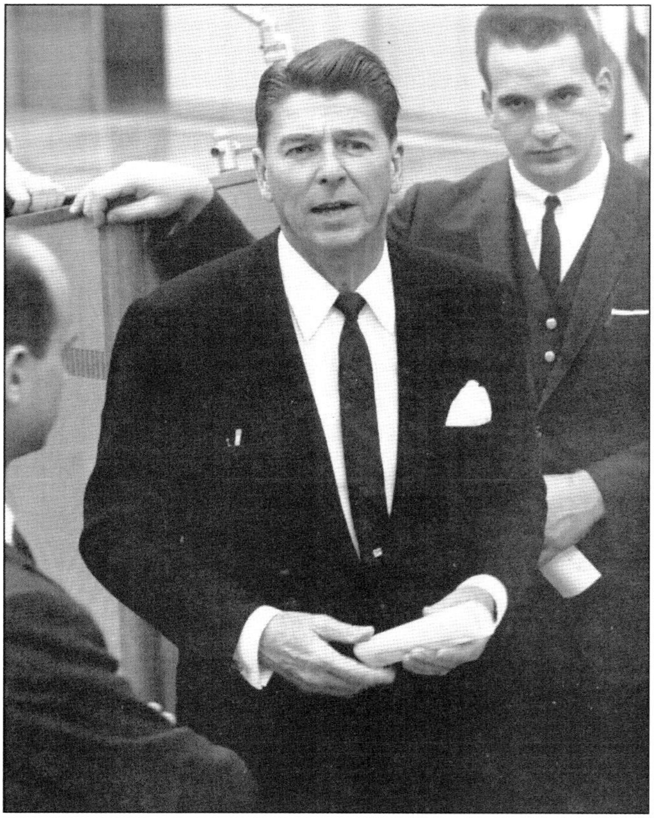

Classroom in the Sky, 1970s. Mount San Antonio College's astro-lunar mission, called Apollo 12, began in 1970. The program took learning to new heights in education with a Boeing 747 that served as a classroom. The flights brought together the study of aeronautics, geography, history and mathematics. Gov. Ronald Reagan visited Mount San Antonio College in 1973 to honor the college for this program. During its 10-year run, the program drew worldwide attention for its unique approach to higher education.

Walnut City Council Helps Kick-Off Relays, 1971. From left to right are council members Dick Laughter, Louise Huff, unidentified, Mount San Antonio College president Marie Mills, Mayor Bill Cheek, and council members Bill Wentworth and Joe Dyer.

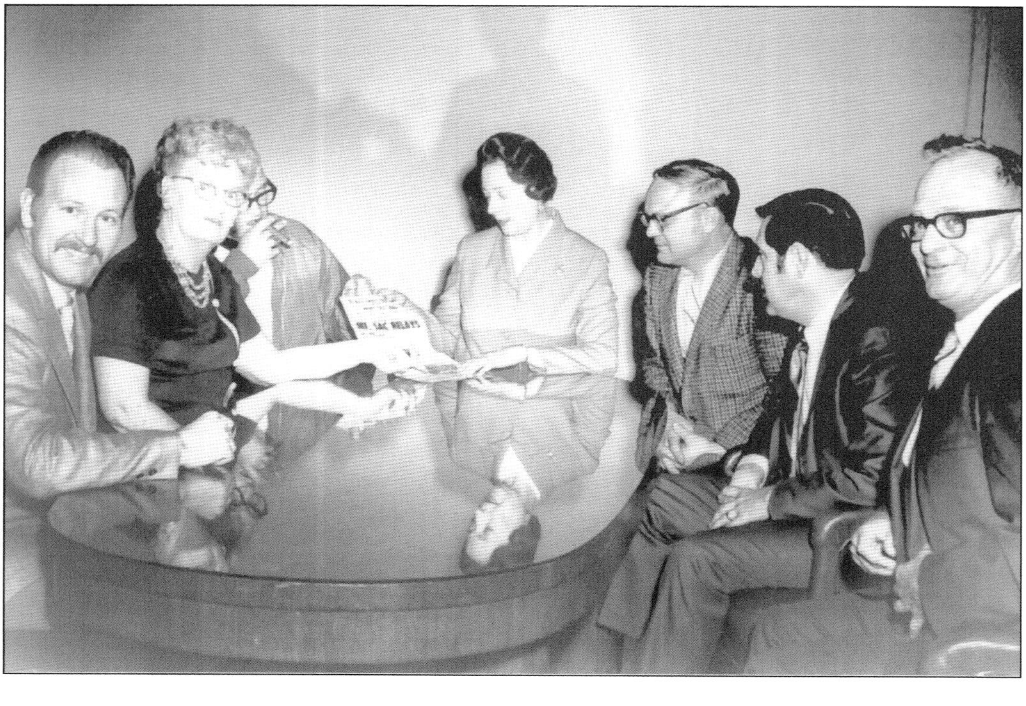

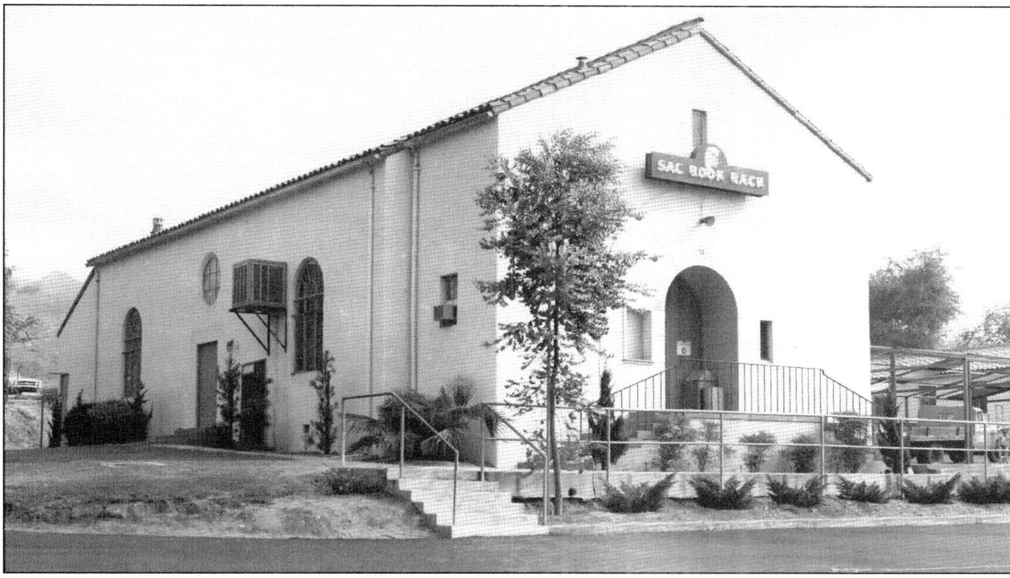

BOOK RACK, 1940S. At the opening of the college, the bookstore was used as a chapel for concerts, meetings, and plays. In 1972, the building was torn down to make room for the art center. The chapel was used in 1947 as the official site for the college dedication overseen by college president Dr. George Bell.

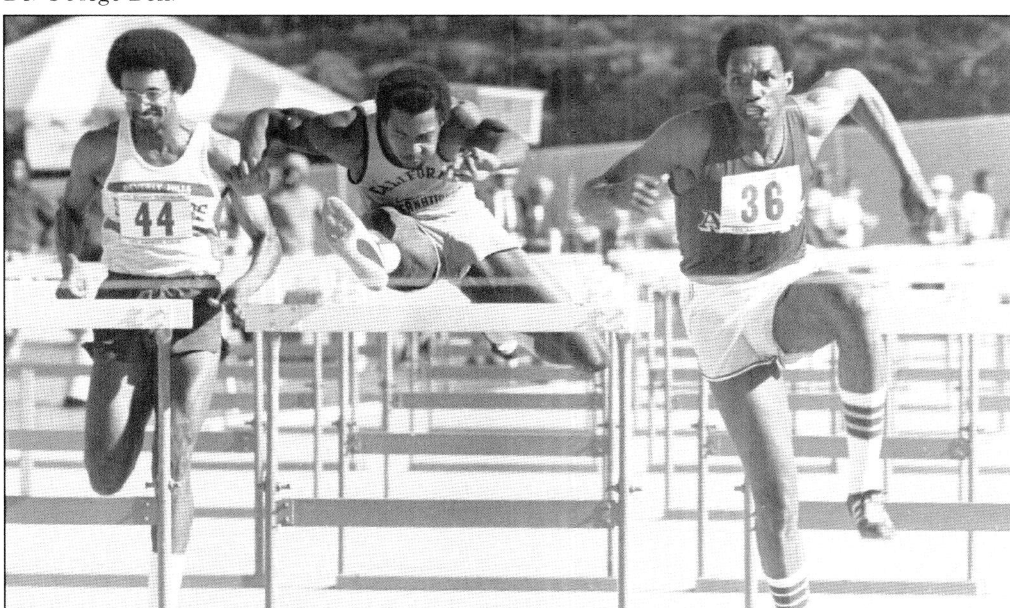

OLYMPIC ATHLETES, 1960S. From left to right, athletes Tommie Lee White, Charles Rich, and Tom Hill were joined by University of California, Los Angeles' James Owens and Willie Davenport at the Mount San Antonio Relays. One of the first hurdle competitions took place at the 1977 relays. Willie Davenport was honored with induction into the Mount San Antonio College Hall of Fame. Willie Davenport, who has competed in the relays since 1968, won an Olympic gold medal in 1968. During his preparation for the 1968 Olympics, Willie won his first relays title.

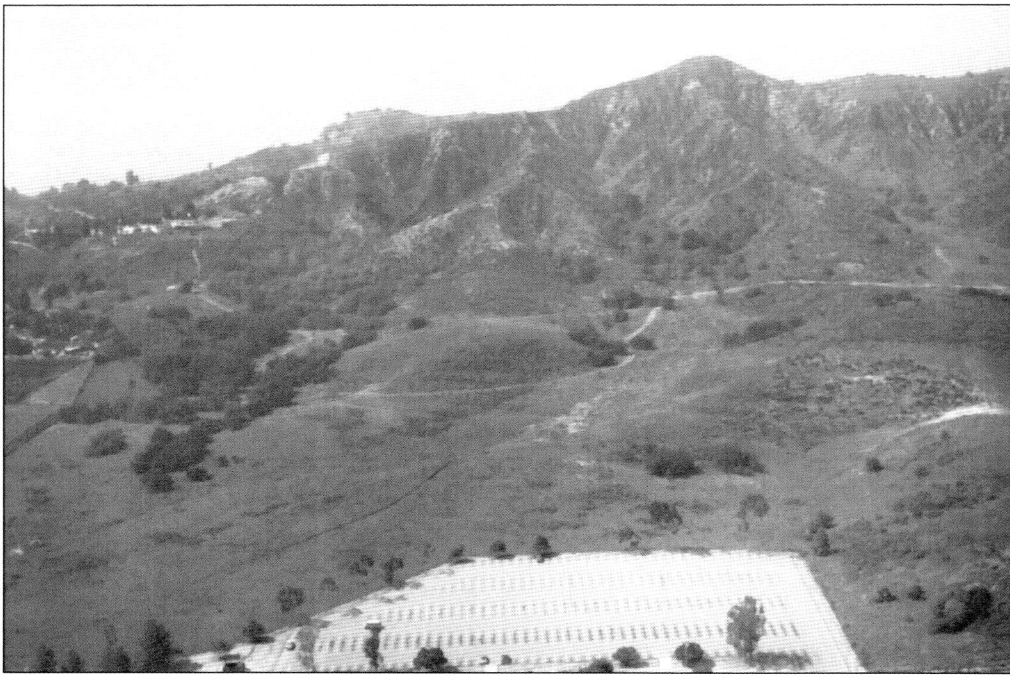

BUZZARD'S PEAK, 1980S. The area of Walnut north of Mount San Antonio College is now home to Timberline, a housing development built in the late 1980s or early 1990s. The peaks of the mountains can be seen above Timberline and are part of Walnut's open space. In 2011, Walnut had 90 acres of parks, 2 miles of bridle trials, and over 425 acres of open space. The city is 95 percent residential, 5 percent commercial and industrial, and 98 percent built according to the zoning ordinances.

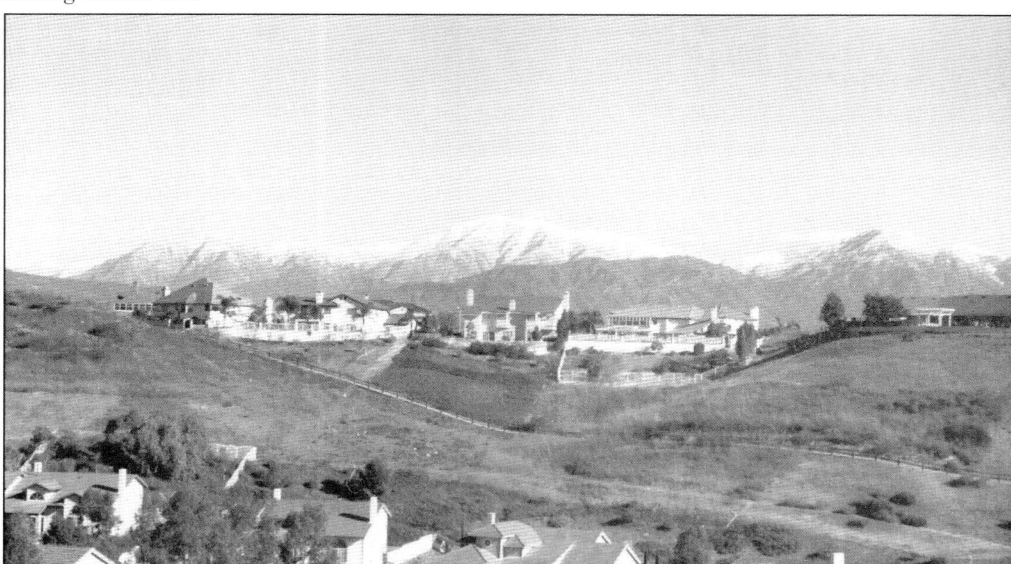

MOUNT BALDY, 1980S. Nicknamed "Mount Baldy," snowcapped Mount San Antonio can be seen from all areas of Walnut. Residents and visitors enjoy magnificent views during the wintertime.

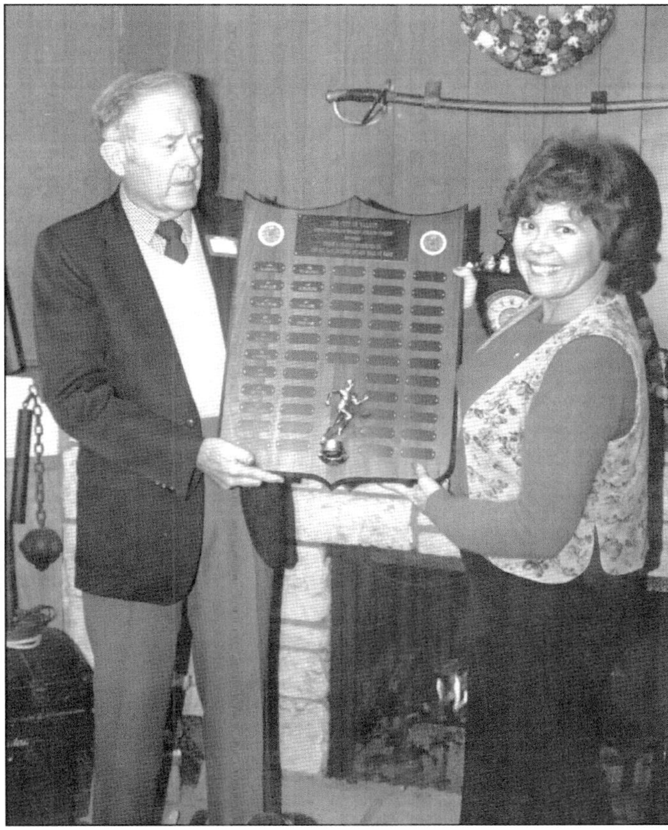

Larry Stout Honored, 1983. The City of Walnut honors athletes, coaches, and relay committee members who are in the Mount San Antonio Relays Hall of Fame. In 1983, Walnut mayor Harvey Holden presented the Hilmer Lodge Memorial Plaque honoring Larry Stout for outstanding contributions by a relay committee member.

Mount San Antonio College 60th Anniversary, 2006. From left to right are Pres. Chris O'Hearn and trustees Fred Chyr, David Hall, Judy Chen Haggerty, Rosanne Bader, and Manuel Baca.

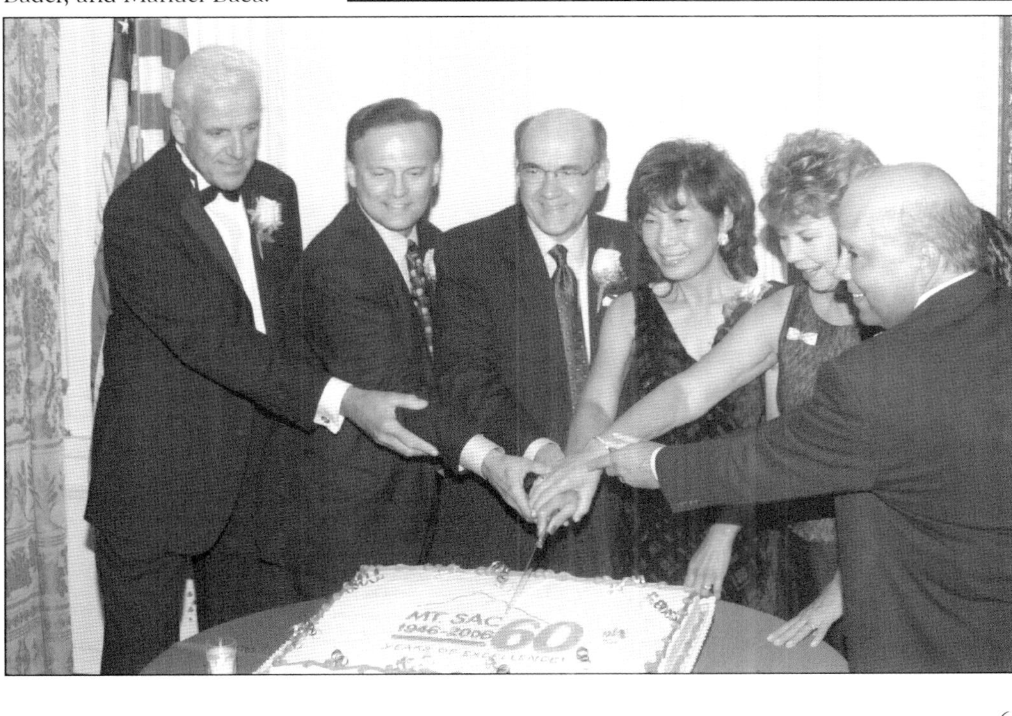

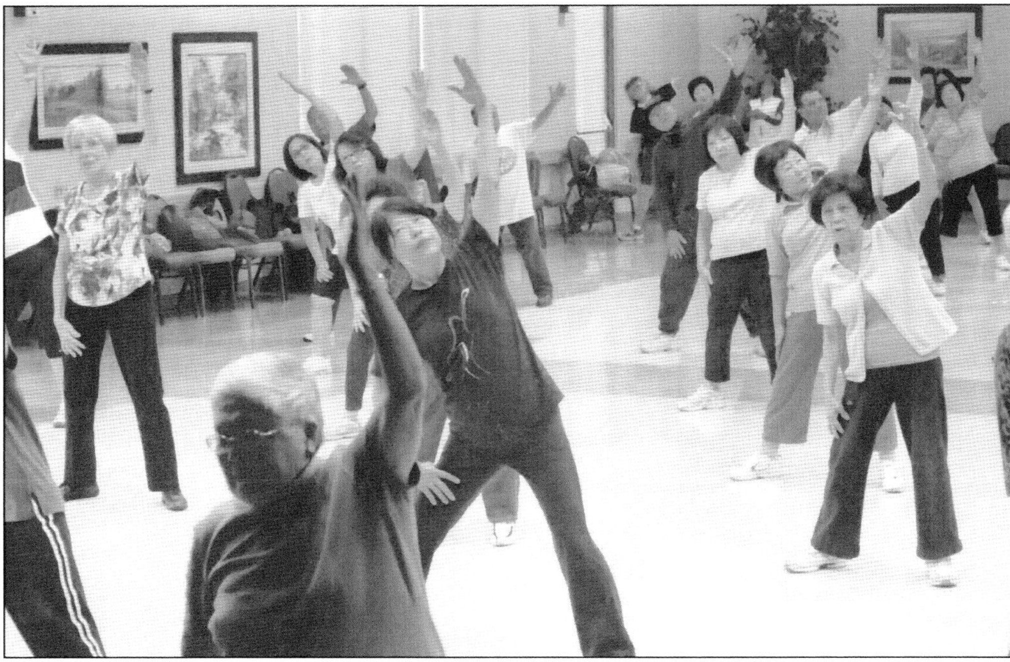

COMMUNITY SERVICES DEPARTMENT, 2011. In 1971, Mount San Antonio College developed the Community Services Department to provide cultural and educational programs to the local community. In 1978, the program expanded to include new areas of education, including basics skills, English as a second language (ESL), older adult, disabled, parent education, and health and fitness. Community enrichment and fee-based classes were part of the division's expansion as well. The Continuing Education Division has grown to one of the largest noncredit programs in the state of California.

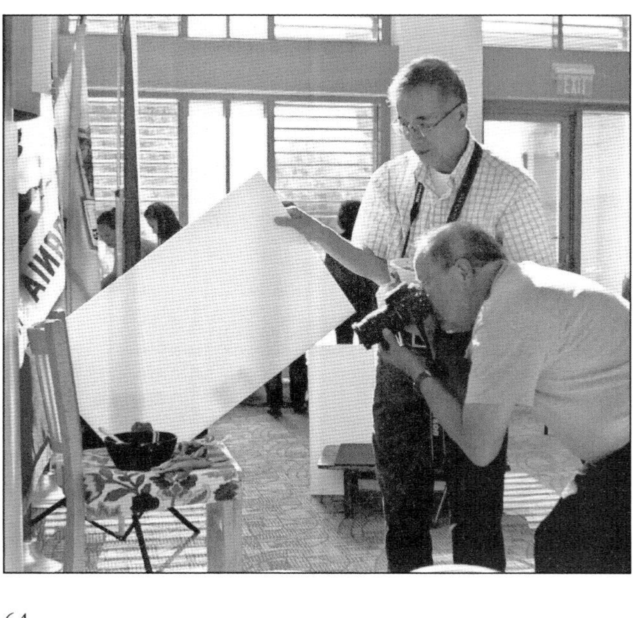

OLDER ADULT PROGRAM, 2011. Mount San Antonio College has many older adult classes in addition to the health and wellness class offerings. Popular classes among the seniors are computing and digital photography. Learning how to become a stylist and then do a photo shoot with their cameras was taught by instructor Linda Chang at the Diamond Bar Community Center. The Older Adult Program has approximately 6,000 seniors enrolled in various activities. These classes are held off campus at various locations, including the Senior Center in the City of Walnut.

Five

How It All Began

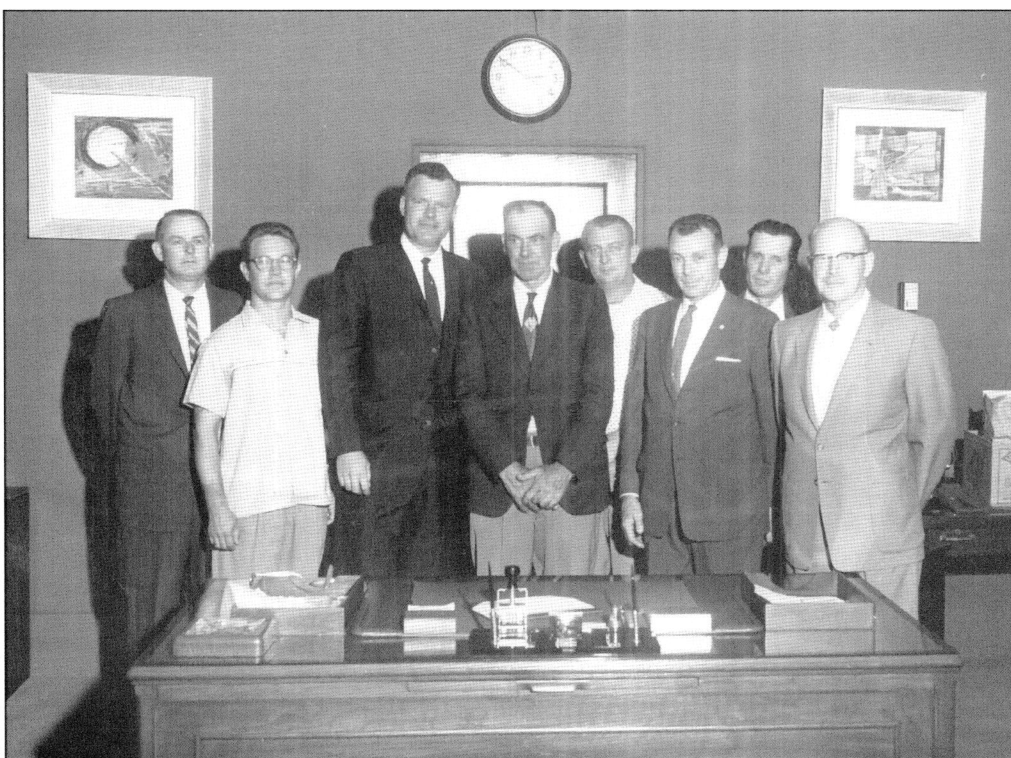

First City Council, 1959. From left to right are unidentified, City Clerk John Tapp, unidentified, Mayor Pete Bourdet, council members Max Fiegles, Leroy Coates, and Robert Carrey, and Vice Mayor Leonard Westhoff. The men roused a population of 934 into a successful incorporation movement in 1958, when area residents became concerned over City of Industry and West Covina annexing large parcels of land. Not wanting to be part of either city, they incorporated into their own city and named it Walnut.

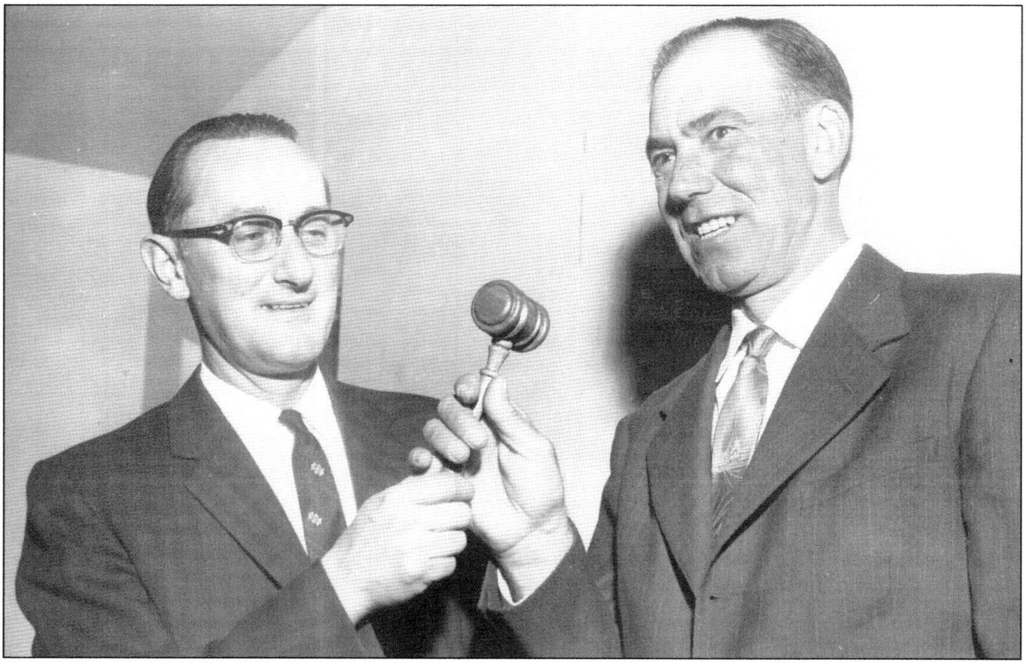

MAYOR PETE BOURDET ACCEPTS GAVEL, 1959. The City of Walnut was incorporated at 3:23 p.m. on January 19, 1959, with a population of less than a thousand and a budget of $10,000. Born and raised in Walnut, Pete Bourdet (right) became Walnut's first mayor and served in that position for three and half years. Seen here, the official city certification ceremony took place at Mount San Antonio College.

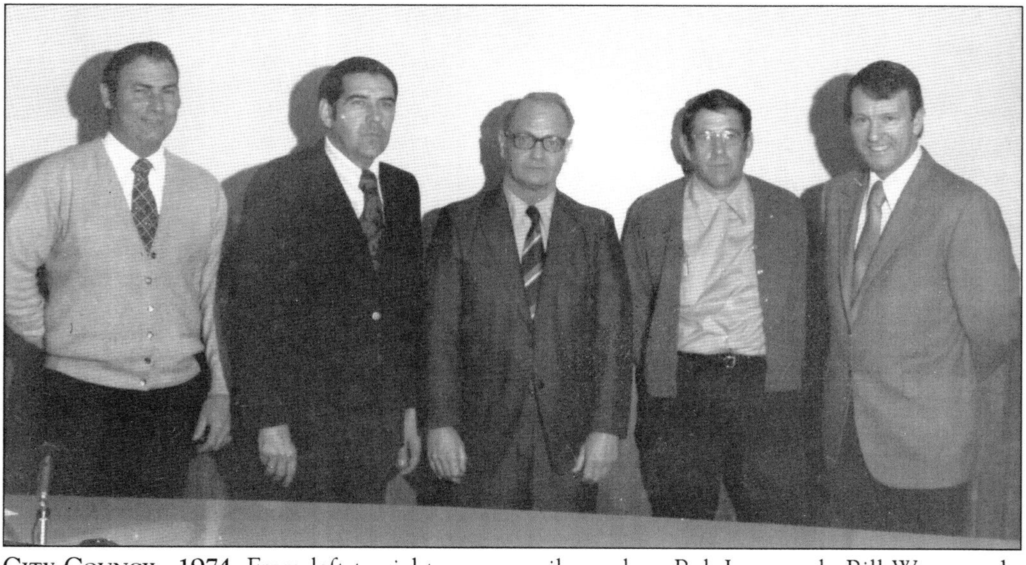

CITY COUNCIL, 1974. From left to right are council members Bob Lovemark, Bill Wentworth, Mayor Pro Tem Joe Dyer, council member Bill Cotton, and Mayor Dick Laughter. The council at this time worked on a more conducive land use plan to fit the rolling hills surrounding the city. Walnut was envisioned as a city of 60,000 to 90,000 people, but this belief changed in the 1970s. In 2011, Walnut has a population of more than 29,000—the city's maximum zoning density.

RAISING THE FLAG, 1959. The City of Walnut's first council meetings were held in the mayor's office. An old door placed over two cardboard boxes served as a meeting table. The public looked through windows to give testimony during oral communications. Here, Mayor Pete Bourdet supervises the raising of the flag in June 1959.

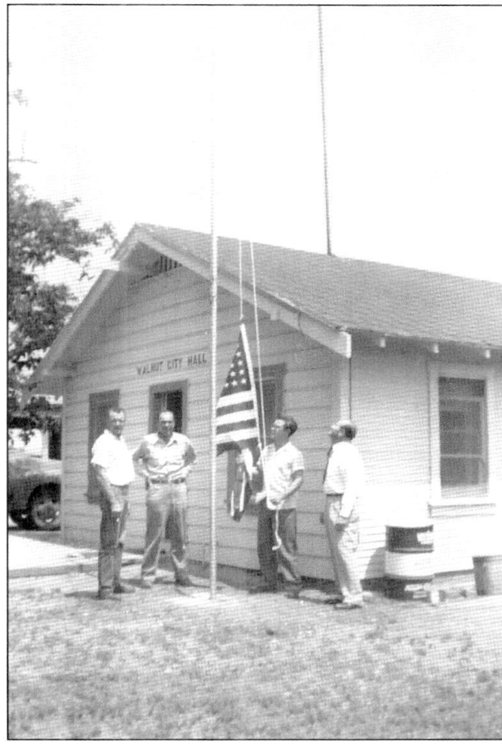

CITY HALL, 1960S. The second city hall, which faced Carrey Road, was a donated house transported and placed on leased property for $1 a year. The room on the west side of the home was used as a council chamber; it housed the planning staff when no council or planning meetings were being held. The east side consisted of offices—one for the city manager, who also acted as city clerk; treasurer; and deputy city clerk. Another room was used by additional staff and a counter for the public. The small house had a kitchen and a bathroom. The County of Los Angeles provided police and fire services.

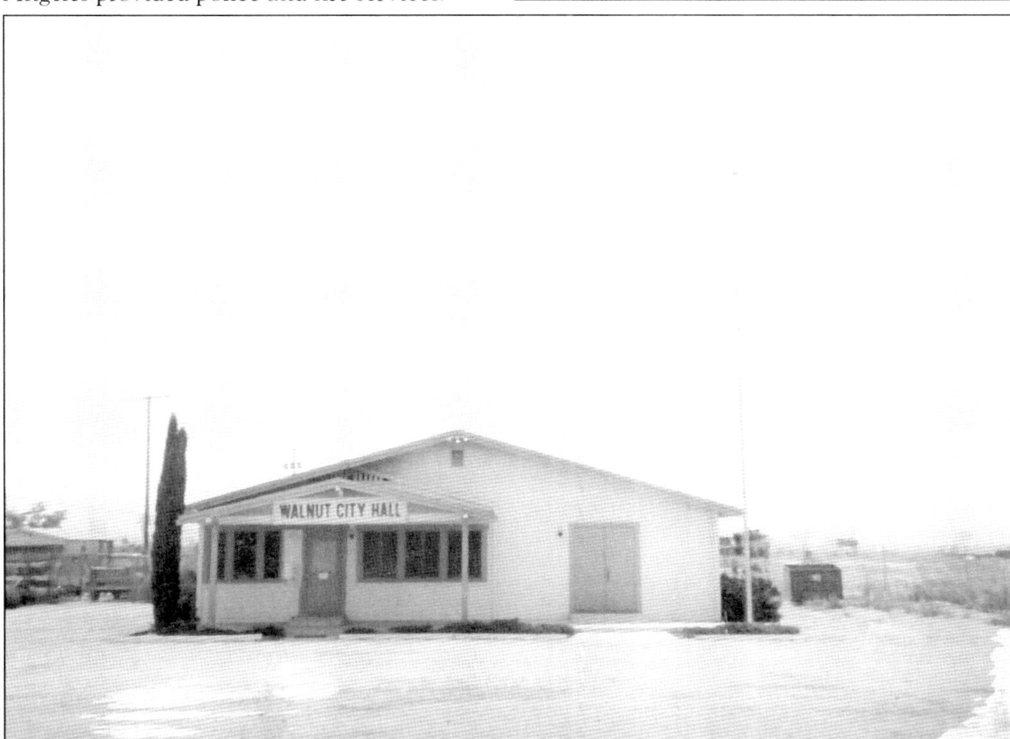

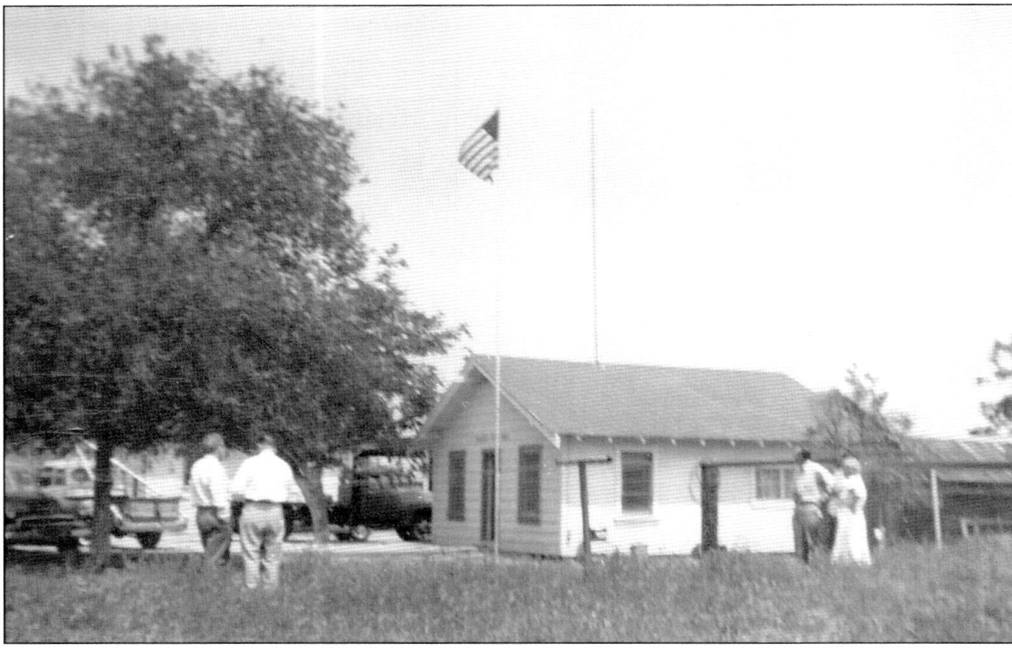

City Clerk John Tapp and Treasurer Peggy Davis, 1959. City hall was a converted 12-foot-by-20-foot garage donated by the Carrey family. Despite its tiny size, the office proved adequate for the staff of two, except for popular meetings, which included three public hearings on a new zoning ordinance. The hearings were held at Walnut School on Lemon Avenue, which was not within the city boundaries.

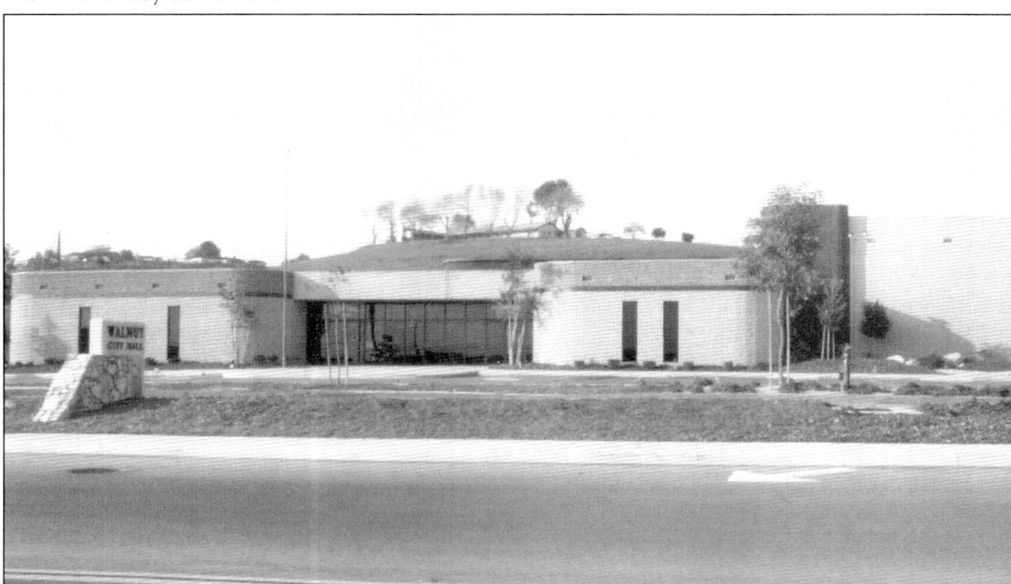

City Hall, 1982. Located on La Puente Road, the one-floor building contained a community room for city functions. It was torn down in 2001 to make room for a new city hall. The staff was moved to an industrial location on Lemon Avenue and Valley Boulevard for a year during construction. Council meetings were held in the Walnut Senior Center on La Puente Road.

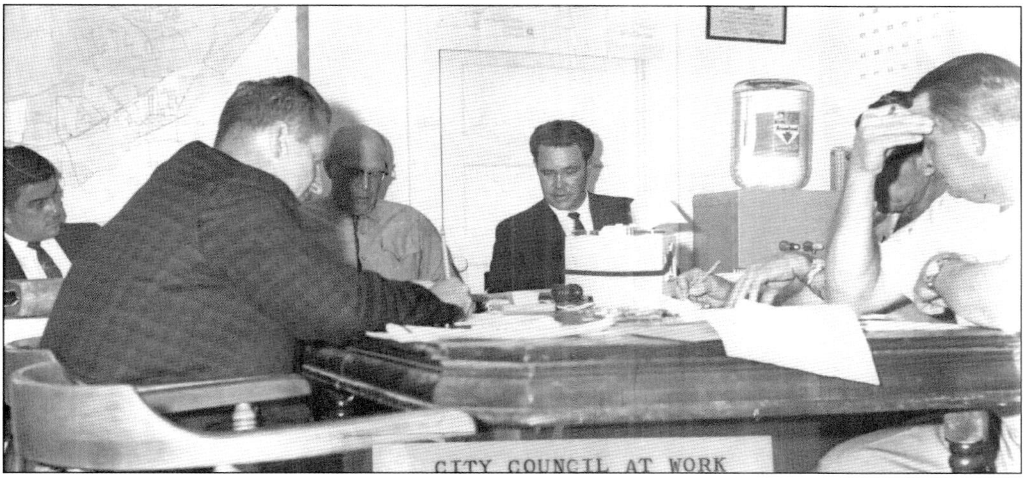

CITY COUNCIL, 1963. The council is hard at work discussing future plans for the city. From left to right are council member Dick Sears, city attorney Howard Black, Mayor Leonard Westhoff, city clerk John Tapp, and council members Leroy Coats and Max Feigles. Zoning ordinances for land use, streets, sewer, and water supplies were high on their list for consideration.

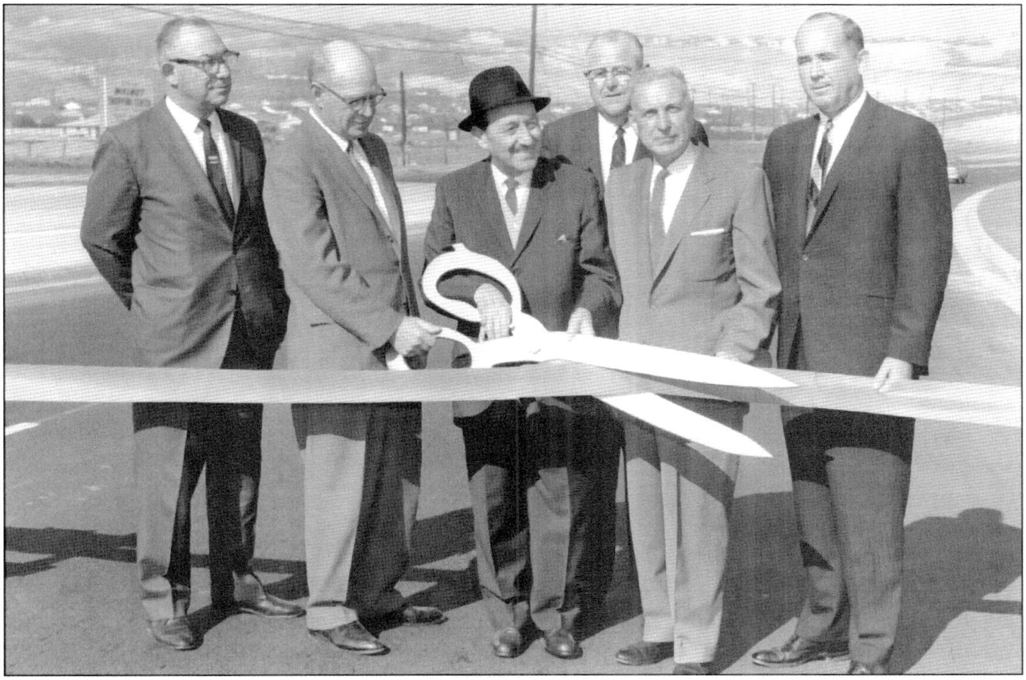

GRAND AVENUE GRAND OPENING, 1964. From left to right are Mount San Antonio College president Dr. Oscar H. Edinger Jr., Mayor Leonard Westhoff, supervisor Frank Bonelli, unidentified, Mount San Antonio College trustee Fred Harnsen, and unidentified. Grand Avenue going north was a small two-lane road that was widened to four lanes to accommodate traffic in front of Mount San Antonio College. According to Oscar Edinger, "It is a first step in a long-awaited move to provide access via Grand Avenue from the San Bernardino Freeway to Valley Boulevard, eliminating San Jose Hills Road, which was considered to be a narrow, winding two-lane road which constitutes a serious hazard."

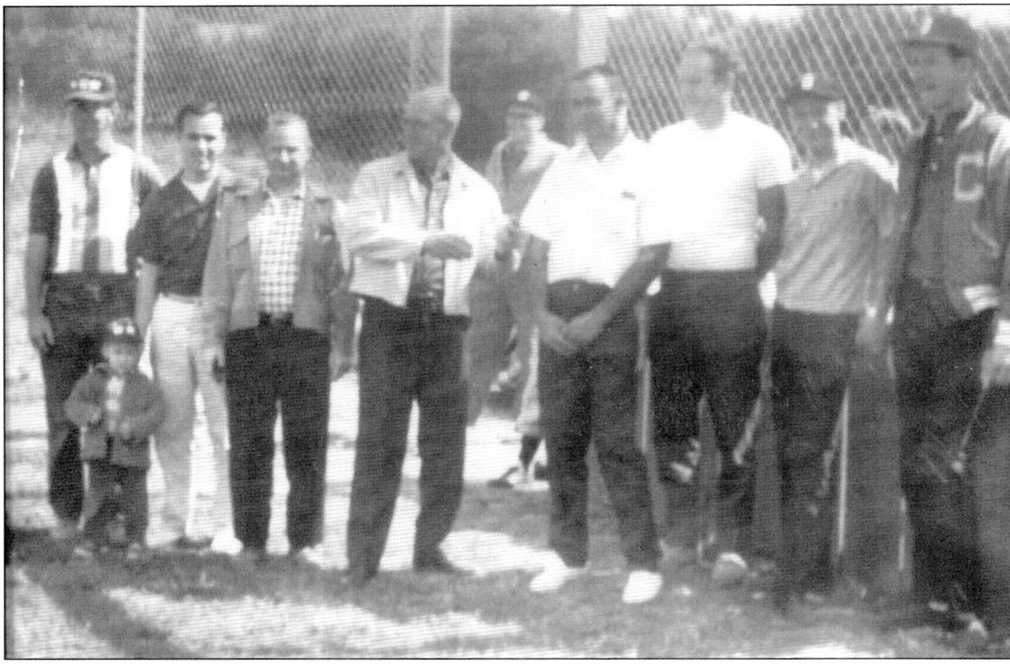

Pony Baseball, 1964. Walnut mayor Leonard Westhoff throws out the first ball for Walnut Valley Pony Baseball League in 1964 at Suzanne Park. He is joined by Pony Baseball team managers and council members Don Risk and Max Feigles.

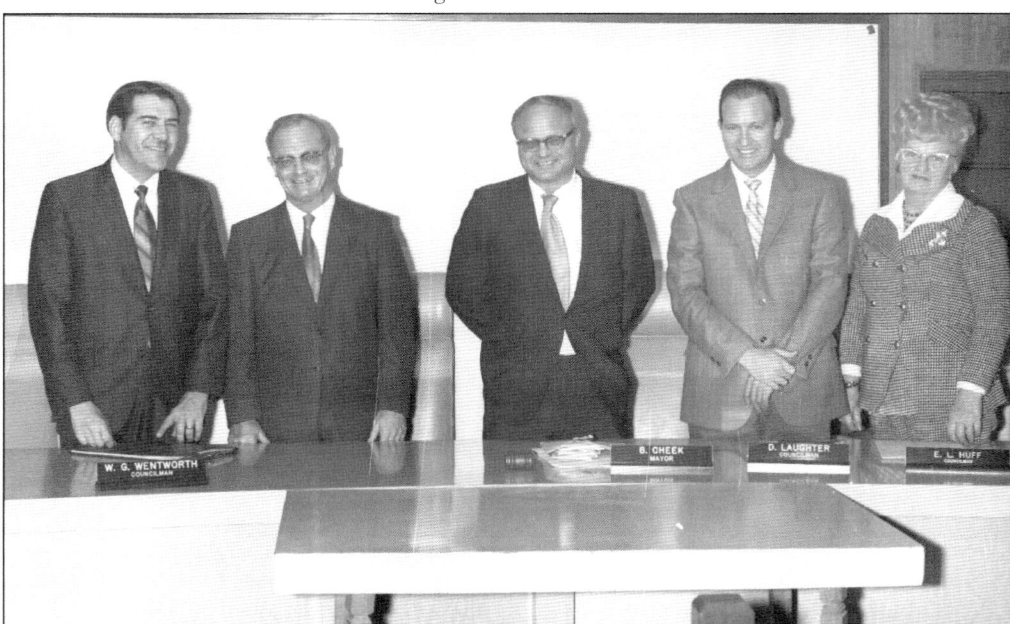

City Council, 1970. From left to right are Mayor Pro Tem Bill Wentworth, council member Joe Dyer, Mayor Bill Cheek, and council members Dick Laughter and Louise Huff. The council welcomed Joe Dyer in December 1970 to replace Bill Daley, who resigned and moved out of the city.

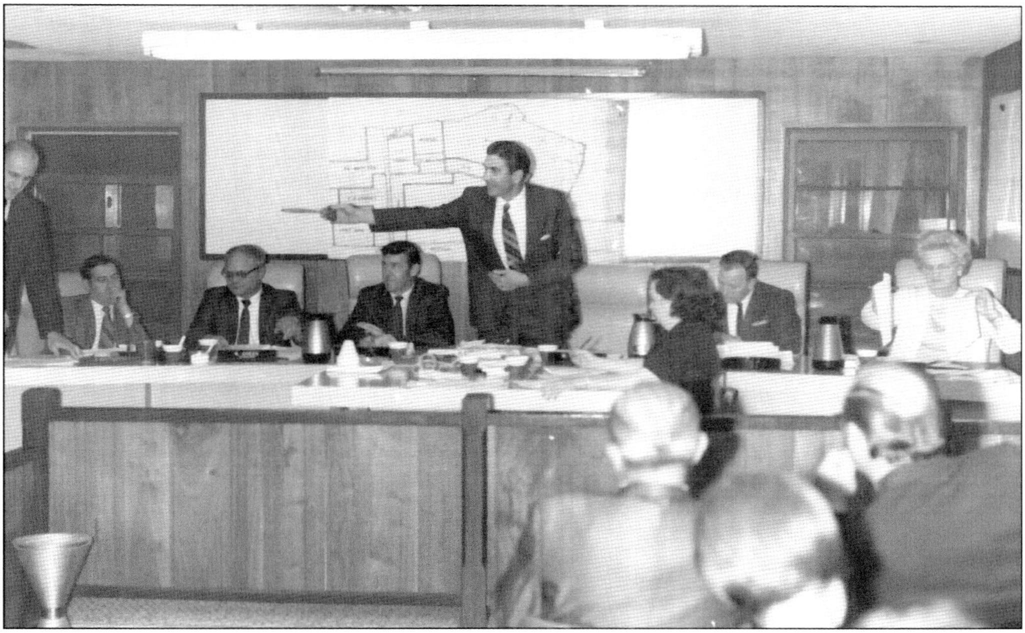

CITY COUNCIL, 1970. From left to right are city manager Andy Lazaretto, council member William Wentworth, Mayor Pro Tem Bill Cheek, city attorney Michael O'Shea, Mayor Bill Daley, council members Dick Laughter and Louise Huff, and secretary Evelyn Ivins (in front of the table). The council gets ready to change hands and elect a new mayor.

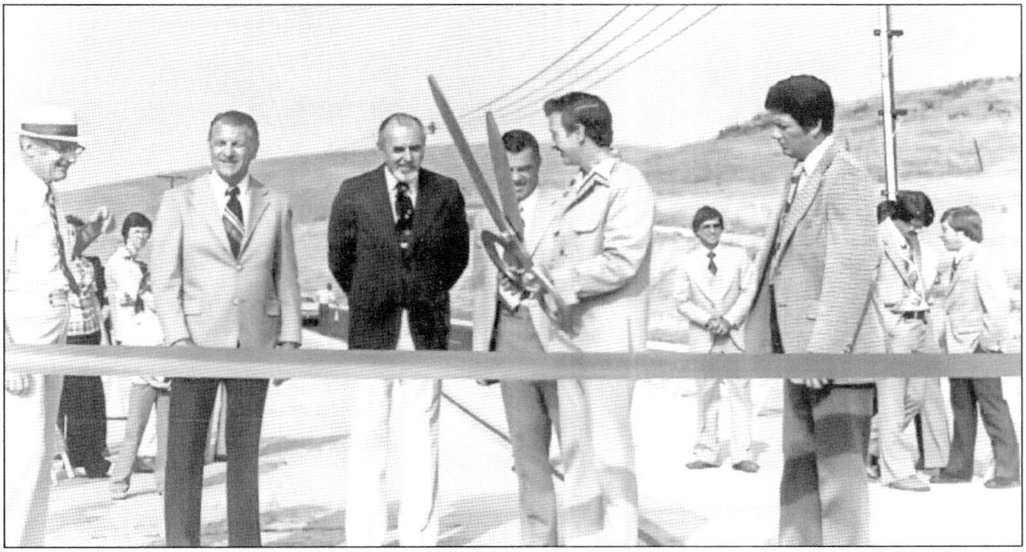

RIBBON CUTTING, LATE 1970S. Mayor Joe Hahn and council members Dick Laughter and Paul Williams attend the ceremony for the realignment of La Puente Road. When the council adopted the Residential Planned Development (RDP) ordinance for Shea property off Grand Avenue and Valley Boulevard, part of the ordinance was to rezone the property into C3, which included the realignment of La Puente Road. This gave Shea a piece of land on both corners of the streets to build a large shopping center. In the early 2000s, Majestic Realty built a commercial center called The Village.

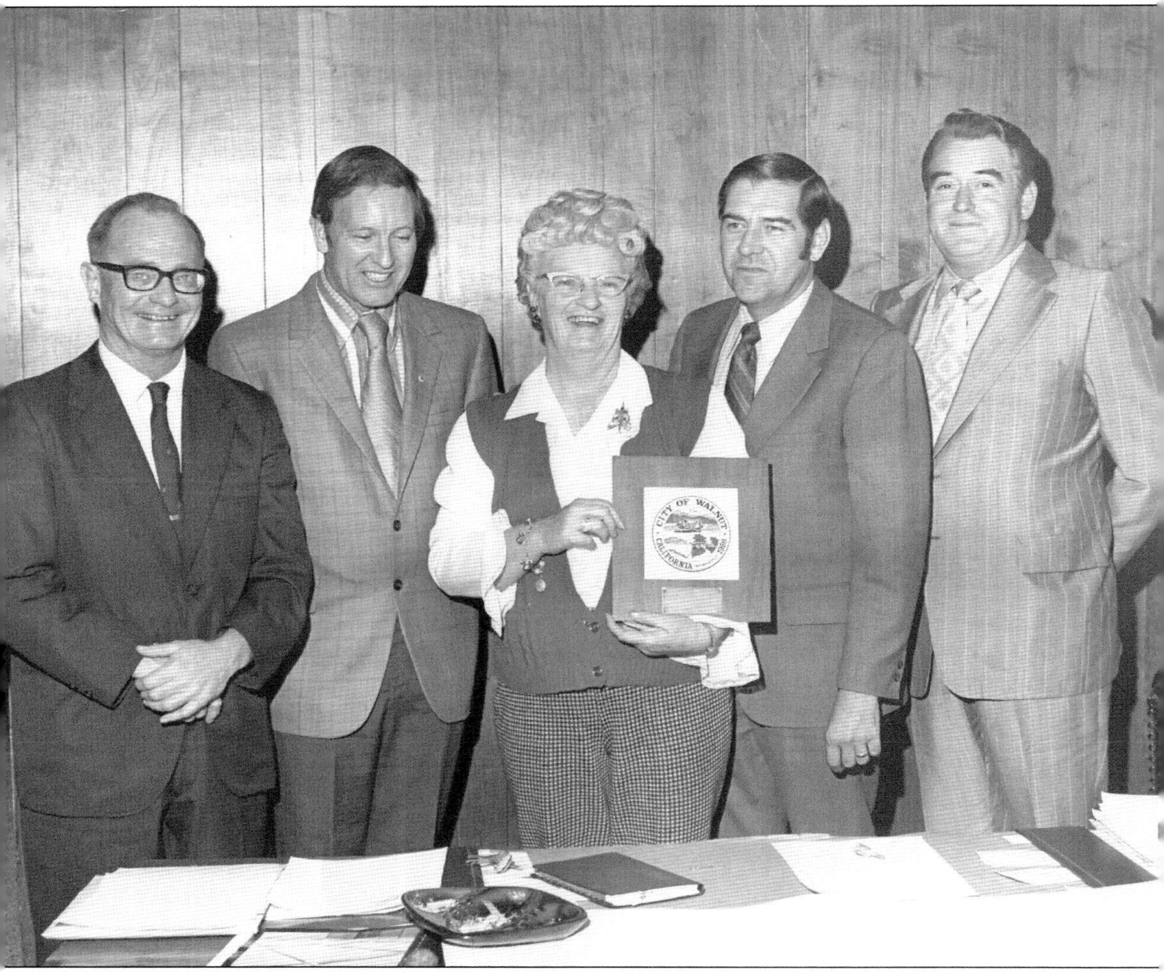

CITY COUNCIL, 1972. From left to right are council member Joe Dyer, Mayor Pro Tem Dick Laughter, Louise Huff, Mayor Bill Wentworth, and council member Bob Beck. The council congratulates outgoing council member Louise Huff; she served as mayor in 1971.

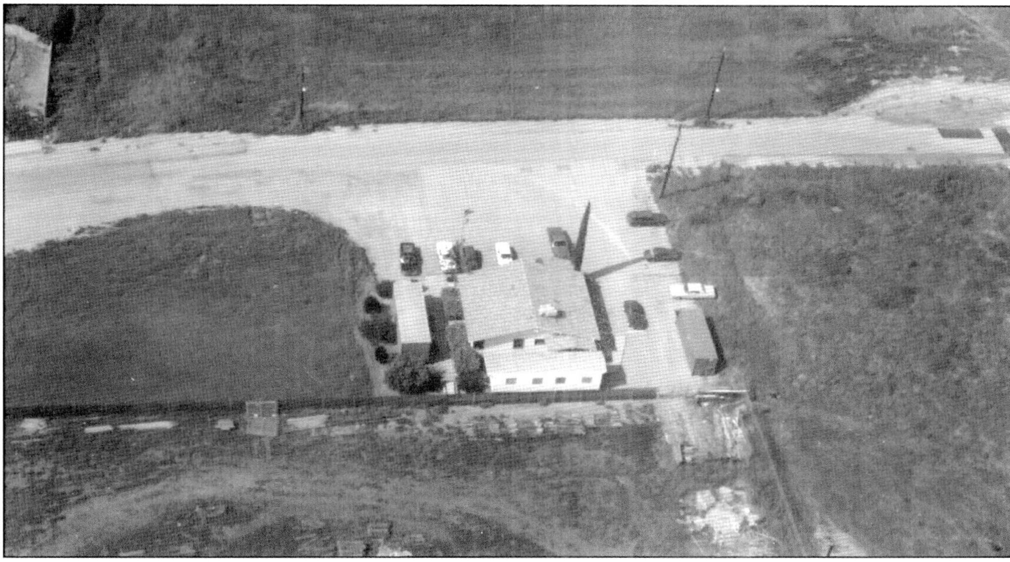

CITY HALL, 1980. The building began to expand as trailers beside and behind the structure helped house city staff for 20 years. The city was growing, and additional space was needed to accommodate more staff.

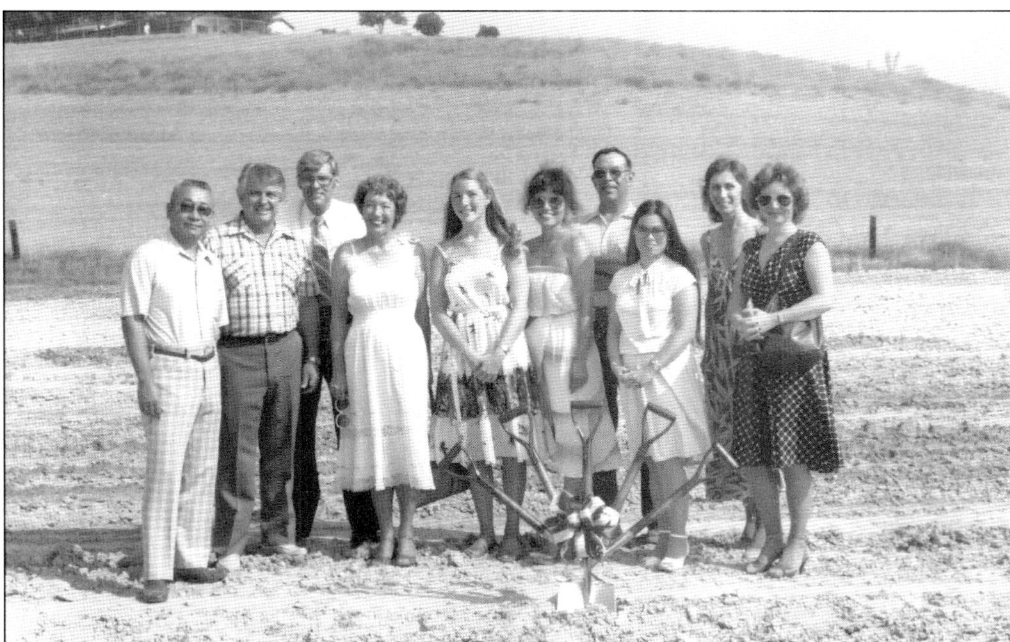

CITY STAFF, 1981. Pictured are, from left to right, planning director George Shindo, city engineer Ron Kranzer, city manager Don Kemp, city clerk Beverly Sherwood, intern Chris Horn, finance department member Lorraine Sanchez, maintenance department member Manny Velenzuela, planning department secretary Donna Interlicchia, assistant city manager Clarice Johnson, and city manager secretary Linda Kimbro. Staff attended a ground-breaking ceremony for the new Walnut City Hall on La Fuente Road.

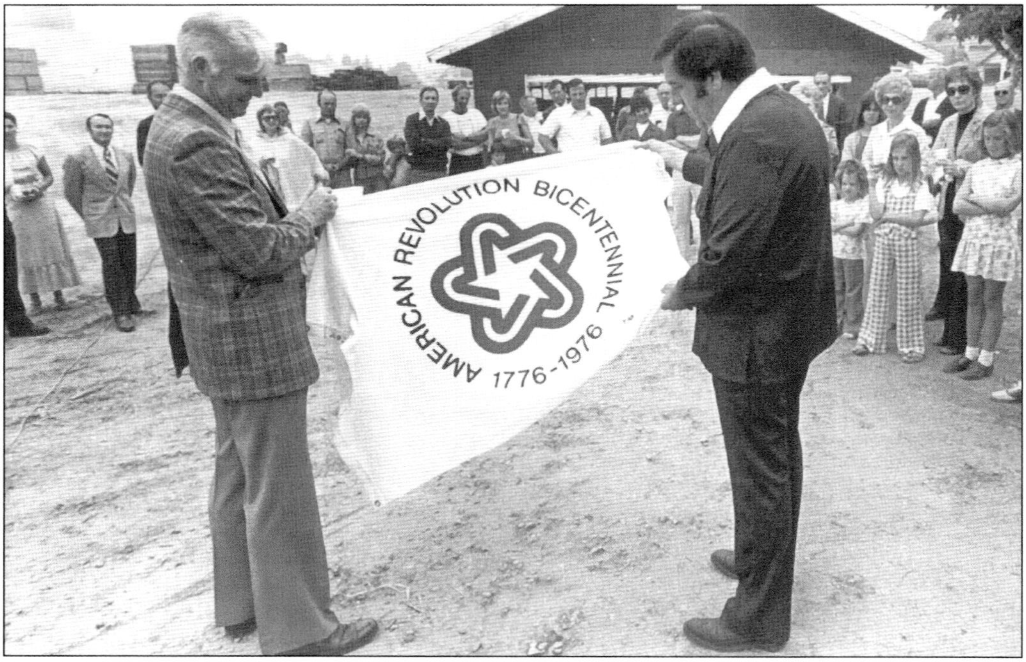

FLAG DAY CELEBRATION, 1975. On June 14, 1975, the celebration at Lemon Creek Park was the official start of the city of Walnut's observation of America's Bicentennial. Congressman Jim Lloyd presented the flag to Mayor Bill Wentworth and Bicentennial Commission representative Leonard Westhoff.

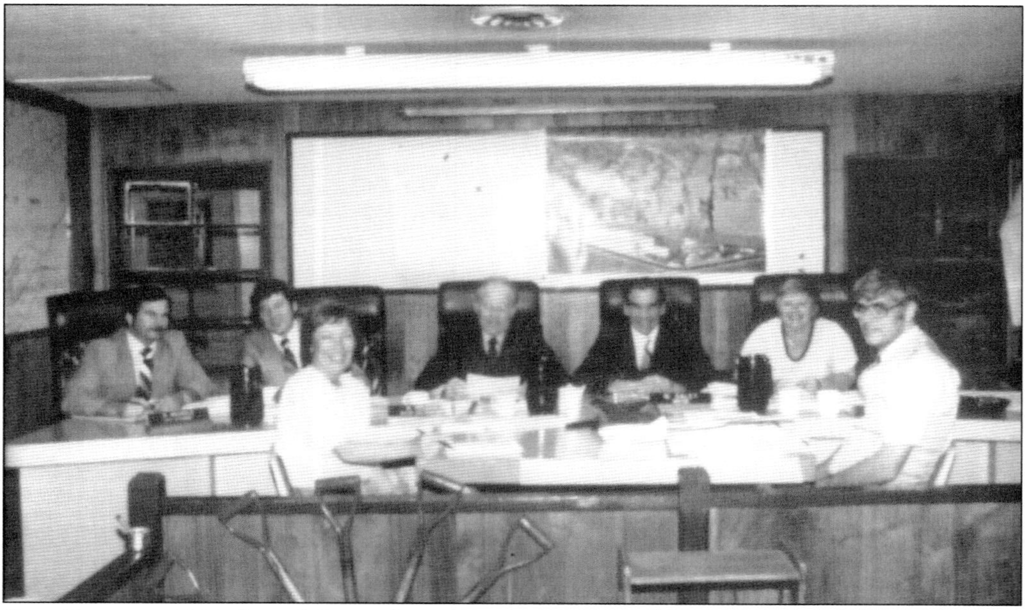

CITY COUNCIL, 1982. From left to right are attorney Scott Nicholas, council member Jim Zamary, city clerk Beverly Sherwood, Mayor Pro Tem Harvey Holden, Mayor Bill Daley, council member Bert Ashley, and city manager Don Kemp. This is the last meeting of city council before moving from Carrey Road to the new city hall on La Puente Road.

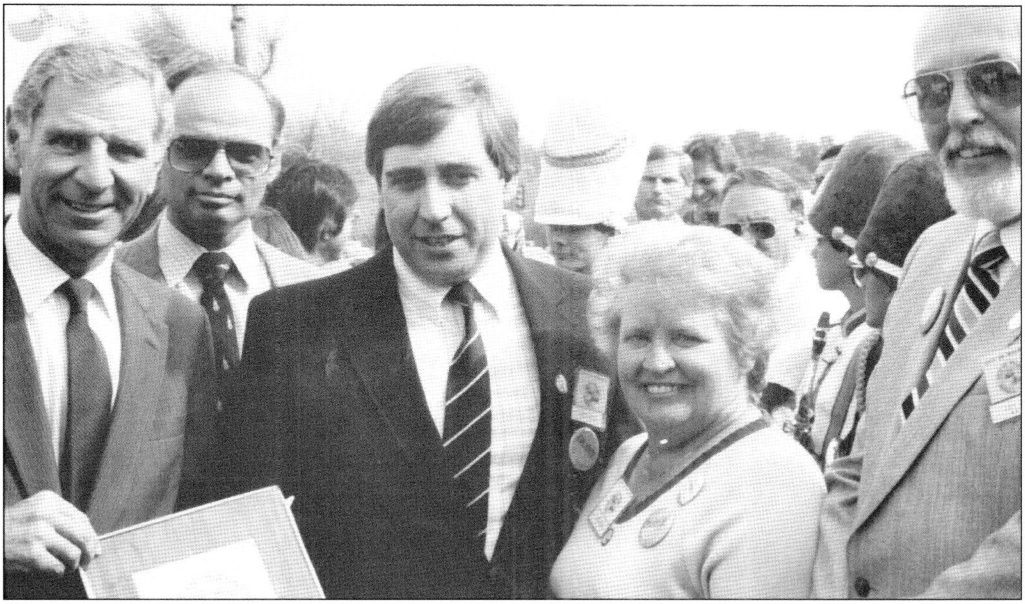

City Council, 1984. Walnut welcomes Gov. George Deukmejian (left). From left to right, council member Chuck Richardson, Mayor Drexel Smith, Mayor Pro Tem Bert Ashley, and council member John Hahn made the presentation. The Walnut High School band provided the musical entertainment.

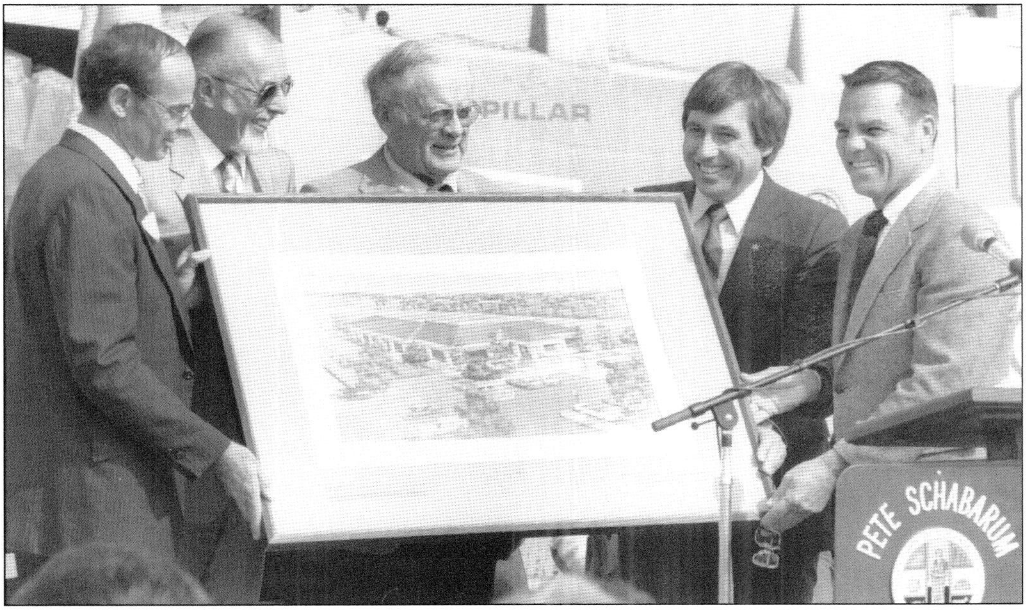

Sheriff's Station, Late 1980s. From left to right, Walnut city council member Chuck Richardson, Mayor Pro Tem Joe Hahn, Mayor Harvey Holden, council member Drexel Smith, Supervisor Pete Schabarum, and Sheriff Sherman Block (not pictured) attend a ground-breaking ceremony for the Walnut Sheriff Station at 21795 Valley Boulevard. The $8-million station was built to serve the growing population of Walnut, Diamond Bar, and Rowland Heights. The station opened on September 23, 1987, with Capt. Thomas Vetter as the new station commander.

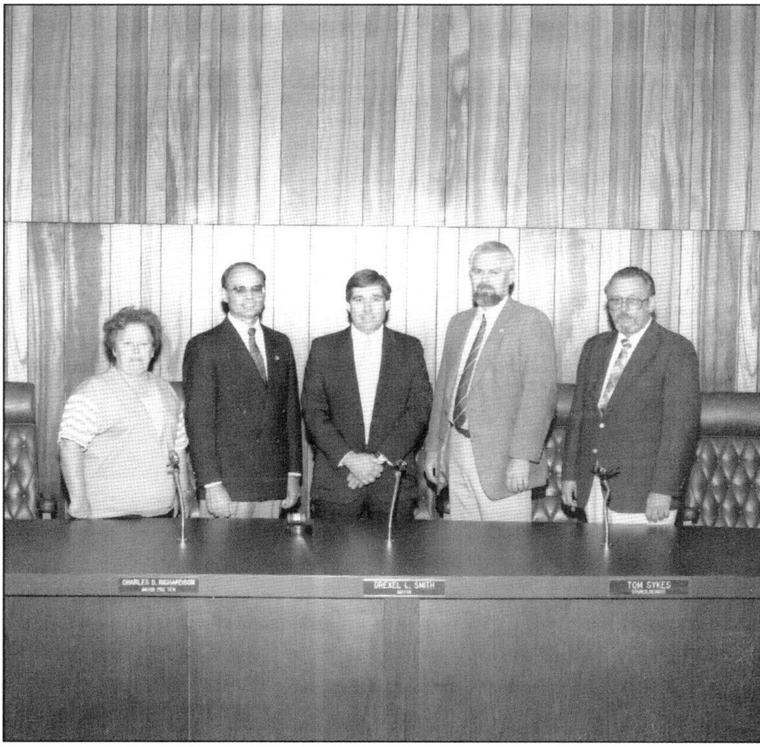

City Council, 1988. From left to right are council member Bert Ashley, Mayor Pro Tem Chuck Richardson, Mayor Drexel Smith, and council members Tom Sykes and Ray Watson.

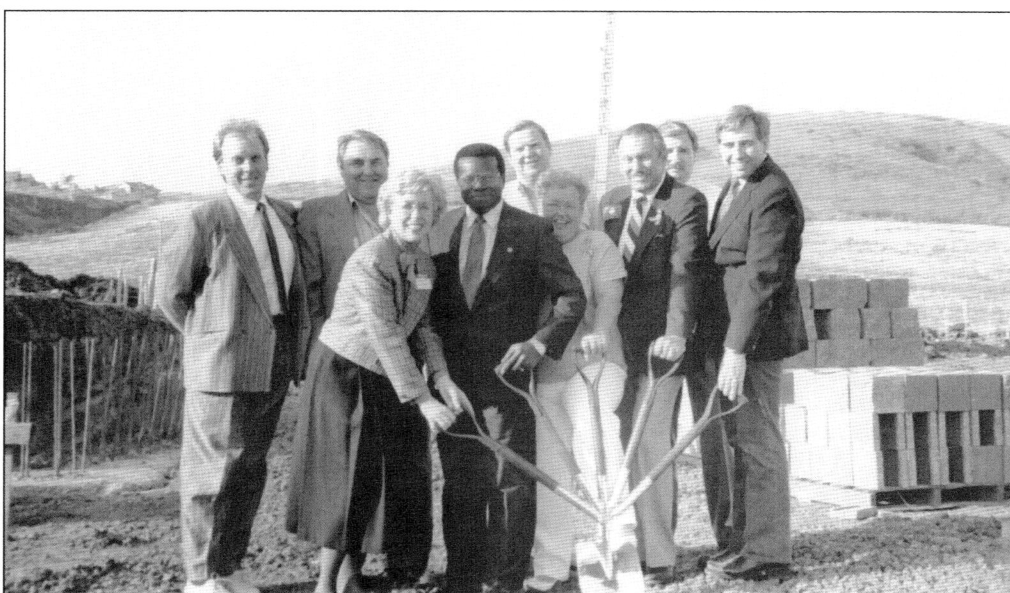

City Council, 1991. Pictured are, from left to right, (first row) city manager Linda Holmes, council members Bill Choctow and Bert Ashley, Mayor Ray Watson, and council member Drexel Smith; (back row) city engineer Bob Morgenstein and two unidentified. This photograph shows the ground-breaking ceremony for the City of Walnut Maintenance Department and Recreation Services building on Valley Boulevard next to the Walnut Sheriff Station.

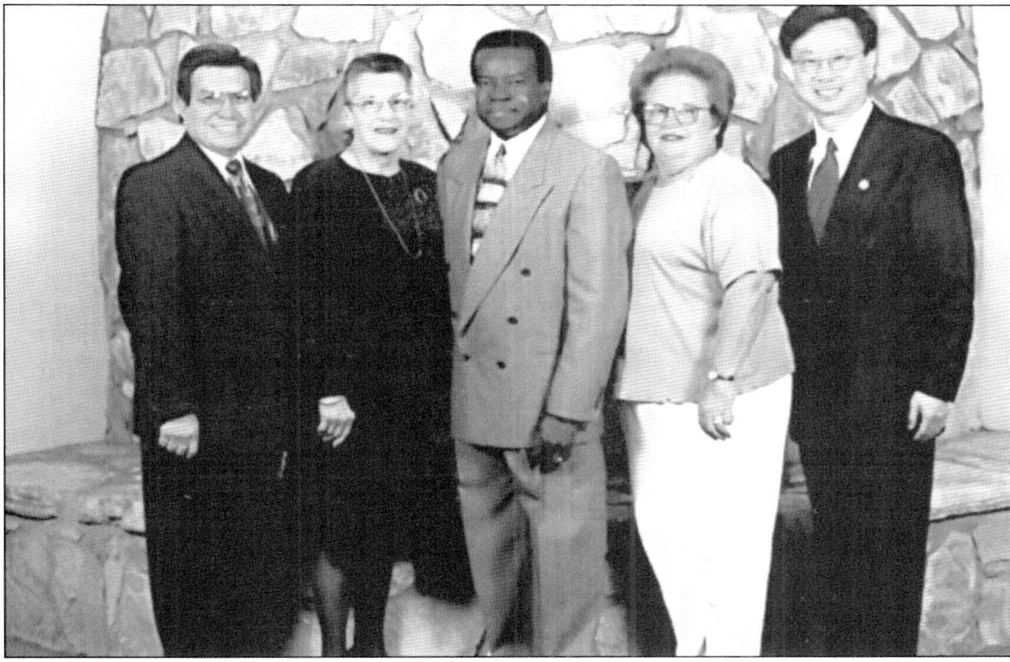

City Council, 1996. From left to right are council member Robert Pacheco, Mayor June Wentworth, Mayor Pro Tem Bill Choctow, and council members Bert Ashley and Joaquin Lim.

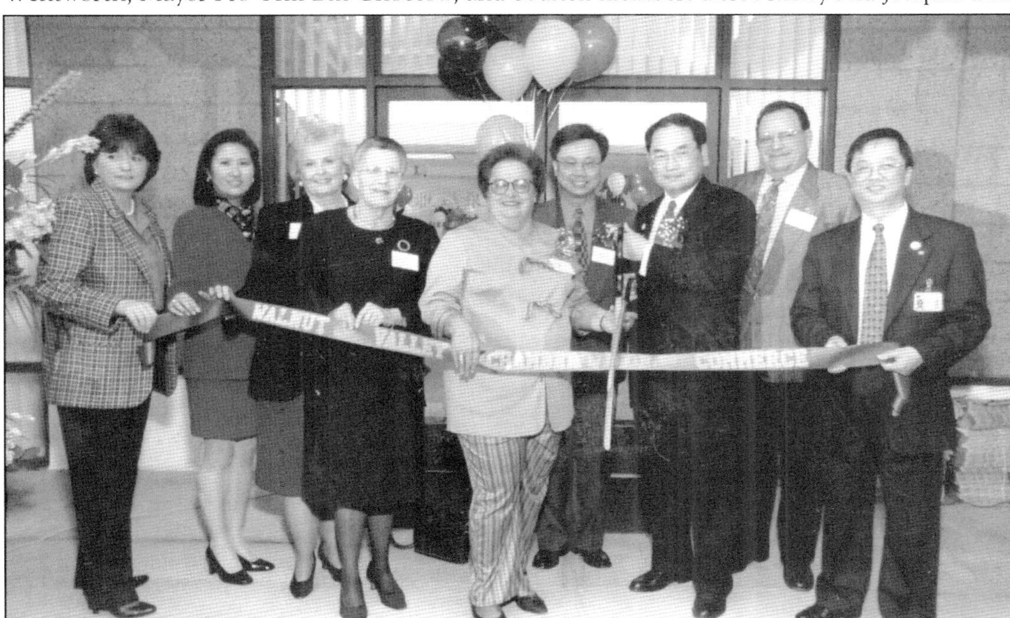

East West Bank Grand Opening, 1998. Cutting the ribbon from the Walnut City Council are Mayor Bert Ashley, council members June Wentworth and Dan Marostica, and Mayor Pro Tem Joaquin Lim. Joining them are members from the Walnut Valley Chamber of Commerce. The growing Asian population saw a need for culturally diverse banks in the area. In 2011, Walnut's Asian population had grown to 57.3 percent of the city.

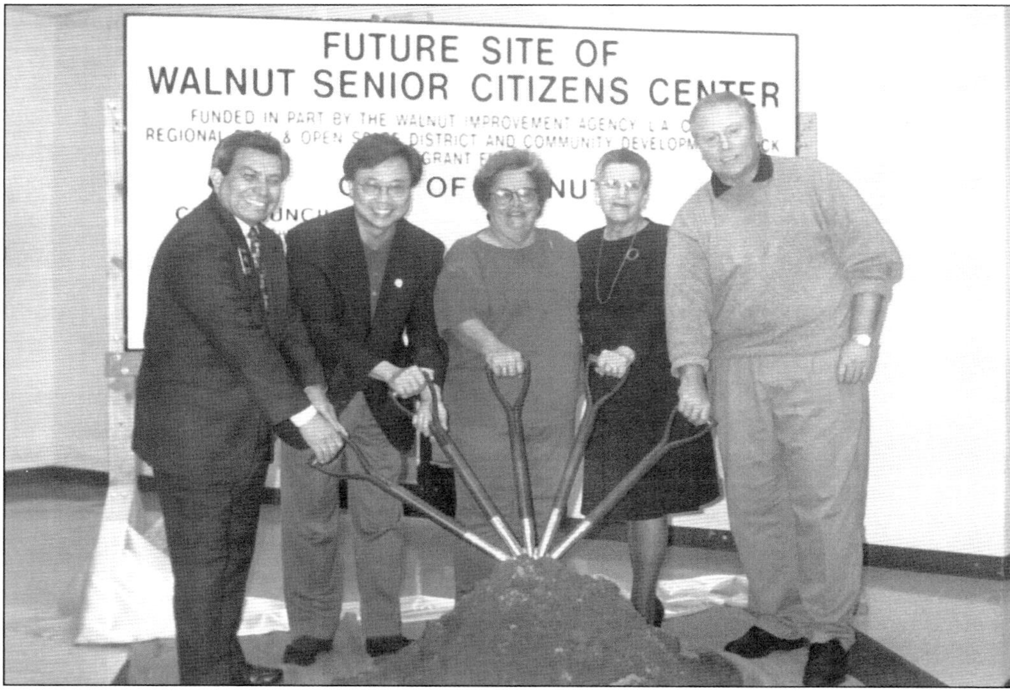

Senior Center Ground-Breaking, 1998. From left to right are council member Robert Pacheco, Mayor Pro Tem Joaquin Lim, Mayor Bert Ashley, and council members June Wentworth and Larry Waldie. The official dedication of the senior center, located on La Puente Road, and its opening took place on October 1, 1999.

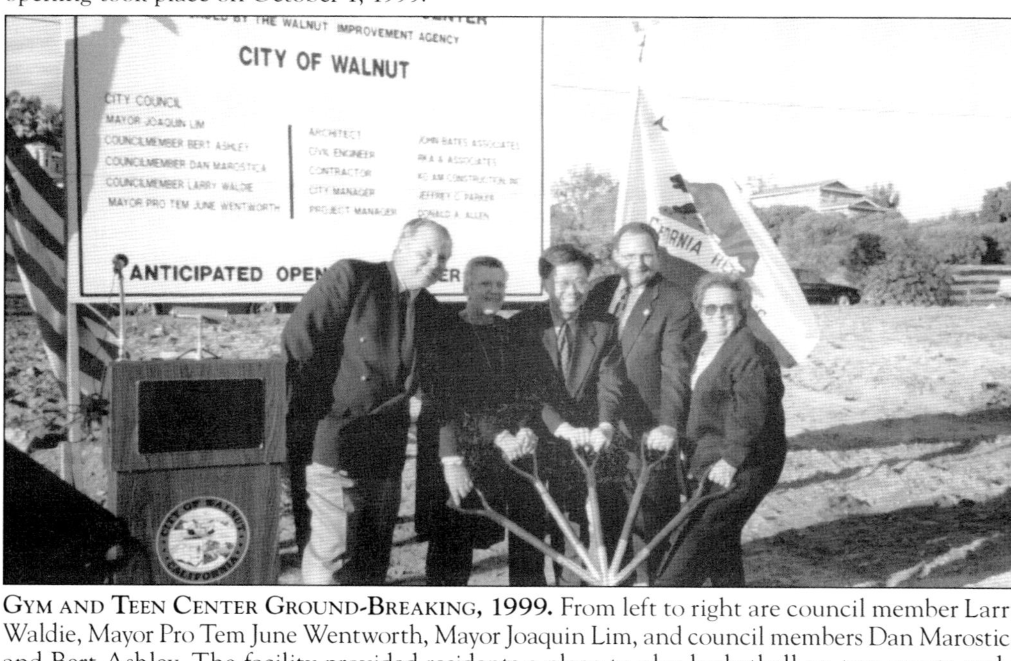

Gym and Teen Center Ground-Breaking, 1999. From left to right are council member Larry Waldie, Mayor Pro Tem June Wentworth, Mayor Joaquin Lim, and council members Dan Marostica and Bert Ashley. The facility provided residents a place to play basketball on two courts and a teen center for youth.

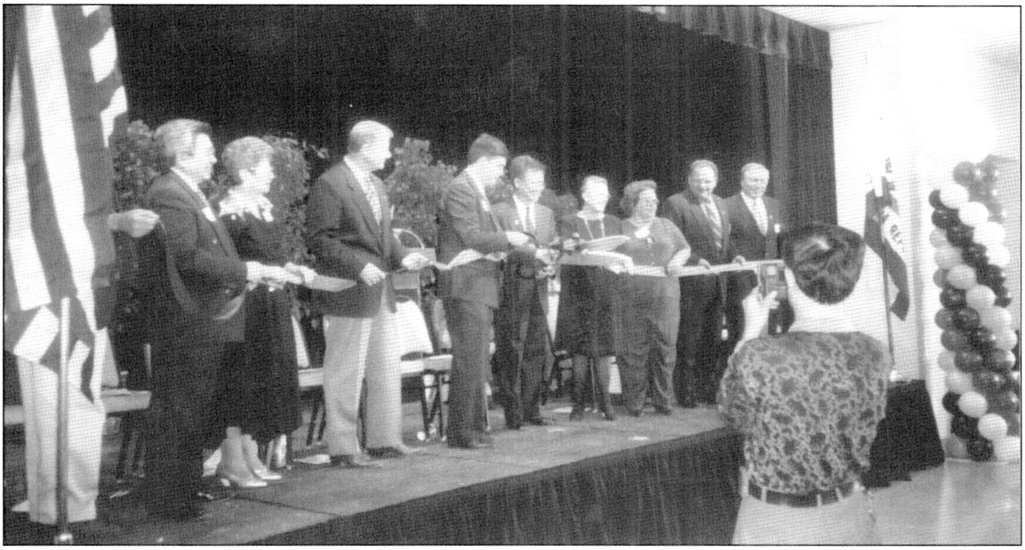

Senior Center Ribbon Cutting, 1999. From left to right are assembly member Bob Pacheco, Walnut Senior Club president Rose Erickson, community service director Don Allan, city manager Jeff Parker, Mayor Joaquin Lim, Mayor Pro Tem June Wentworth, and council members Bert Ashley, Dan Marostica, and Larry Waldie. On October 9, 1999, the council officially cut the ribbon and dedicated the new senior center.

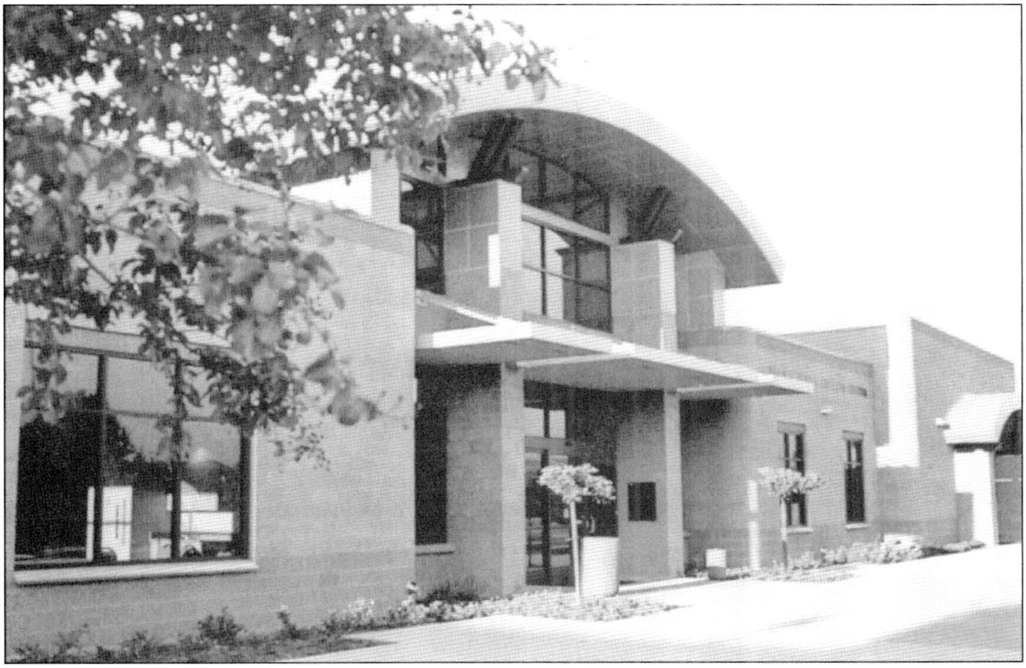

Senior Center, 2011. The facility now serves between 900 and 1,000 people a month with various activities for the senior community. Mount San Antonio College offers many classes through its Older Adult Program, which includes aerobics, tai chi, stretch and balance, and computer classes. Also, many personal development classes are offered, including a lunch program, senior bingo, trips, and supportive services.

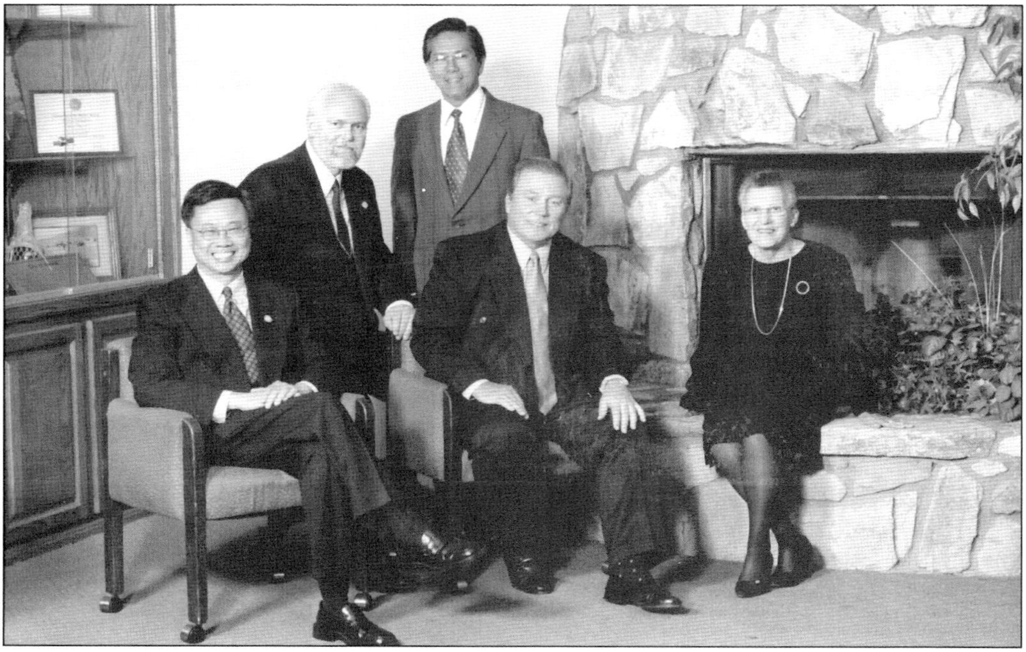

CITY COUNCIL, 2001. From left to right are council members Joaquin Lim, Tom Sykes and Tony Cartagena, Mayor Pro Tem Larry Waldie, and Mayor June Wentworth. June served as personnel commissioner for the Walnut Valley Unified School District from 1970 into the 21st century. Larry Waldie served as undersheriff for Los Angeles County from 2005 to 2011.

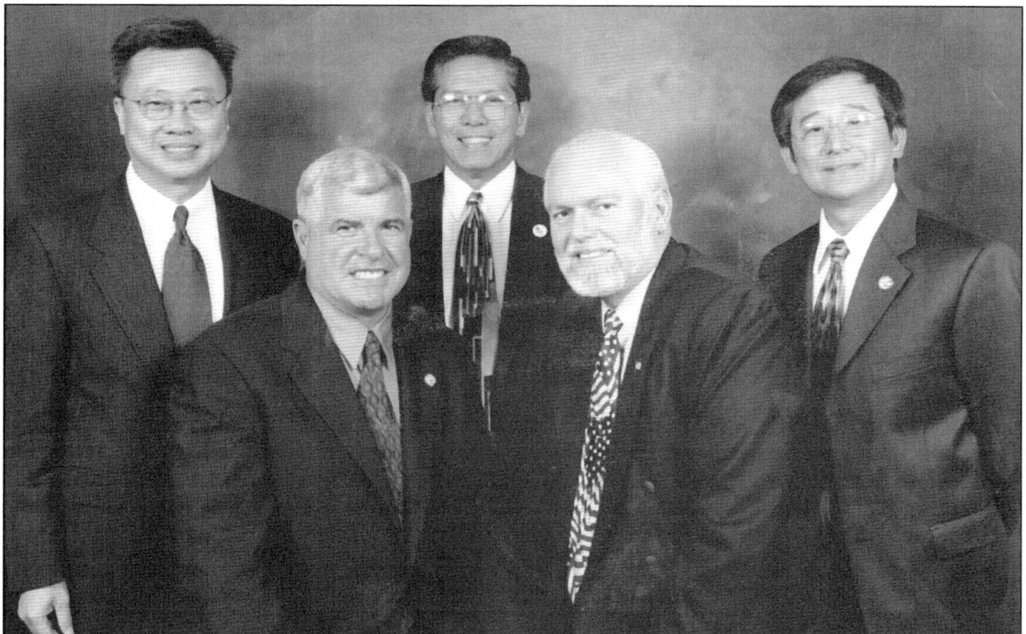

CITY COUNCIL, 2002. From left to right are council members Joaquin Lim and Tom King, Mayor Tony Cartagena, Mayor Pro Tem Tom Sykes, and council member Miles Nam.

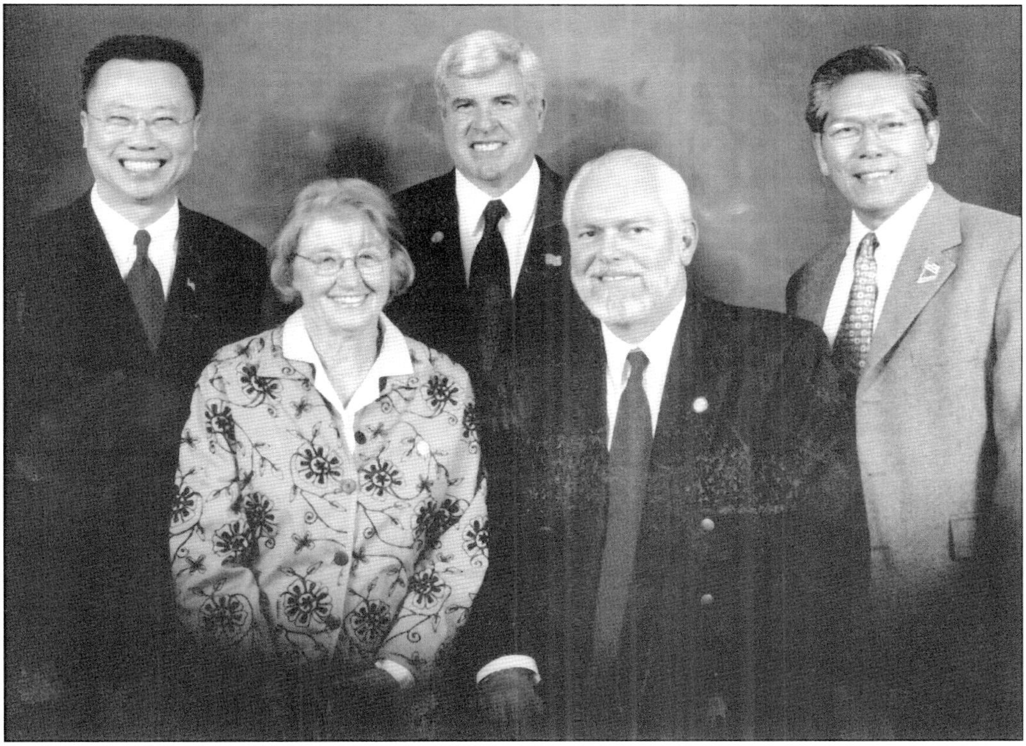

CITY COUNCIL, 2003. From left to right are council members Joaquin Lim, Katy Rzonca, and Tom King, Mayor Pro Tem Tom Sykes, and Mayor Tony Cartagena.

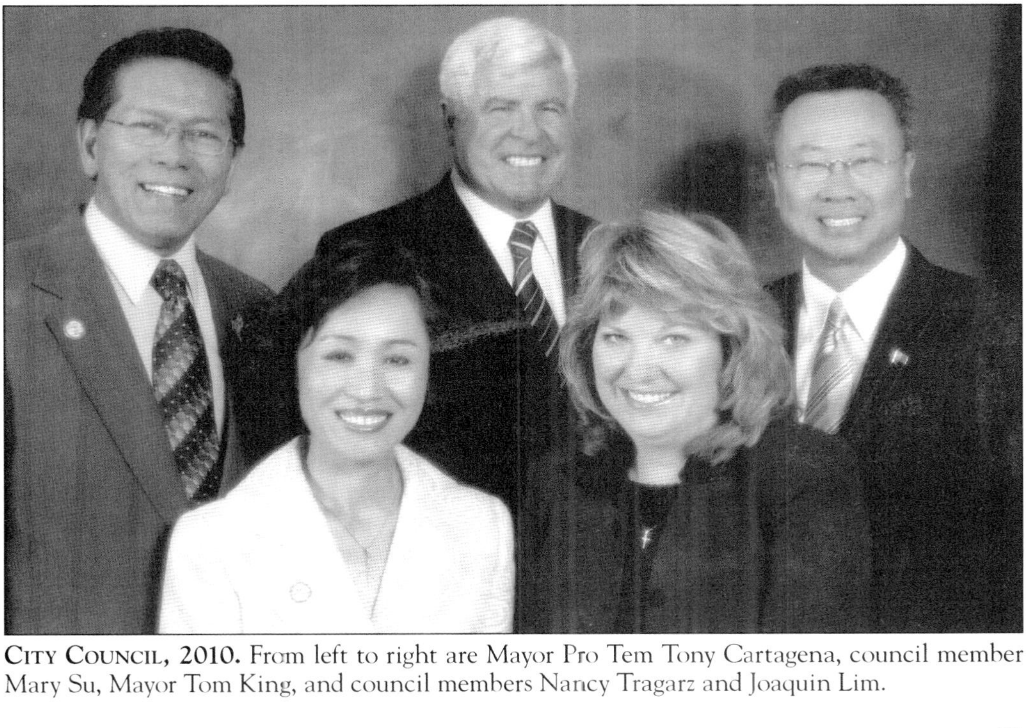

CITY COUNCIL, 2010. From left to right are Mayor Pro Tem Tony Cartagena, council member Mary Su, Mayor Tom King, and council members Nancy Tragarz and Joaquin Lim.

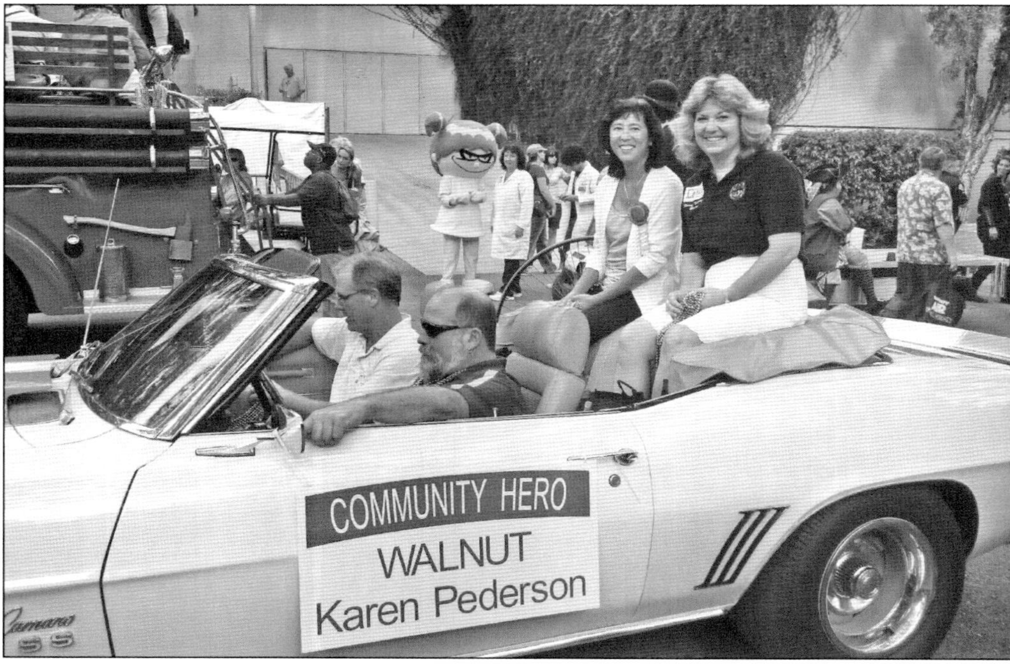

Day at the Fair Parade, 2011. Mayor Nancy Tragarz (right) rides with "Walnut Community Hero" Karen Pedersen. Karen was recognized for her dedicated community service. Nancy is a longtime Walnut resident who attended Collegewood Elementary, Suzanne Middle School, and Walnut High School.

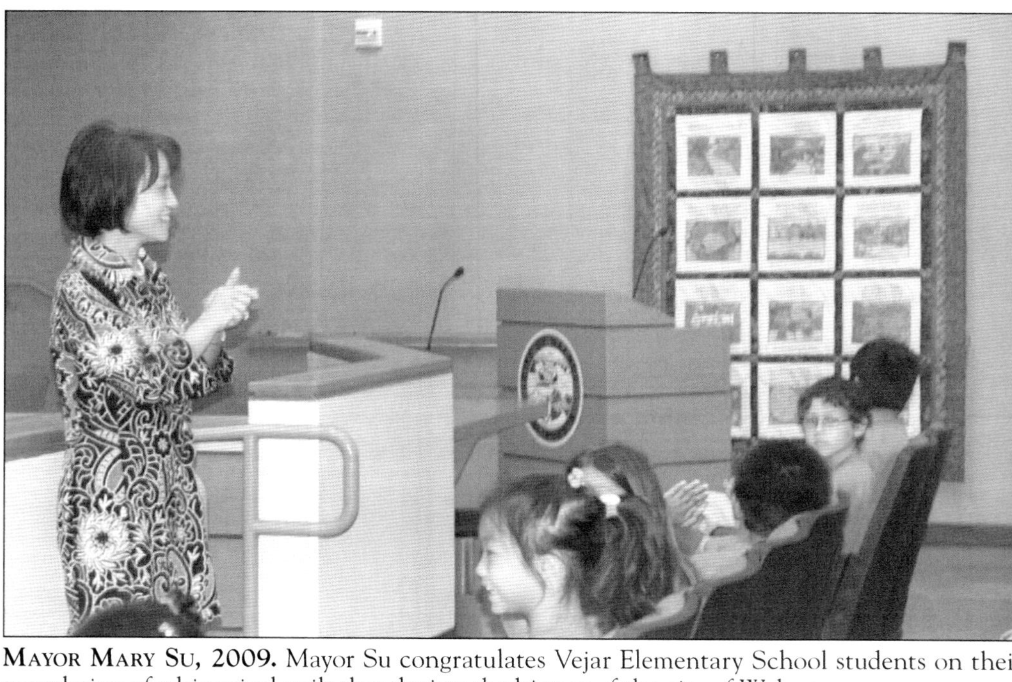

Mayor Mary Su, 2009. Mayor Su congratulates Vejar Elementary School students on their completion of a historical quilt that depicts the history of the city of Walnut.

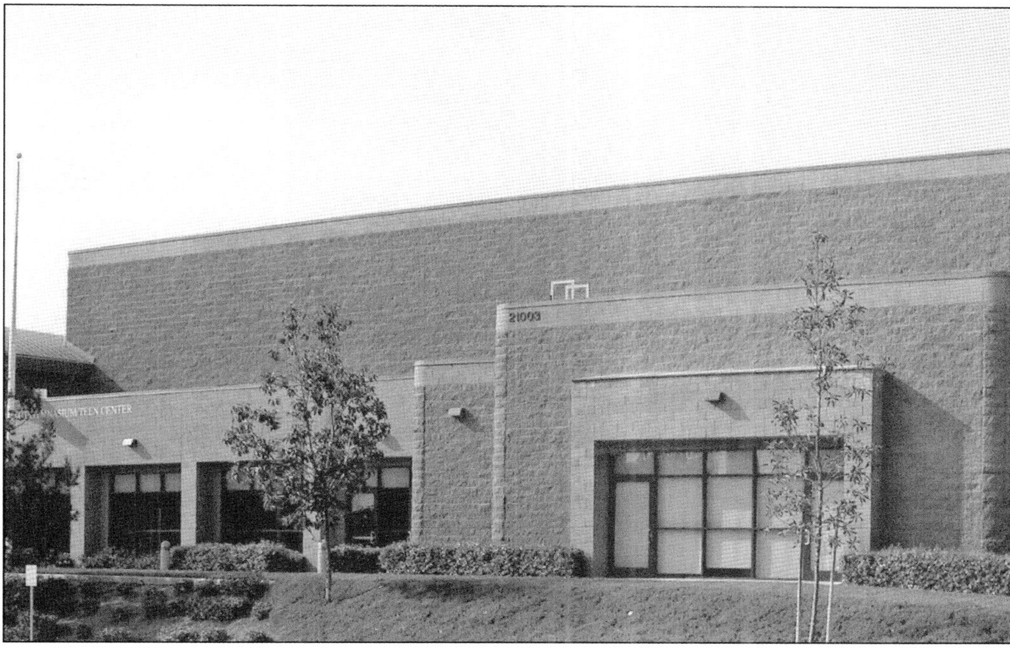

TEEN CENTER, 2002. The facility has two basketball courts and a multipurpose room. The center provides scheduled fitness and youth-related classes, badminton, volleyball, table tennis, and a teen center. The teen center offers a variety of educational, recreational, and supportive programs. It has a computer room and Ping-Pong tables and provides after school tutoring.

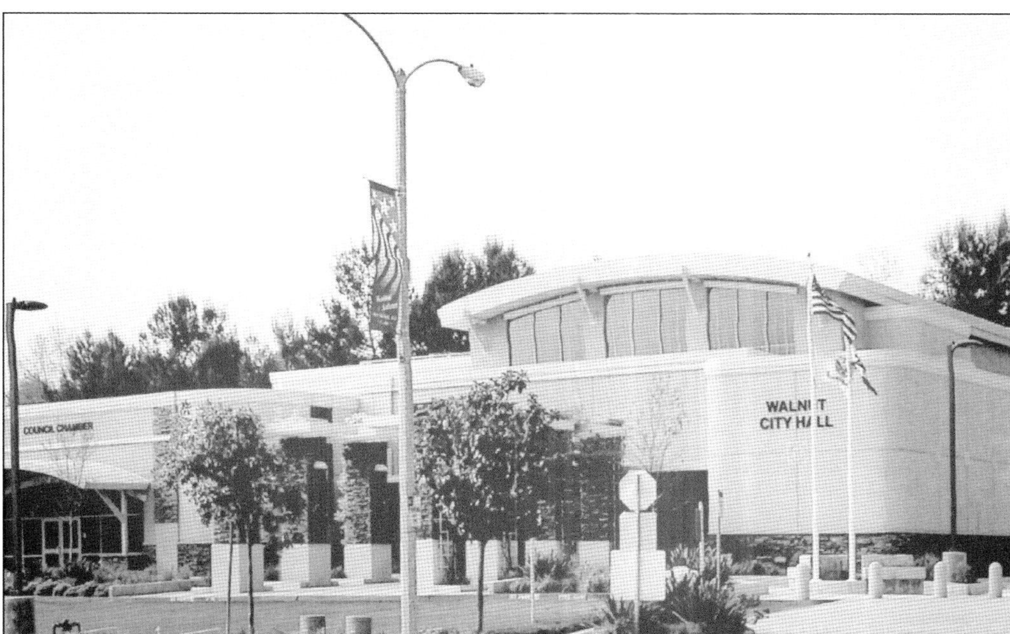

CITY HALL, 2003. On June 2003, Walnut opened a new city hall on the site of the former city hall on La Puente Road.

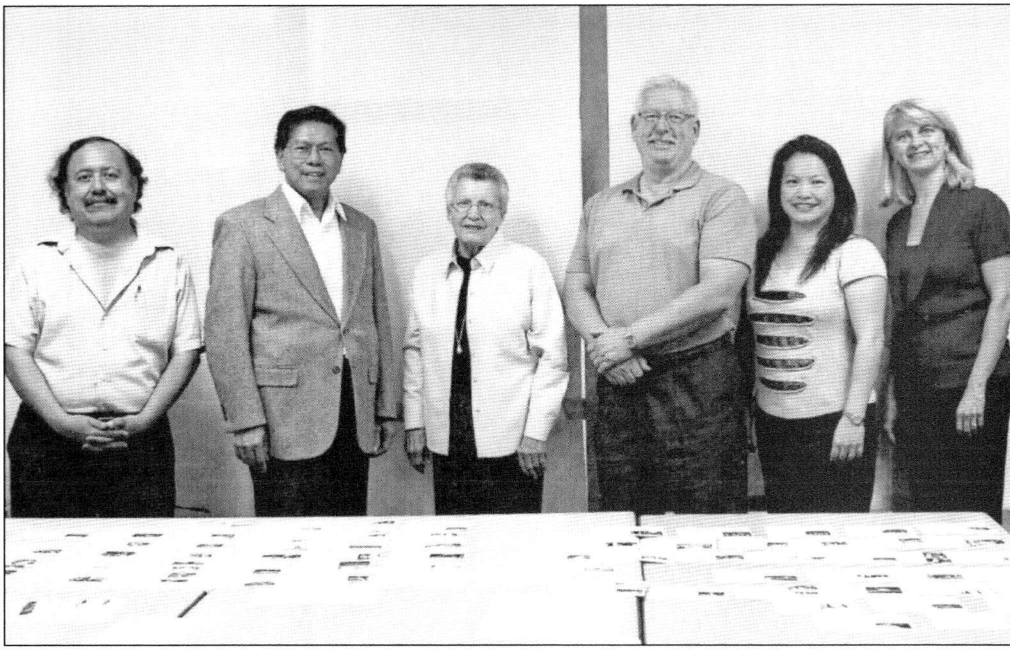

Walnut Historical Society, 2011. As the first project, the historical book brought together dedicated community members through the Walnut Historical Society. From left to right are Albert Garcia, council member Tony Cartagena, June Wentworth, Chris Rae, Walnut Valley Water District board member Scarlett Kwong, and Sandy Olson. Not pictured is Debra Martin.

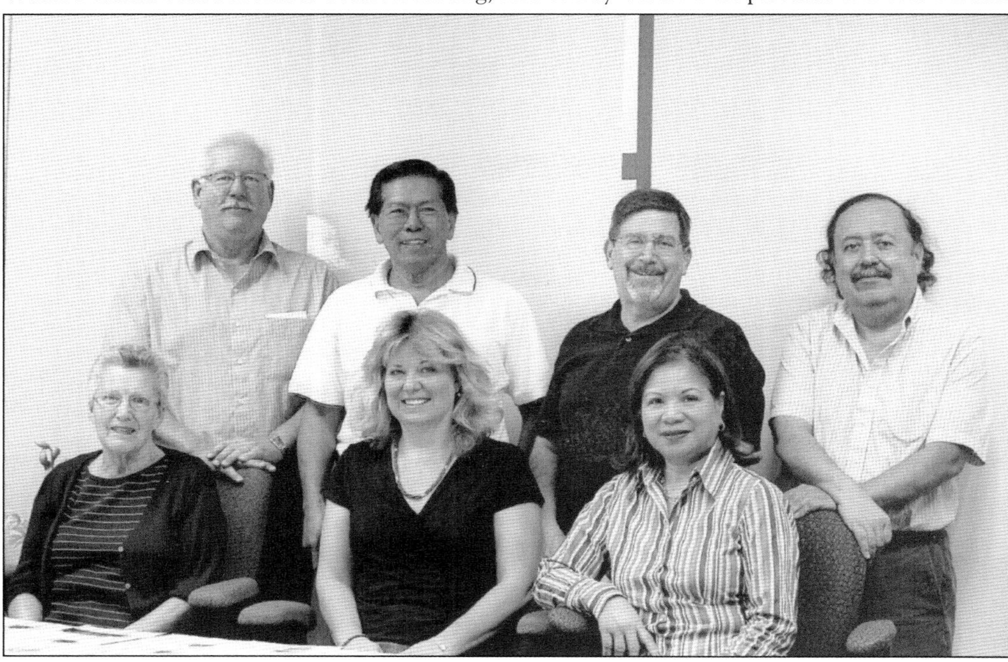

History Book Committee Members. From left to right are (first row) President June Wentworth, Walnut mayor Nancy Tragarz, and Bella Cristobal; (second row) Chris Rae, council Member Tony Cartagena, Mark Maki, and Albert Garcia.

Six

Bringing Community Together

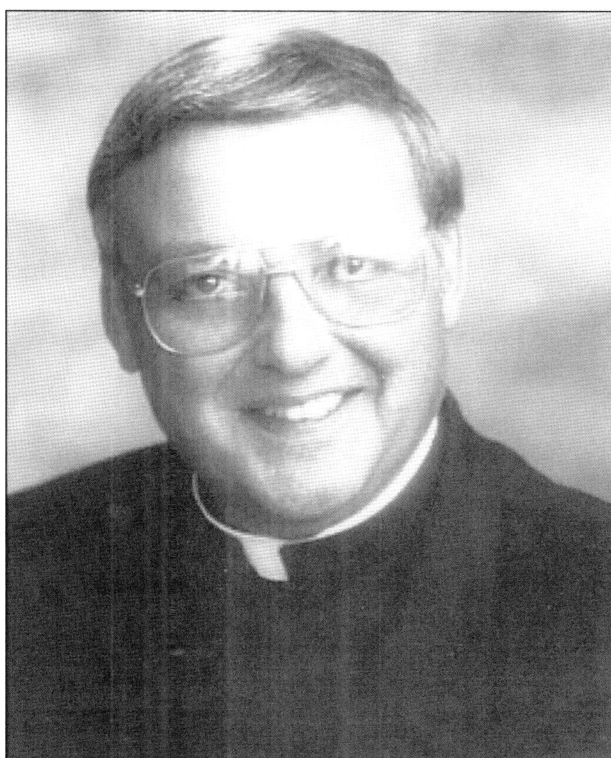

St. Lorenzo Ruiz Parish Community, 1990s. Fr. Dennis Vellucci was the first pastor of the St. Lorenzo Ruiz Parish community. He celebrated his first mass on November 22, 1990. On September 8, 1991, Cardinal Roger Mahony issued a decree establishing the parish of St. Lorenzo Ruiz. Father Dennis was installed as the first pastor on October 8, 1991. While services were being held at a warehouse location, he initiated plans for and construction of the St. Lorenzo Ruiz Catholic Parish Community Center on the land bought by the archdiocese on Lemon Avenue and Meadowpass Road. Ground-breaking was held in March 1994, and the first mass was held on March 17, 1996. The land had previously been part of John Rowland's La Puente Rancho, then was owned by the Sentous family, and finally was owned by J.P. Winnett.

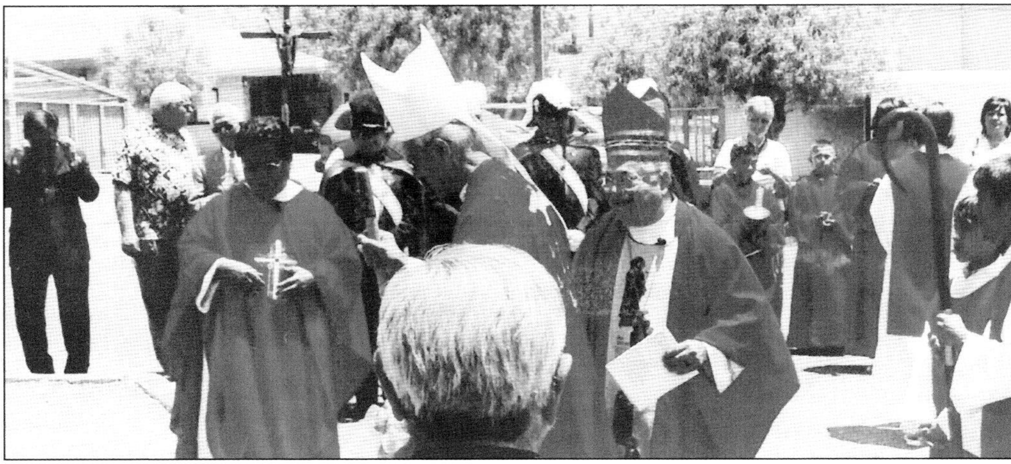

Fr. Tony Astudillo, 2000s. Father Astudillo joined St. Lorenzo Ruiz Catholic Parish Community in July 2005 and was installed as a pastor in August 2005. He continued the plans to build the Church of St. Lorenzo Ruiz at Meadowpass Road and brought it to completion. Phase one of the construction of the church started with the ground-breaking ceremony held on June 29, 2008. Archdiocese of Los Angeles auxiliary bishop emeritus Rev. Joseph Sartoris and San Gabriel Pastoral Region bishop the Most Reverend Gabino Zavala joined the ceremony with parish pastor Fr. Tony Astudillo.

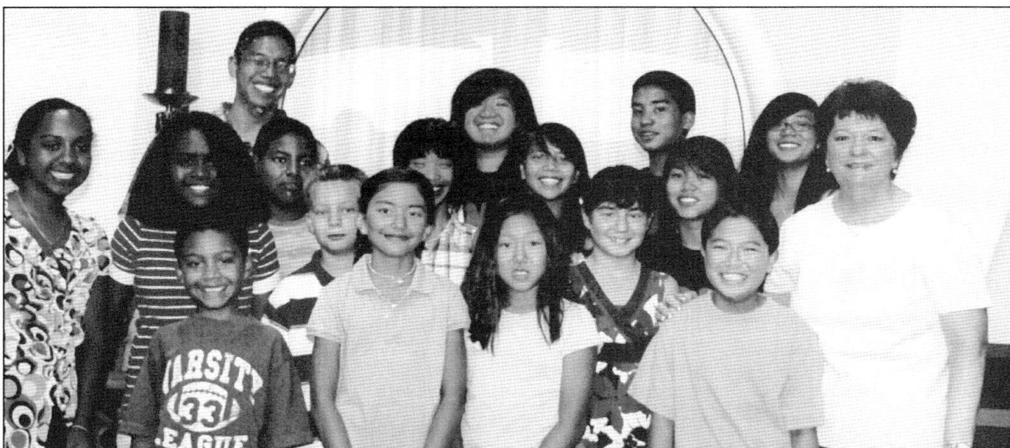

Bob and Gayle Pacheco, 1980–2011. Bob and Gayle Pacheco moved to Walnut in 1985. They became involved in the community with the establishment of St. Lorenzo Ruiz Catholic Church. In 1996, Bob was elected to the Walnut City Council. In 1998, he became the first Walnut resident to be elected to the California State Assembly, where he served until 2004. He received a presidential appointment to the US Naval Board of Visitors and was a senior advisor to the governor until 2011. Gayle served on the Mount San Antonio College Board from 1999 to 2003. As of 2012, she serves on the Walnut Valley Unified School District's Personnel Commission. In addition, Gayle serves as the vice chair of the California Governor's Committee on Employment of People with Disabilities. In 1995, Bob and Gayle established the Walnut Valley Educational Foundation, which has raised over $1 million for student and staff scholarships and has funded classroom and Walnut School District grants for technology, athletics, enrichment, and disadvantaged youths. At St. Lorenzo Ruiz Catholic Church, Gayle has served as director of the youth choir since 1989.

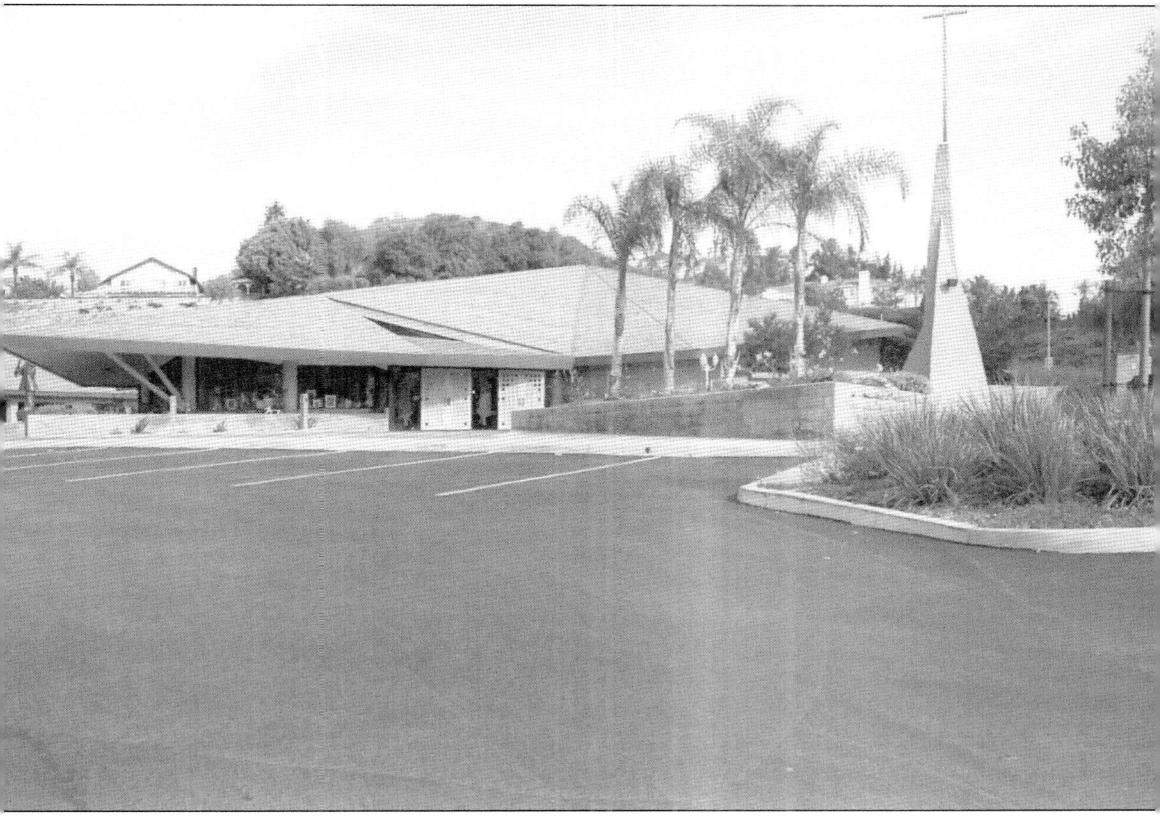

St. Martha's Church, 2000s. Several families attending St. Martha's Parish in Valinda decided that Walnut needed a Catholic church. In 1989, the church allowed Walnut families to hold services as a community. At first, they started at St. Martha's Church, but they soon found a new location at Collegewood Elementary School. The Walnut group soon grew to 300 families. They then found an empty warehouse where services could be held. Fundraising was held for the conversion of the warehouse to a Walnut chapel. The parish met at this location for five years before a temporary church was built on 18 acres of land bought by the archdiocese at Lemon Avenue and Meadowpass Road. A new sanctuary, serving 3,000 families, was built in 2010. The archdiocese had previously owned a piece of land on Pierre Road across from Walnut High School.

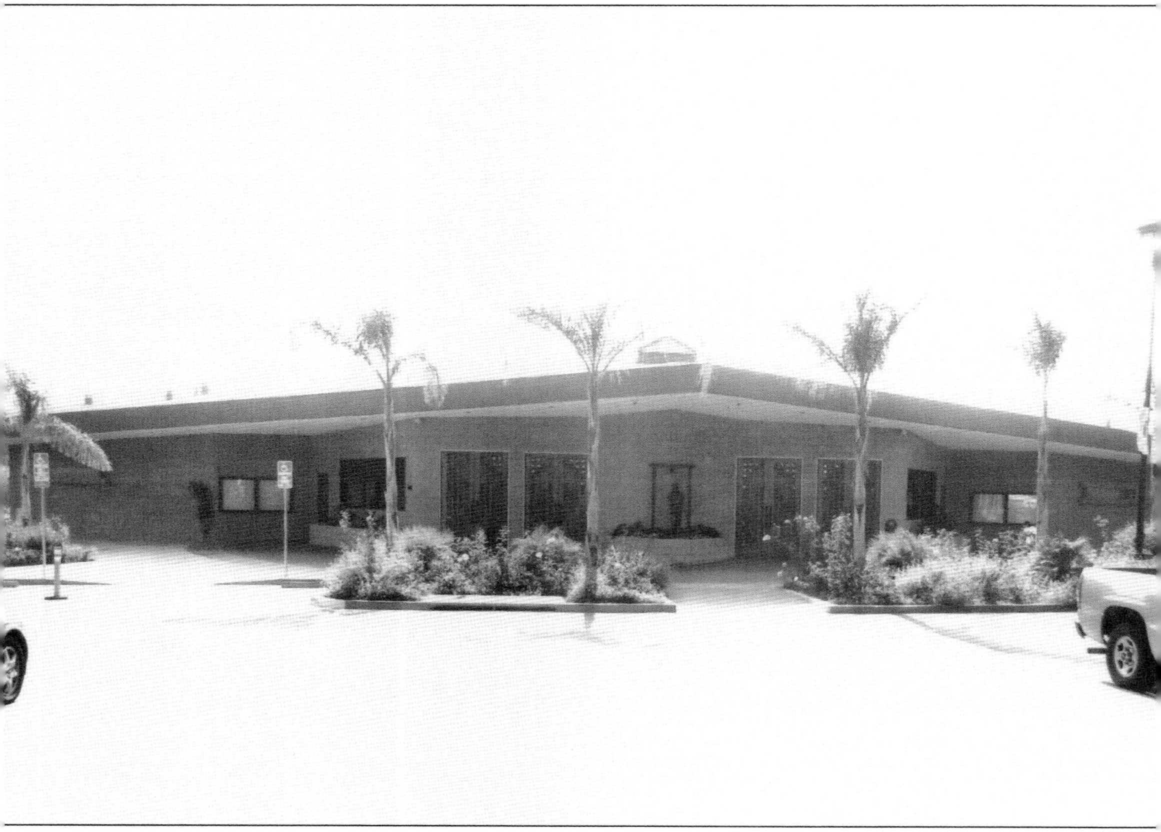

Dedication and Blessing, 2010. The ceremony took place on September 26, 2010, and was blessed by Los Angeles archbishop Cardinal Mahony. Mahony had a long history with the local church. In one of his first actions after being named archbishop, Cardinal Mahony purchased 18 acres on Meadowpass Road and designated it for a new church. He also issued a decree establishing the Parish of St. Lorenzo Ruiz. Father Tony Astudillo said at the dedication of the church that "this is 21 years of building a new church."

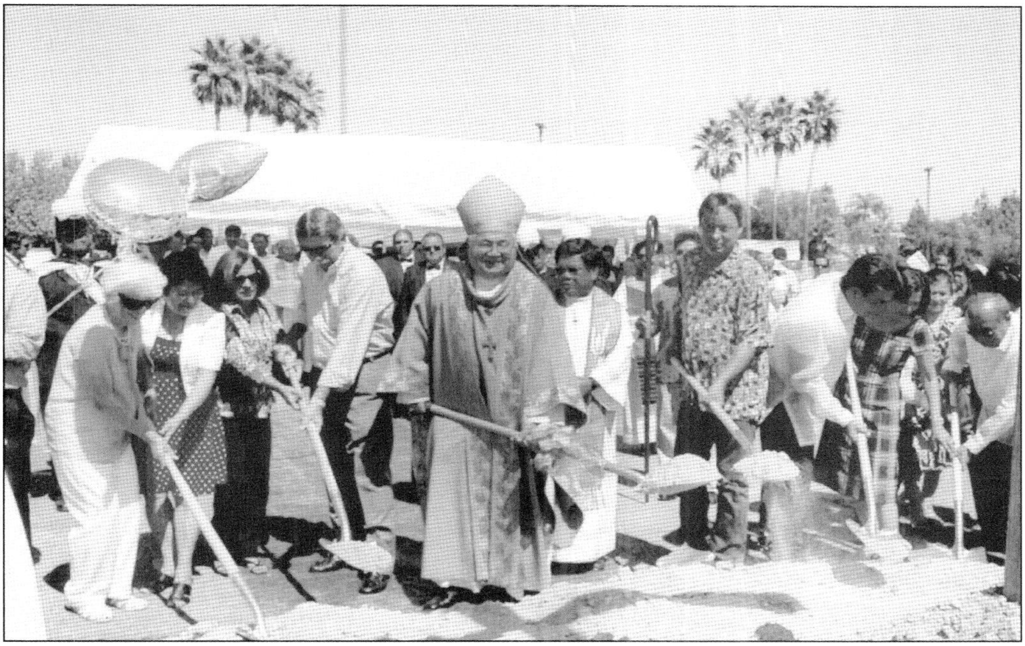

GROUND-BREAKING CEREMONY, 2009. The ceremony for phase two of the St. Lorenzo Ruiz Catholic Church took place on September 20, 2009. From left to right are bishop Rev. Gabino Zabala (center), Fr. Tony Astudillo, and Fr. Hyacinth Kalu, along with parish leaders. This was the first strike of "Holy Ground."

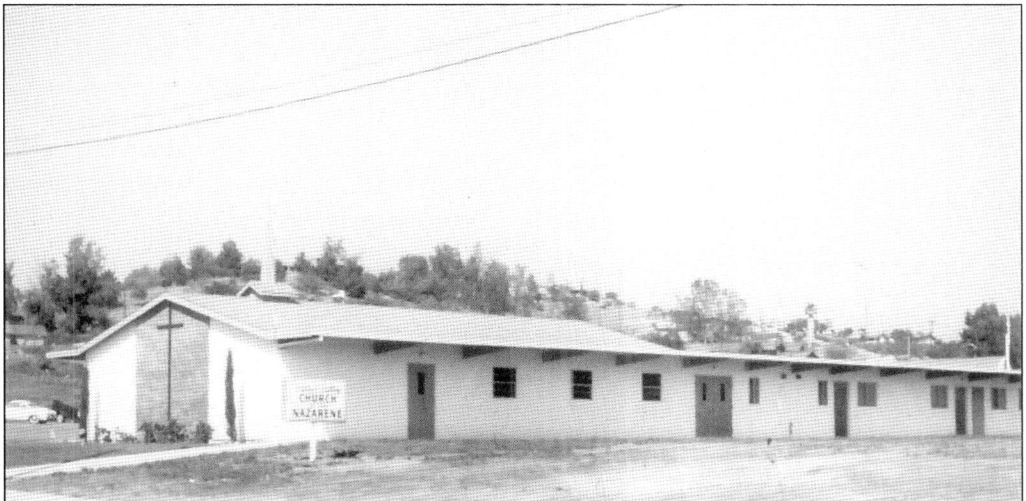

NAZARENE CHURCH, 1971. The Walnut Valley Church of the Nazarene is one of many churches that grace La Puente Road. With the growing Asian population, local churches serve culturally diverse ethnic congregations. In 2011, a growing Korean congregation worships at the location.

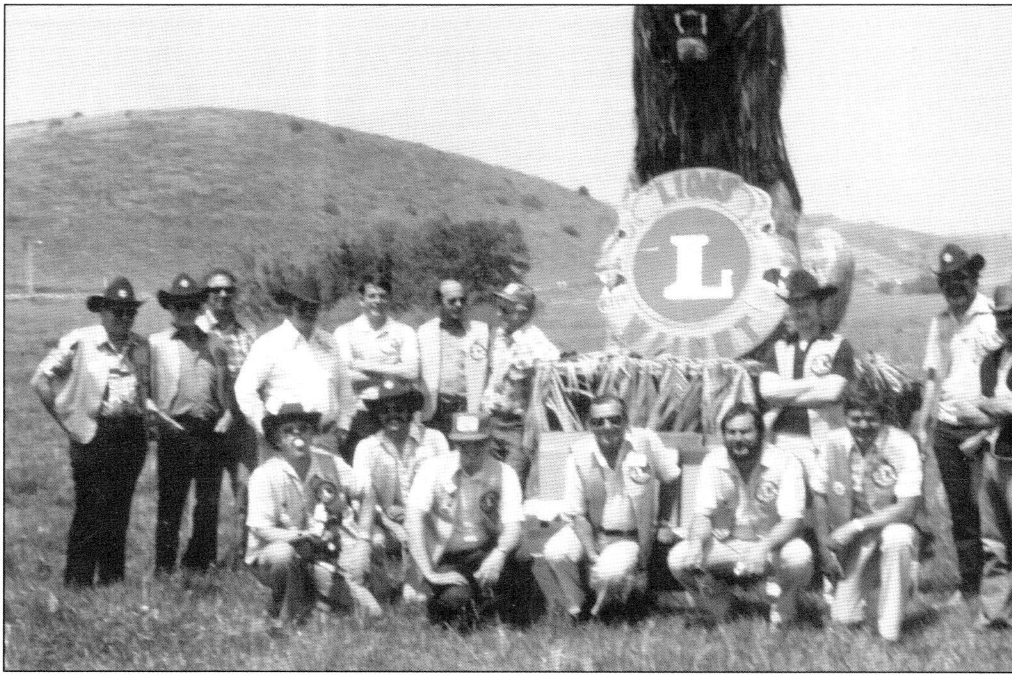

Walnut Lions Club, 1975. The service community was founded and organized in 1975. It is part of many community activities, including an annual Easter egg hunt, Family Festival pancake breakfast, and the Lion International seeing-eye program. In 1982, they built and erected a monument sign for the new Walnut City Hall on La Puente Road. Pictured here are, from left to right, (first row) David Eskridge, Bill Daley Jr., Paul Skidmore, Chet Rzonca, Mike Hormuth, and Bill Hormuth; (second row) Bob Gius, Leonard Westhoff, Dewayne Kelly, Tom Cobb, Ron Chambers, Pete Snider, Jim Schreyer, Bill Steinbrenner, and Bill Ziegenbien.

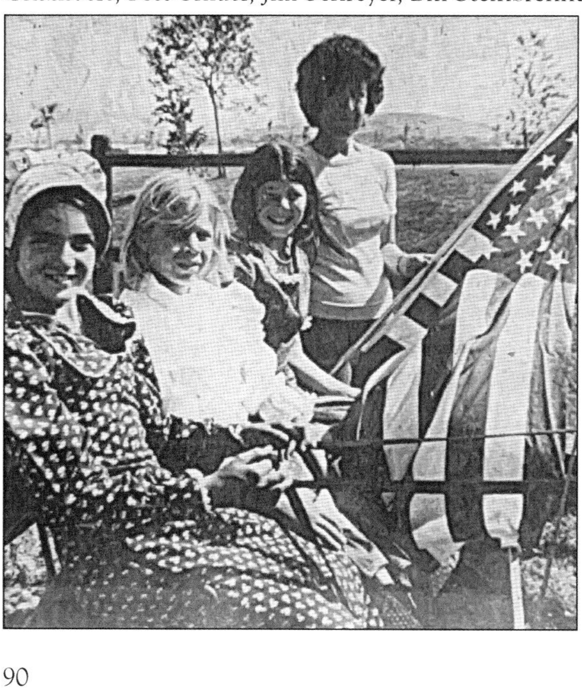

Family Festival, 1976. On July 3, 1976, the Bicentennial festivities for the City of Walnut kicked off with the first Family Festival Parade, sponsored by the Walnut Valley Riders. The parade started at Suzanne Park and ended at Lemon Creek Park. This picture shows, from left to right, Janette Hudson, Marcy Noelte, Regina Kincaid, and Beverly Kincaid riding on their horse and buggy with their American flag.

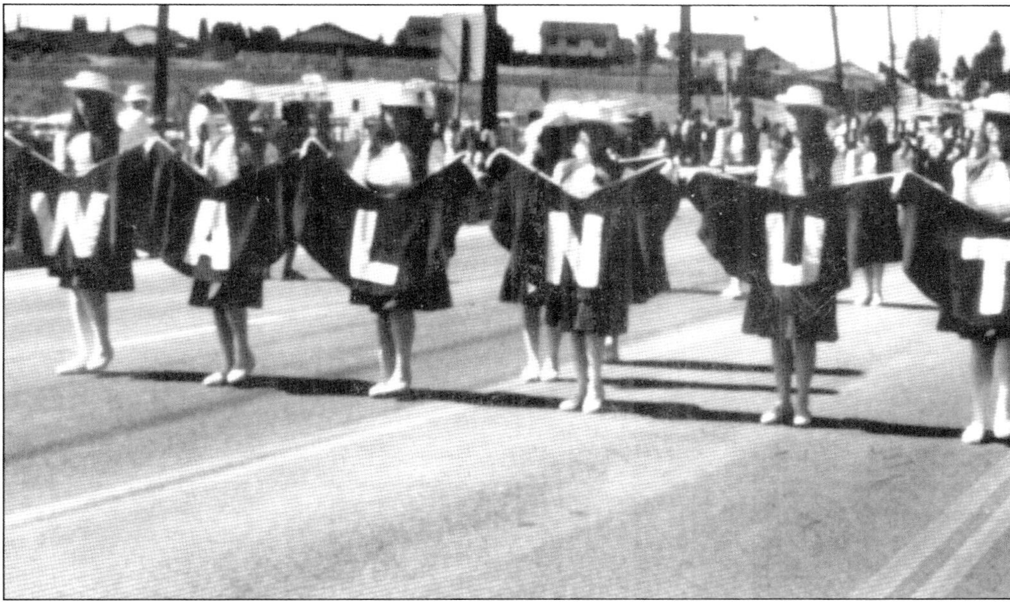

WALNUT HIGH SCHOOL DRILL TEAM AND BAND, 1980S. The band leads the Family Festival parade in the early 1980s. Since July 4, 1976, Walnut has held a Family Festival celebration, many with a fall parade, bringing the community together one day a year. The Von's shopping center, now known as Lemon Creek Village (to the left of the picture), was vacant at the time. Walnut did not have a major shopping center until Von's was built by Larry Armour.

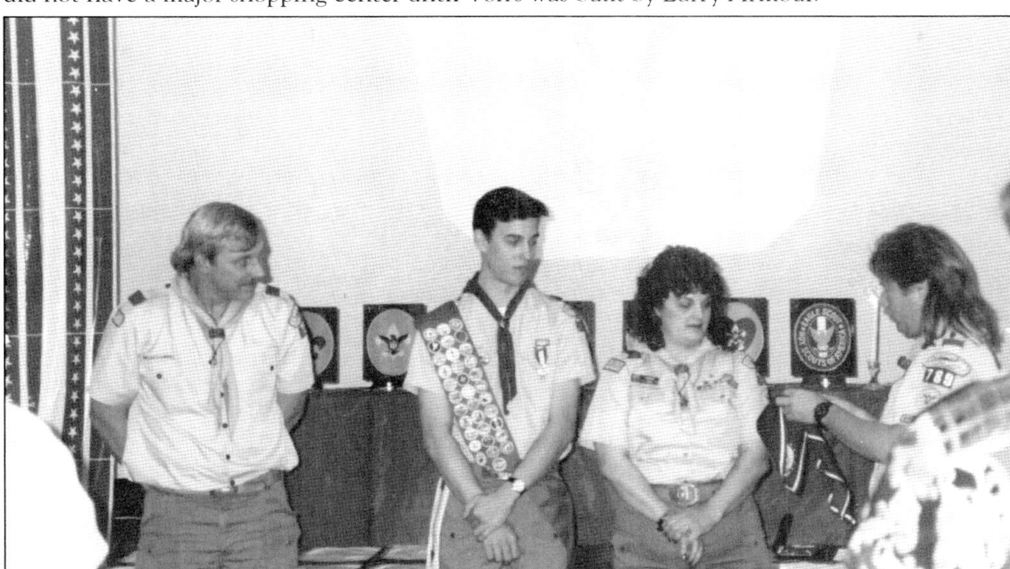

SCOUT TROOP 789, 1993. Scout Kevin Zuk receives his Eagle Scout badge. Kevin's project to attain this Scouting leadership honor was refurbishing the Sunday school trailer for the Walnut Valley Baptist Church on La Puente Road. Kevin directed others in this leadership project, replacing all of the outside walls, which were rotted, with new siding. This project took three weeks to complete. Pictured here are, from left to right, his father, Brian Zuk; Kevin; and his mother, Karen Zuk, at the Eagle Scout Court of Honor.

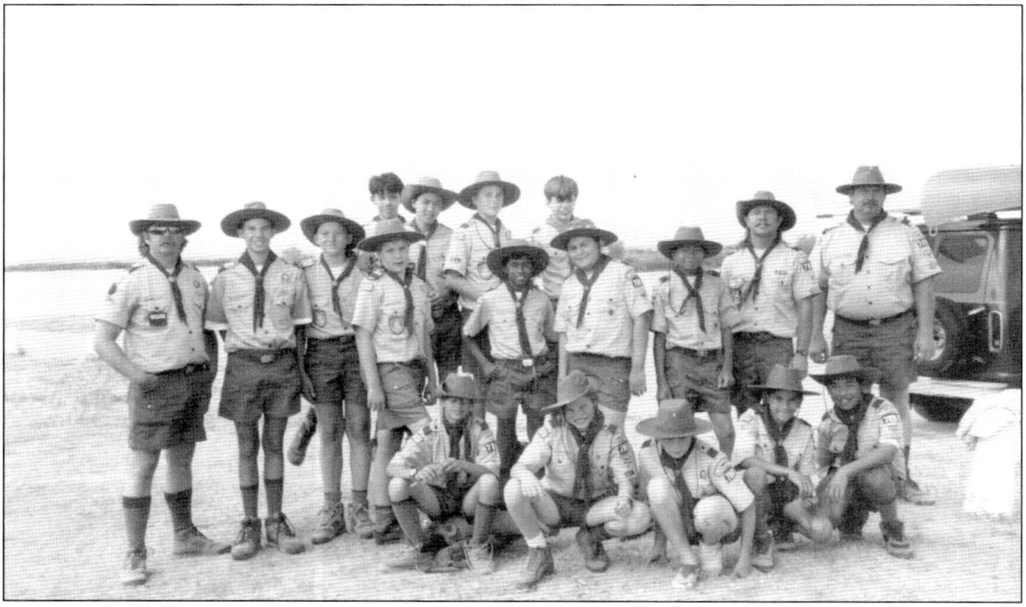

Camping Trip, 1994. On a camping trip to Buena Vista Lake, Boy Scout Troop 789 members include, from left to right, (first row) Tim Madison, James Madison, Danny Watts, Anthony Miller, and David Wu; (second row) Troop Leader Larry Watts, Andrew Courlet, Matt Peterson, Jesse Watts, Isuru Jayaratna, Joel Padilla, Picky Garcia, Richard Crawford, and Troop Leader Roger Madison; (third row) Eric Bonsal, Colin Nakagaki, Scoot Sweeney, and Eric Hoffman.

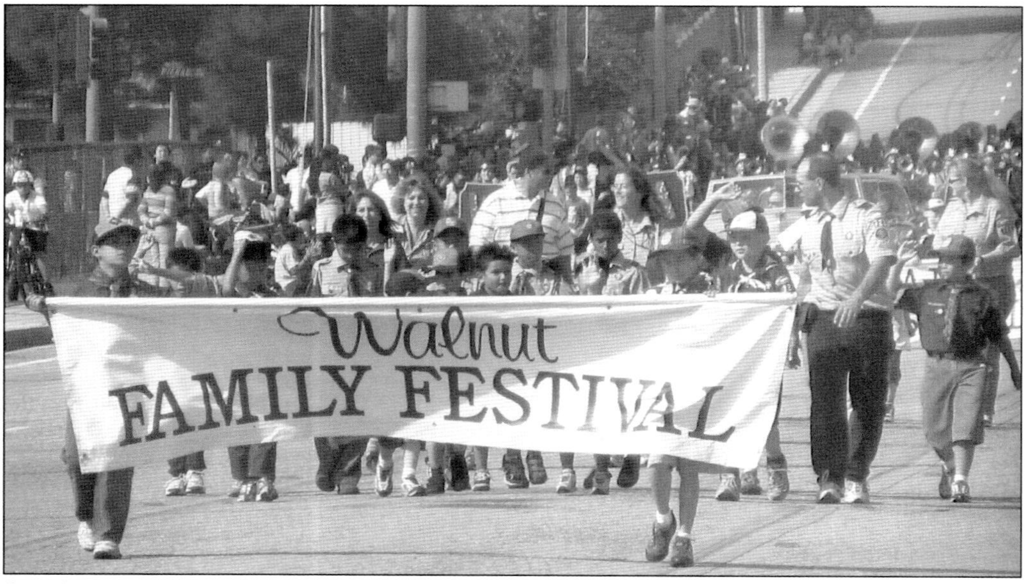

Cub Scout Pack 722, 2005. The Scouts lead the Family Festival Parade. From left to right are (first row) Steven Tragarz and Paul Sonner carrying the banner; (second row) Jackson Deng, Matthew Distante, Joseph Argudo, Christine Vidauri, and John Hernandez; (third row) Cory Chow, Gene Young, Joshua Chen, Somil Patel, Ben Lundblade, and Allen Lin. Adults are, from left to right, (first row) Debbie Dobson, Nancy Tragarz, Paul Vargas, Anne Sonner, Ken Tragarz, and Rae Walker; (second row) Brian Sonner, David Tragarz, and Nick Cook.

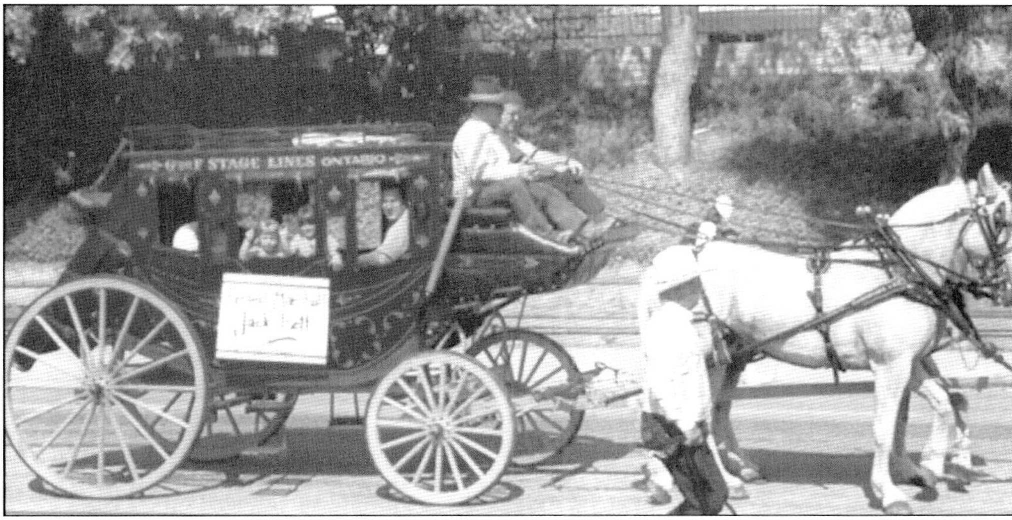

Family Festival Parade, 1996. Former mayor Jack Isett and his family lead the parade in 1996. Mayor Isett plays the grand marshal riding in a stagecoach that in the 1880s would come down La Puente Road. The road in those days was called the road to La Puente Rancho or road to Spadra.

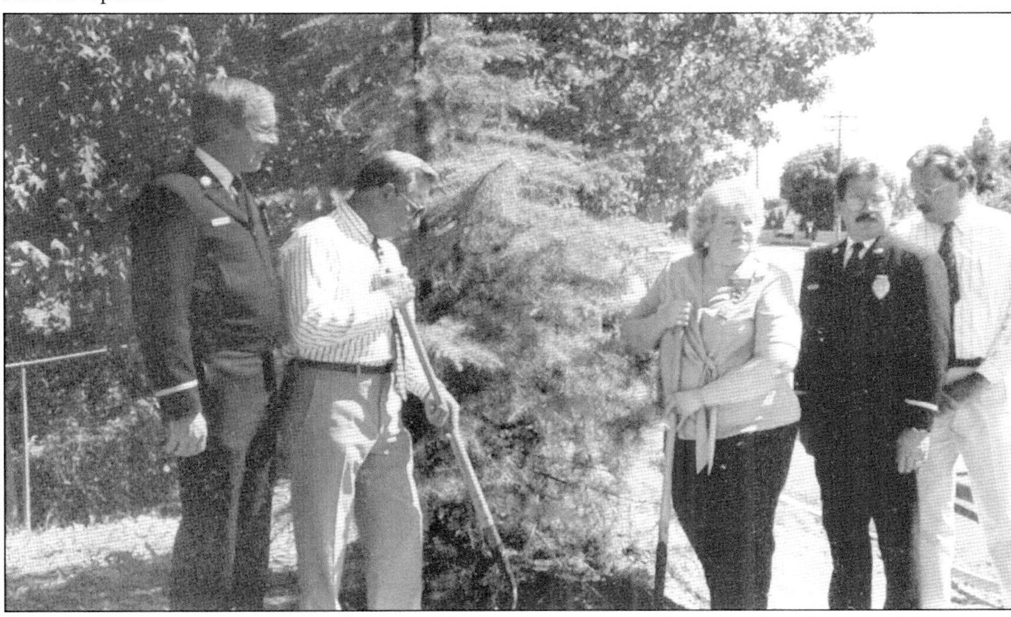

Walnut Valley Women's Club, 1991. The Walnut Valley Women's Club (WVWC) planted a tree in front of Fire Station 61 on La Puente Road. The tree became part of an annual scholarship fundraiser held in December for scholarships awarded to local high school students. The tree is decorated and lit during the Christmas season in Walnut's Christmas tree lighting ceremony. Donations are made to purchase a light or ornament, which is tagged in honor of an individual, the donor, or a family. The "Tree of Lights" raises approximately $6,000 each year. Keith Walton donated the tree and was there to see it planted along with the president of the women's club that year, Joan Hyatt, and Walnut community service director John Davidson. The club celebrated the 20th year of this fund in 2011.

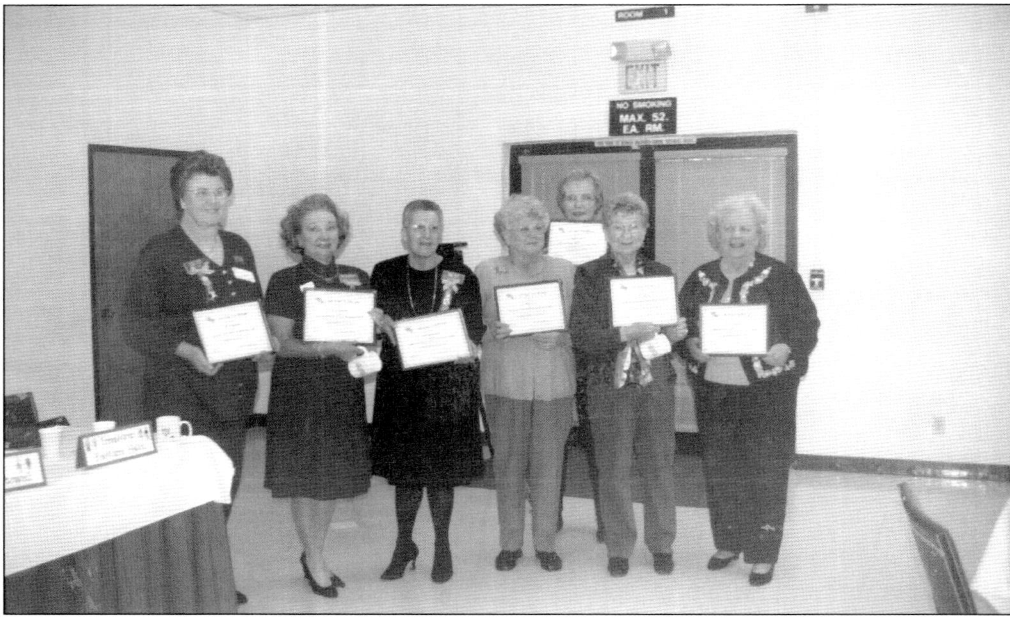

ANNIVERSARY OF WVWC, 1994. The Walnut Valley Women's Club celebrated 25 years of service to the community in 1994. The club was federated in 1964 and incorporated in 1969. Over the years, the club has been committed to community improvement to enrich the quality of life throughout the city of Walnut. One major project was to furnish the inside of the W.R. Rowland Adobe Redwood Ranch House in 1976 at Lemon Creek Park. Collecting money for scholarships for seniors at local high schools has been a top priority. Receiving their certificates of 25 years of service are, from left to right, Jeanne Stowell, Dee Chambers, June Wentworth, Barbara Hahn, Karen Holte, Josie Walker, and Betty Howard.

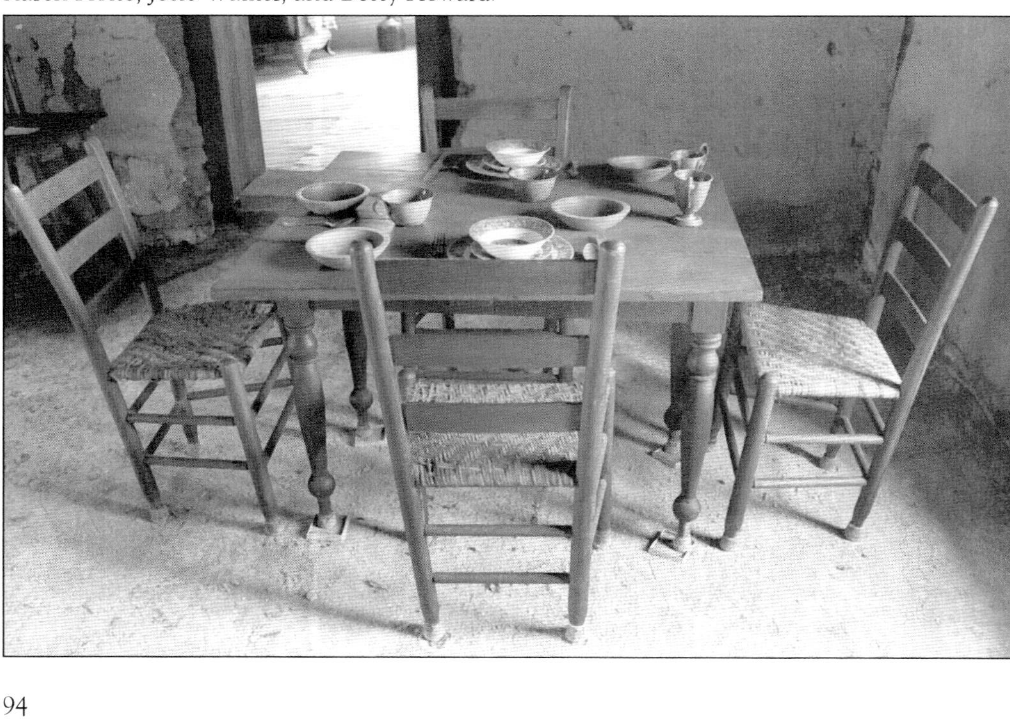

Seven

WALNUT DEVELOPMENT

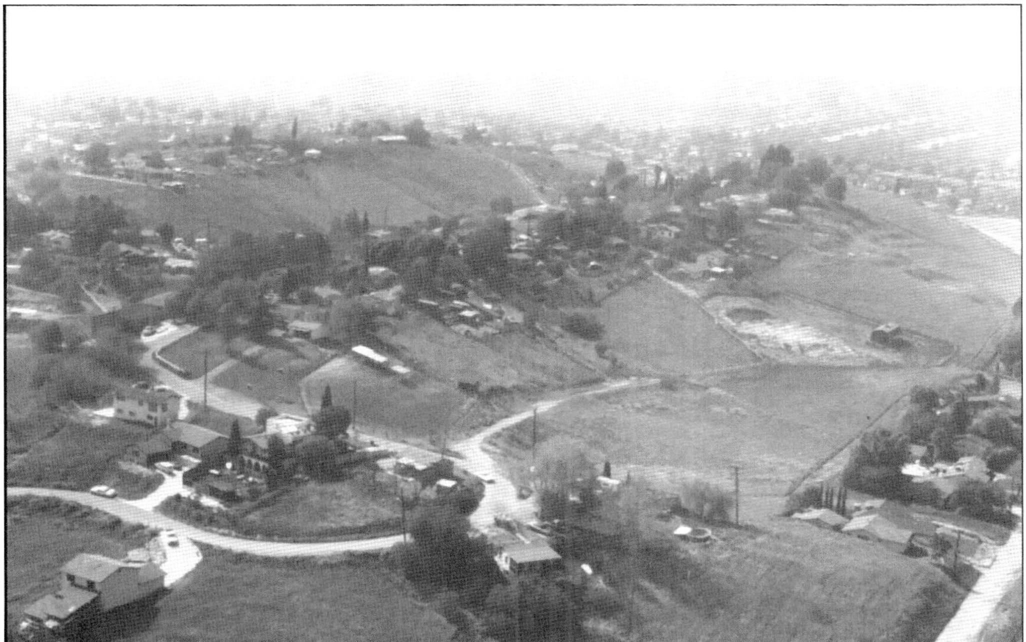

CASTLE HILL DRIVE, 1950S. One of the first streets to be built in the city during the 1950s, Castle Hill Drive was a private road, which it remains today. The road comes off Valley Boulevard and winds up a steep hill. It has a beautiful view of the San Gabriel Valley. It is in a rural overlay zone, and residents still have horses on their property.

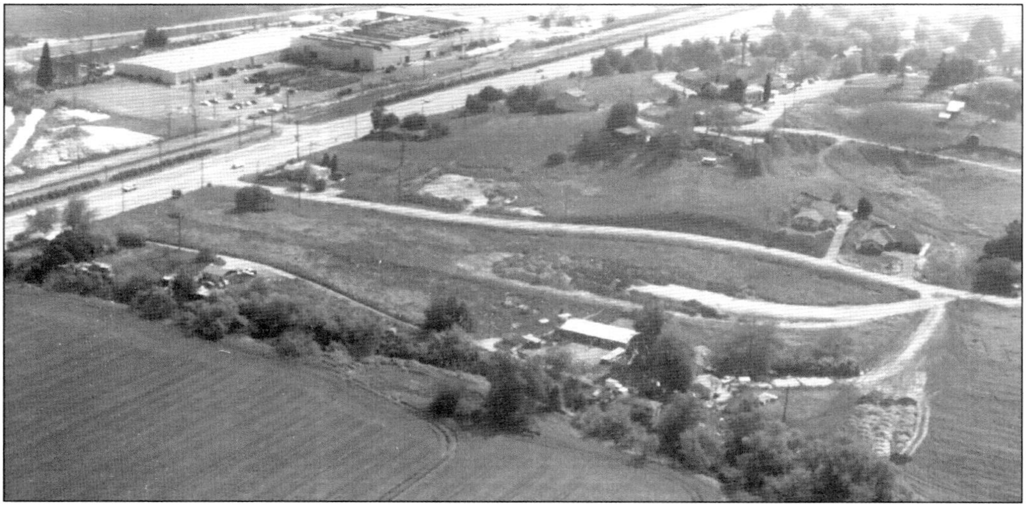

Rowland Manor, 1950s. The manor was located on the southwest boundary of Walnut in the late 1950s. The 250-unit tract contained 95 percent of the 934 residents when the city incorporated in 1959. Clustered on Valley Boulevard were only a few commercial establishments. The tract was built on nonconforming lots and remains that way today. The name was changed during the 1960s to West Walnut.

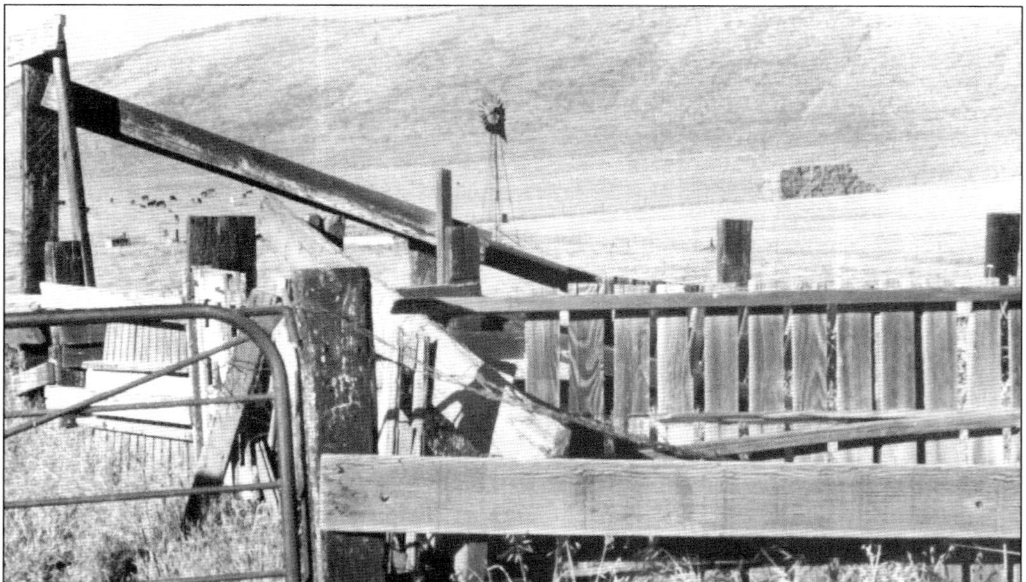

Development, 1980s. Until the late 1980s, Walnut's uneven terrain was almost completely ignored by developers, who preferred sites less costly to grade and with easy access to freeways. The city was hidden by Kellogg Hill and Forest Lawn coming from the San Bernardino freeway. A small two-lane road over the San Jose Hills connected Walnut's Collegewood area and Mount San Antonio College to Grand Avenue to the north. The 60 Freeway was still under construction, and while several developments were completed in this southwestern area of the city, there were still vast areas of undeveloped land. Thus farmers like Randy Bennett and the Carrey family had an opportunity to farm the land and raise cattle until the 1970s.

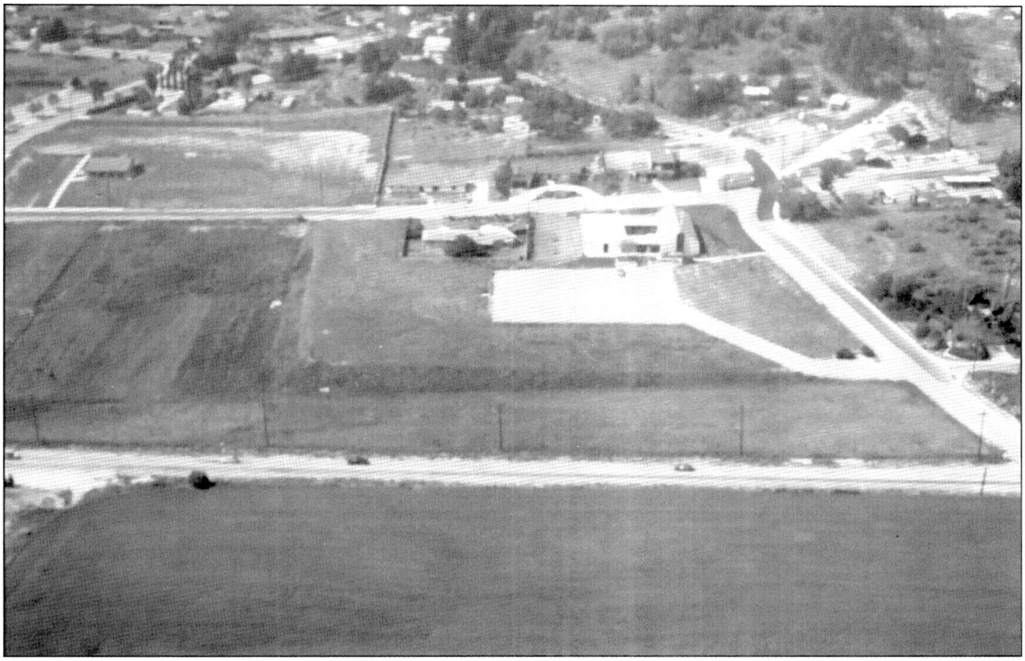

La Puente Road, 1960s. The structure between La Puente Road and Marcon Drive is the Lutheran church, built in the early 1960s. Most of the surrounding land was used for farming hay, grain, and citrus. To the left is part of Suzanne Park.

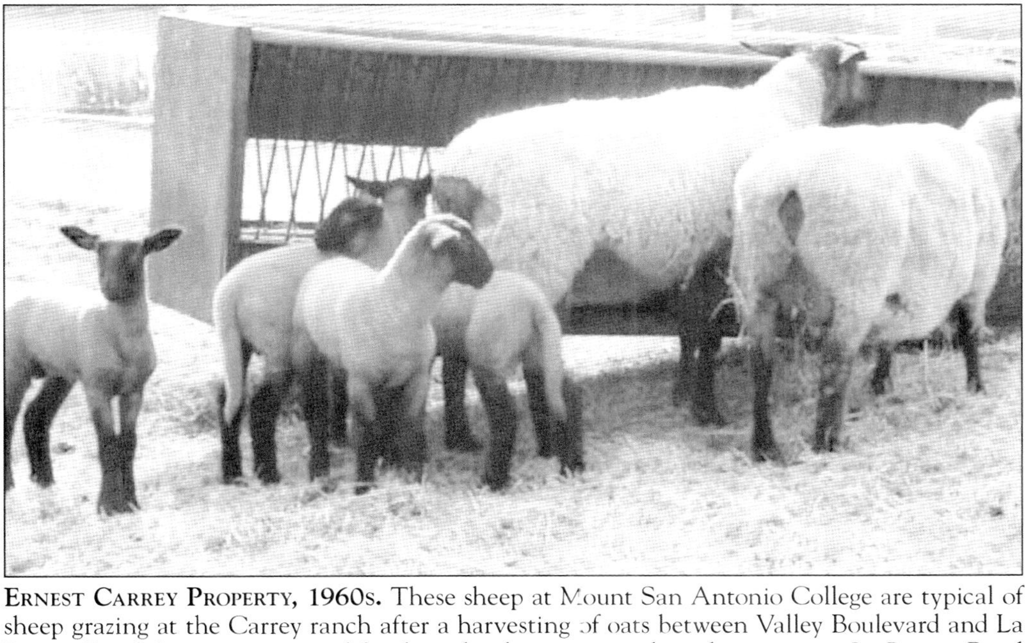

Ernest Carrey Property, 1960s. These sheep at Mount San Antonio College are typical of sheep grazing at the Carrey ranch after a harvesting of oats between Valley Boulevard and La Puente Road. It was not unusual for sheep-herders to move their sheep east on La Puente Road to a new location on any given day. The hundreds of sheep would fill the road; this was when La Puente Road was only two small lanes. These sheep from Mount San Angelo College are typical of the sheep found grazing at the Carrey Ranch.

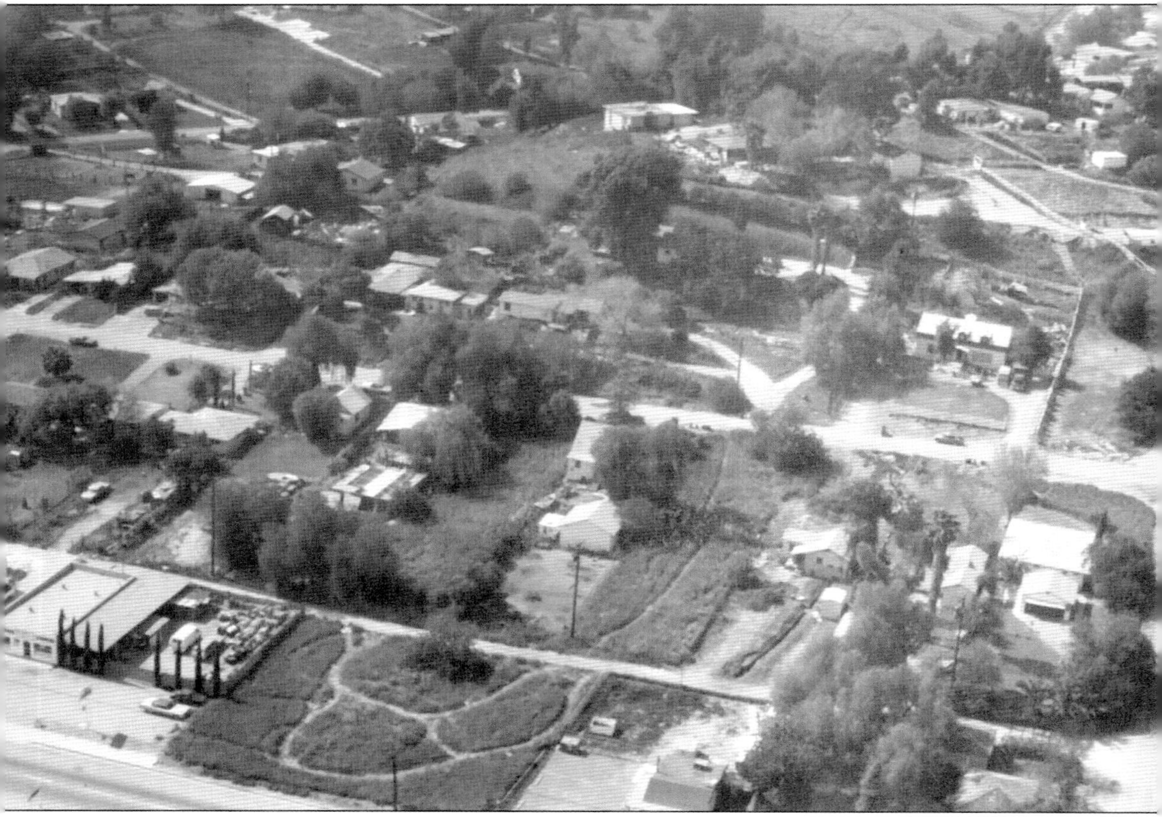

Walnut's Commercial Area, 1960s. Several of the early commercial businesses opened on Valley Boulevard, including a new hardware store. Behind the hardware store is the only alley built in the city, running from Camino De Rosa to Castle Hill Drive. This was Walnut's only commercial area until the late 1960s. In 1910, Valley Boulevard was called San Bernardino Road or Road to San Bernardino.

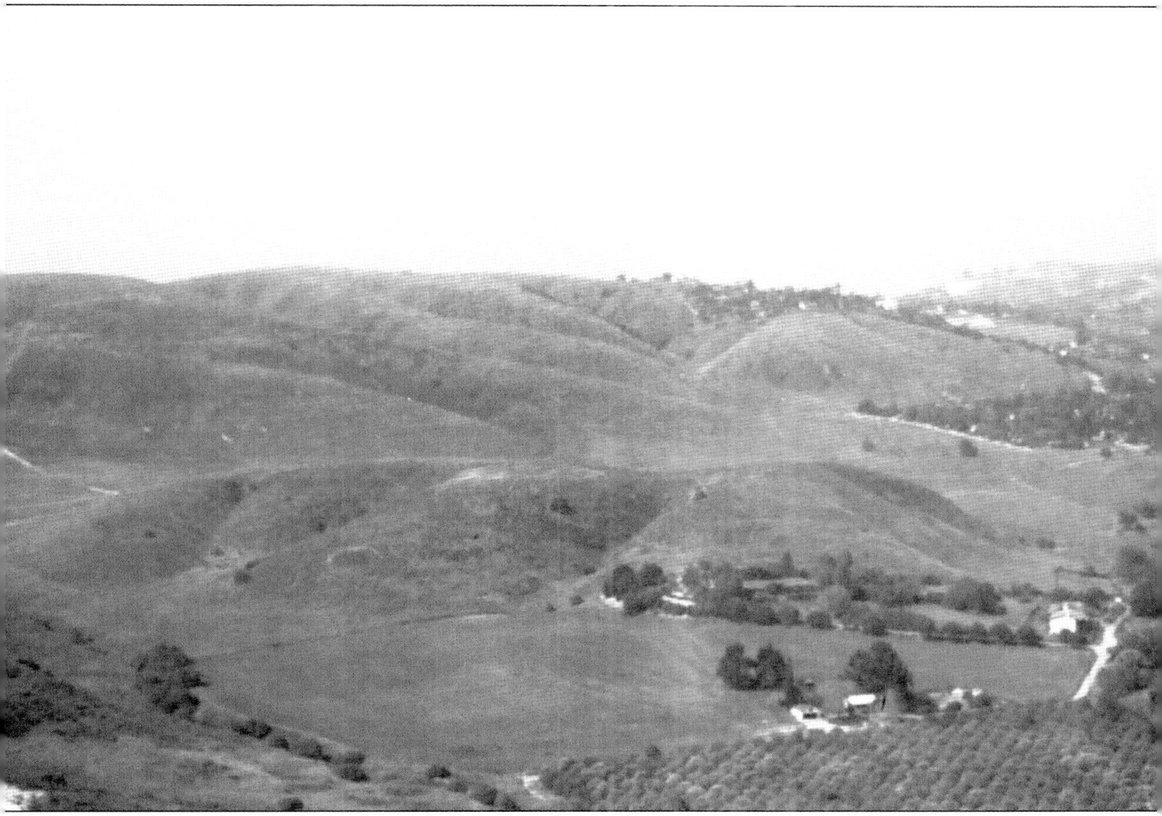

GRIEGORIAN FARM HOUSE AND CHANGE OF DEVELOPMENT, 1960S. The city council was planning to approve major developments, producing a population between 60,000 to 90,000. A general plan was also being studied to include townhouses, duplexes, and apartments, as well as single-family homes. A small group of men, including Bill Wentworth, Bill Daley, and Bill Cotton began a referendum in 1966 to stop the high duplex development that Home Savings and Loan was planning for the area off La Puente Road. Each one of these men was elected to the Walnut City Council and changed the direction of the city. Walnut's population in 2011 was more than 29,000.

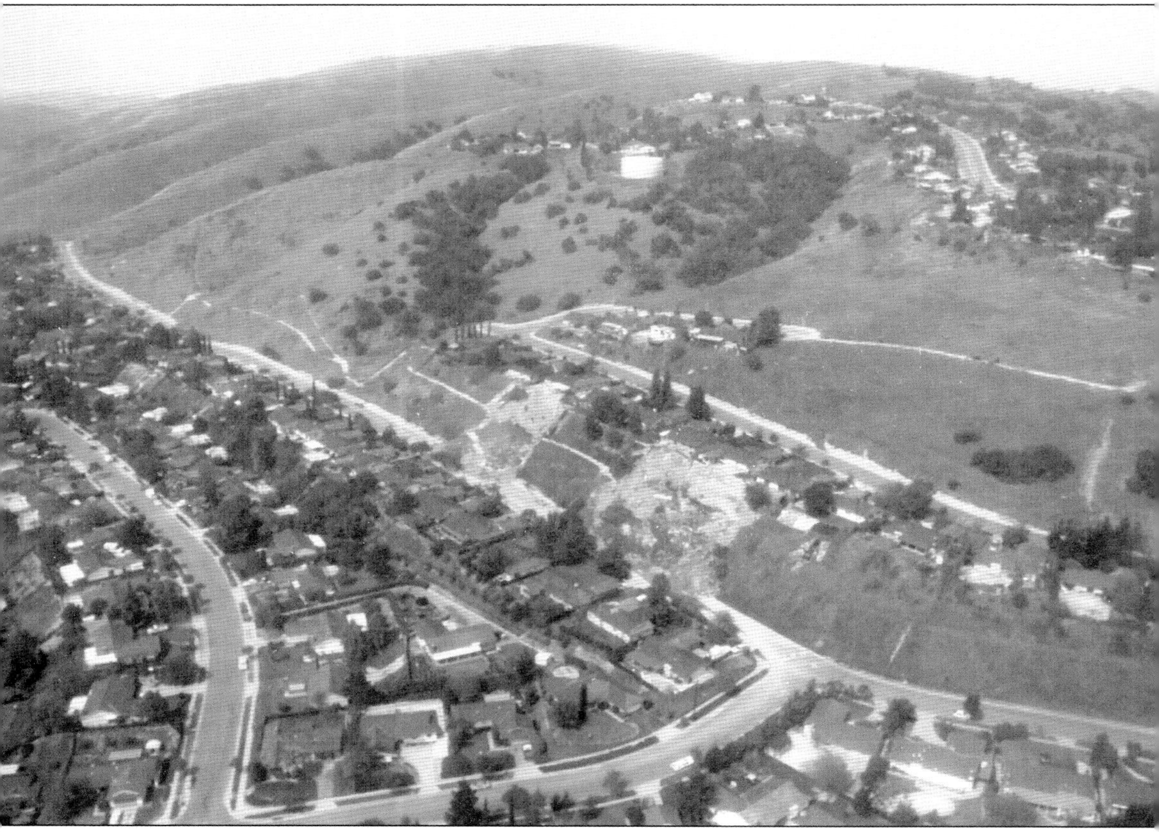

COLLEGEWOOD SLIDES, 1969. The Collegewood development had massive mudslides from the heavy rains that occurred in the spring. Consultants determined the slides were caused by insufficient pad and slope drainage, a previously constructed stabilization blanket with relatively weak bedrocks, and an unusually high groundwater condition that resulted in insignificant excess pore pressure. On Shadow Mount Road, one home slid down the hill, and one home was uninhabited for many years. Many homes on Buckland Drive were left hanging precariously on the side of the hill. This was Walnut's first major hillside development, and many lessons were learned on how to build on the many slopes left to be developed.

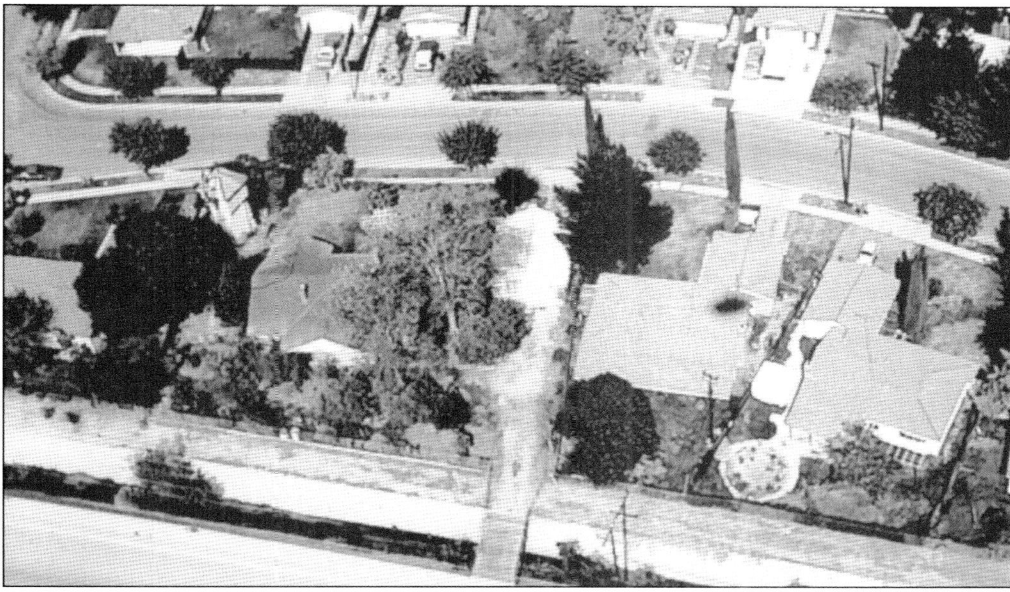

Bourdet Land Development, 1960s. Walnut's first housing tract was built on part of the Bourdet farmland. Pete Bourdet began to sell his land because of high taxes, and homes were built beginning in 1961 around the Bourdet home. The Bourdet home frontage faced Lemon Avenue, and the rest of the tract faced the opposite way. It is the only house in Walnut that faced a major street; all the other homes were built inward.

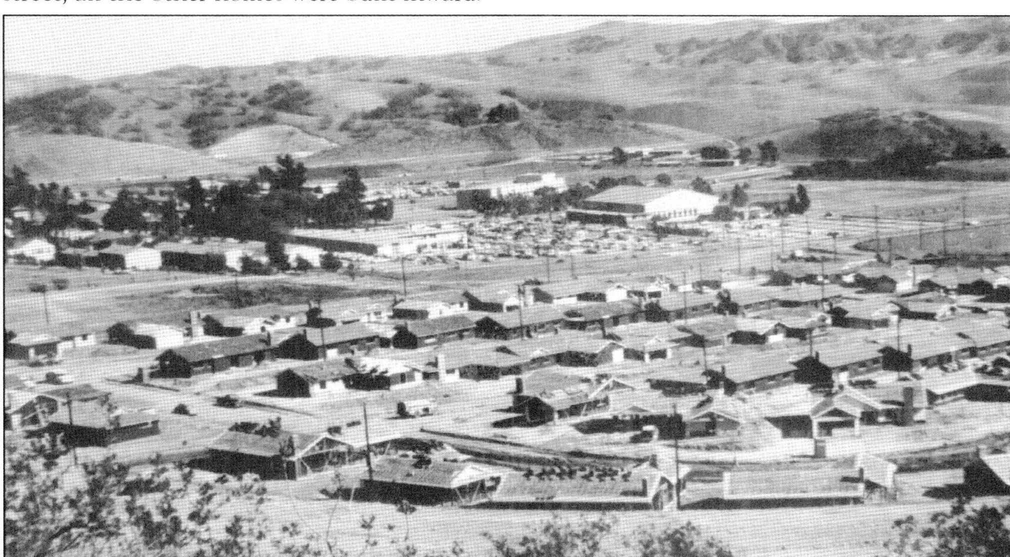

Collegewood Tract, 1960s. Butler Harbour Construction Company began the Collegewood housing tract in 1962 in the northeastern part of the city, across the street from Mount San Antonio College. Butler Harbor was also scheduled to build a multi-million-dollar shopping center in this area, but the plans never came to fruition. The land stayed vacant until the late 1980s, when a major shopping center was built by a different company. Only a small number of stores provided shopping opportunities for the area across from Mount San Antonio College a few years earlier.

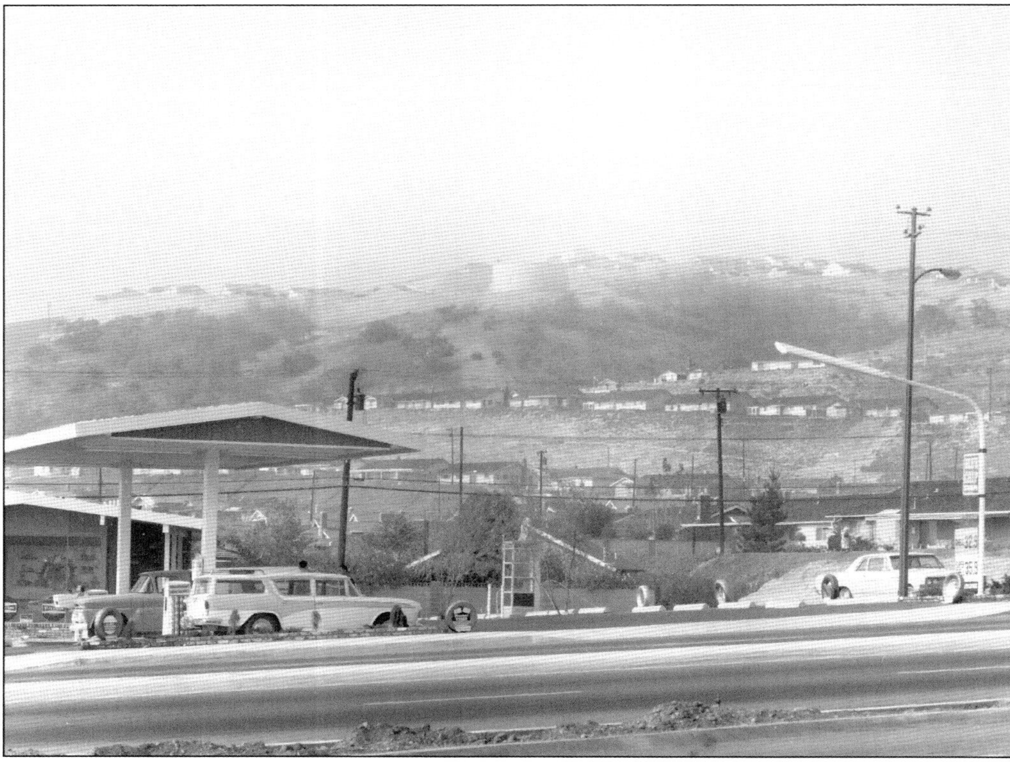

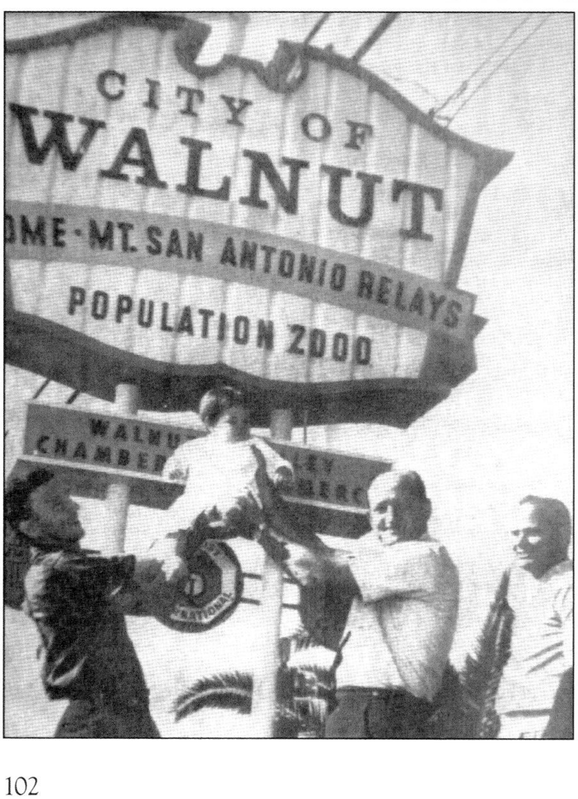

First Gas Station, 1964. Built on the corner of San Jose Road and Grand Avenue, the Shell station does not exist today. Gas sold for 32¢ a gallon. The Walnut Valley Water District's new water tank can be seen behind the station.

Chamber of Commerce Sign, 1964. From left to right are Walnut Valley Chamber of Commerce president Bud Kelso, Sarah Harvey, postmaster Henry Davis, and Walnut School Board president Larry Wallin. Located on the corner of Lemon Avenue and Valley Boulevard, the sign advertised the city and the Mount San Antonio Relays. By 1966, Walnut's population had grown to 2,000. Sarah Harvey (the baby) was the daughter of Betty and George Harvey. Leonard and George Harvey ran a small grocery store on Valley Boulevard at Camino De Gloria. It was the only grocery store in town.

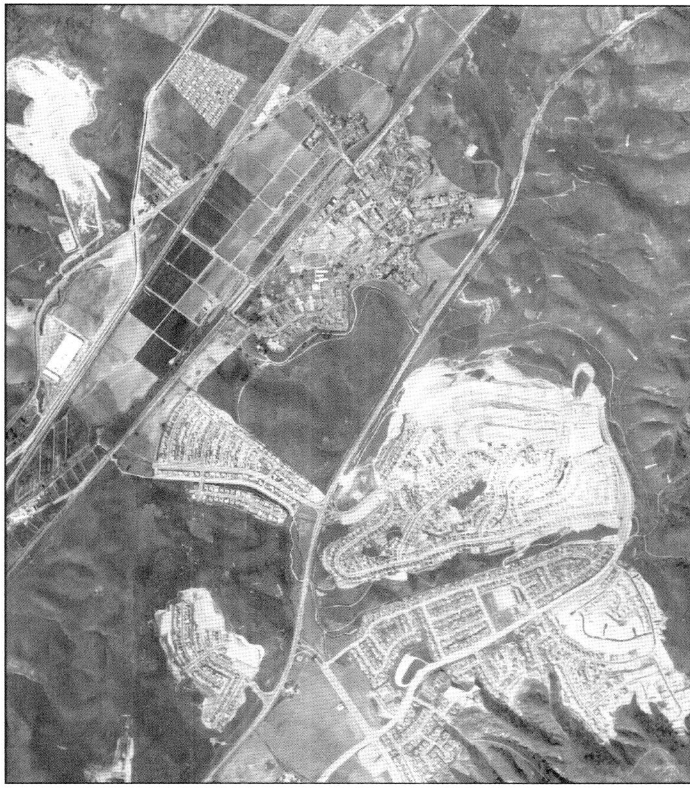

CITY OF WALNUT, 1966. The map shows that very little growth had occurred since the city incorporated in 1959. Walnut's population in 1966 included 3,000 people.

DUBUQUE AVENUE, 1960s. In the hills in the city's northeastern area, construction of homes was held pending the adoption of Walnut's general plan.

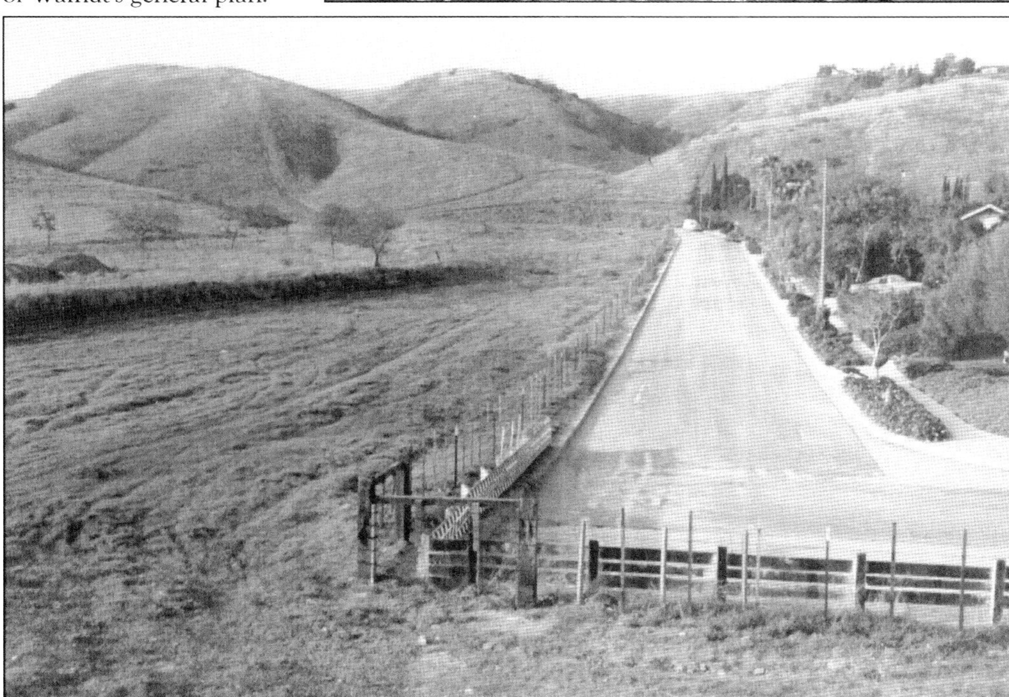

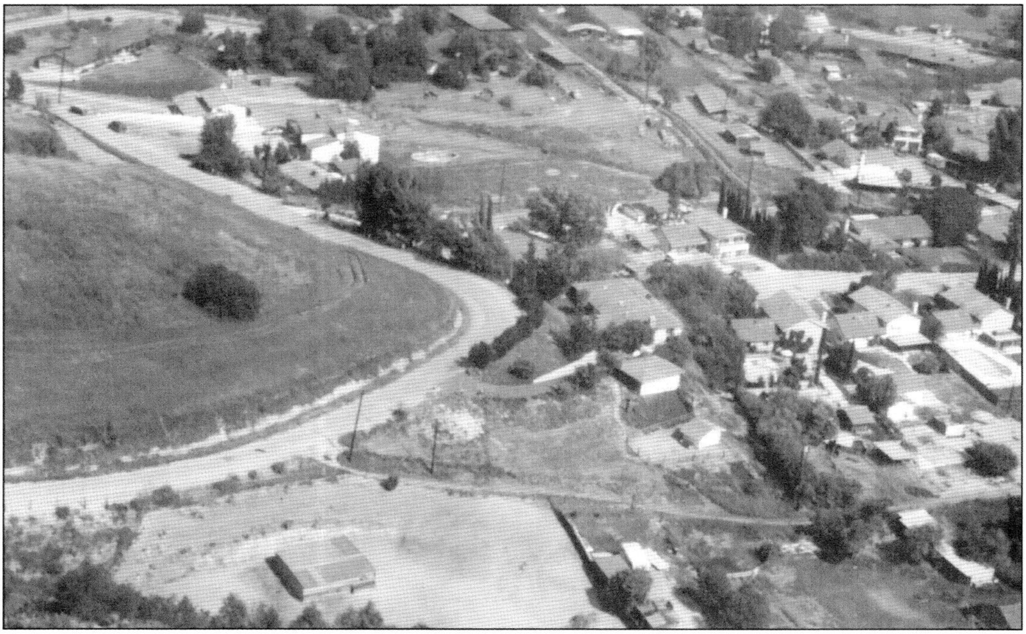

Gartel Drive, 1960s. The private road runs east to west and has large lots and big houses. The road is long and narrow with no curbs or gutters. It is not a city street; it is maintained by the residents living there. Many of the residents kept horses and barns in the 1960s and 1970s due to the rural overlay zone.

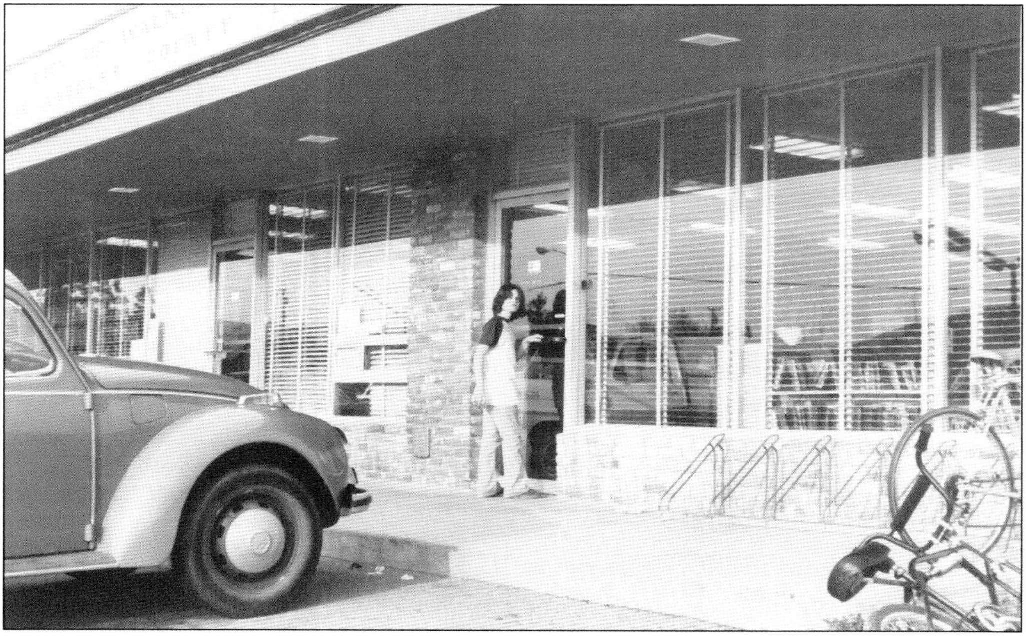

The Liquorette, 1960s. The first commercial development in Walnut was built on Pierre Road off Valley Boulevard. The Walnut Public Library, operated by Los Angeles County, opened here in 1970 along with a Bank of America branch. In the 1980s, Bank of America moved locations to its present building on Lemon Avenue.

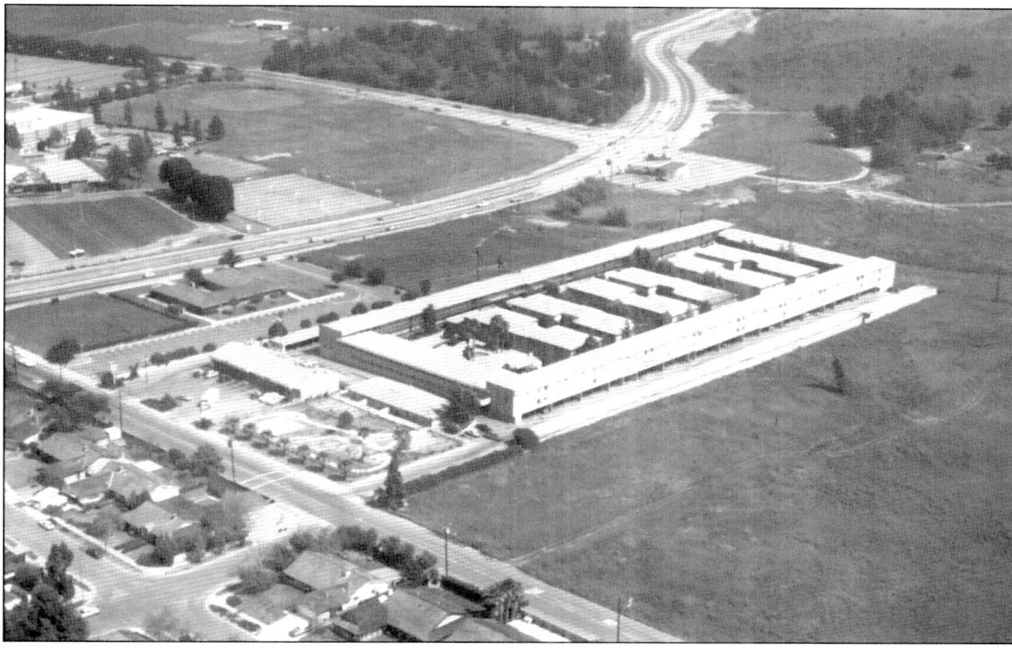

Grand Avenue and Temple Avenue, 1964. At this time, Walnut had very few commercial buildings on Grand Avenue. In this area was Mount San Antonio College, the wildlife sanctuary, a gas station, the Institute of Religion for the Church of Latter-day Saints, and Walnut's only apartment building. When the general plan was adopted in 1978, it did not have zoning for apartments.

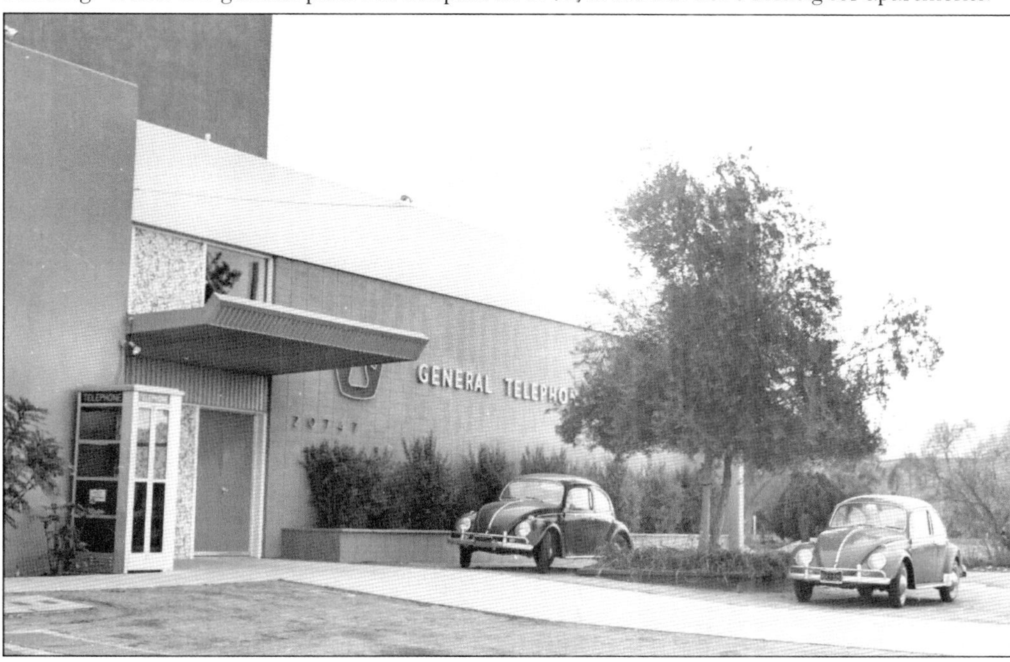

General Telephone Storage Building, Early 1970s. The building stood alone for many years on Valley Boulevard until the industrial area surrounding it began to develop in the 1980s. In 2011, it is still an electrical storage building for General Telephone on Valley Boulevard.

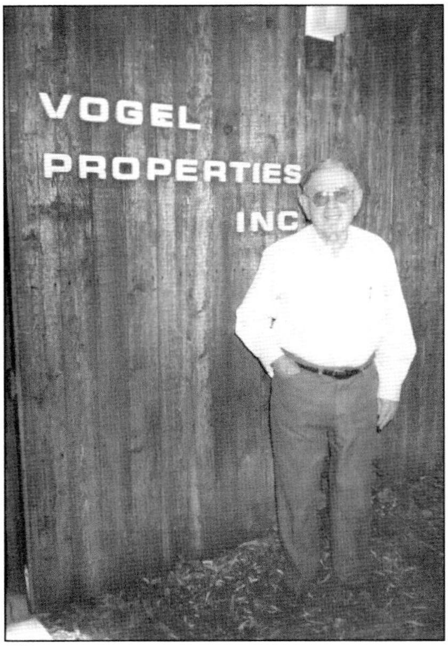

Bill Vogel, Early 1970s. Bill Vogel bought 20 acres of vacant land on Valley Boulevard and Lemon Avenue. He developed it into small industrial buildings and completed his project in 1976. He then purchased adjacent land and built larger industrial buildings. Before the property was developed, he grew corn and sold it from the back of a pick-up truck on Valley Boulevard. Vogel would also let the city hold public meetings in some of his buildings, where important subjects such as Walnut's general plan were discussed. The general plan designated 141 industrially zoned acres, which included Vogel's property. Vogel, his wife, Carmen, and sons, Robert and William, moved to Walnut in 1983.

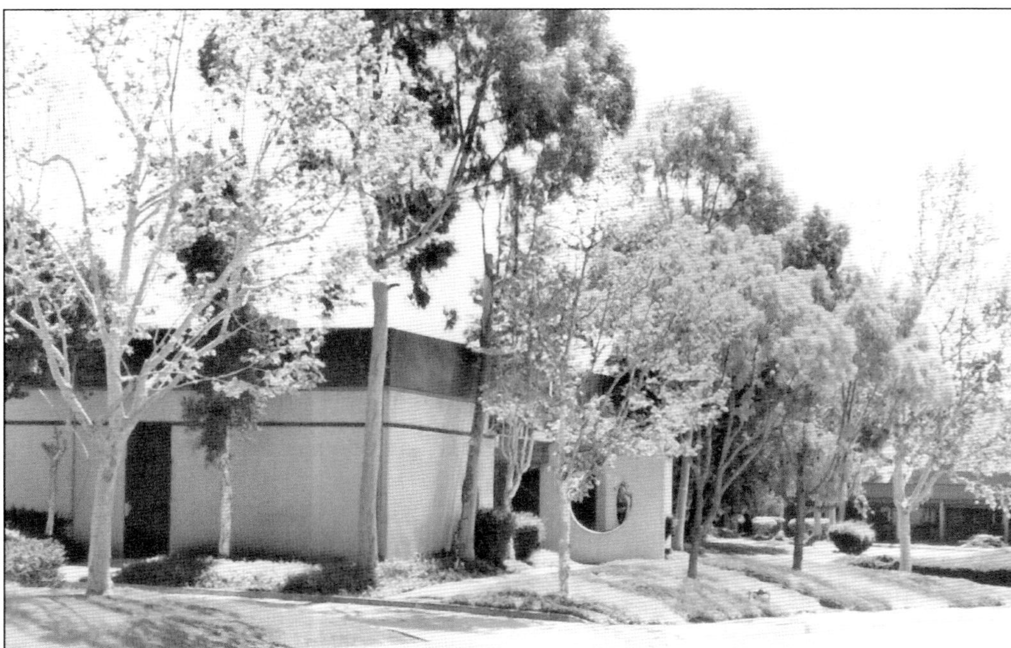

Bill Vogel's Development, 1970s. While developing his property on Valley Boulevard and Lemon Avenue, Vogel received offers from fast-food companies and liquor stores for his corner property. He felt this would cheapen his industrial park and did not accept their offers. He wanted prestige for his development with a bank or financial institution; therefore, he kept this corner undeveloped while he worked toward his goal. The corner has had several banks located on it. The City of Walnut wanted Spanish names as street names; Vogel gave the streets in his development names such as Paseo Sonrisa (Happy Trail), Paseo Del Prado (A Walk through the Meadow) and Paseo Tesoro (Treasurer Trail).

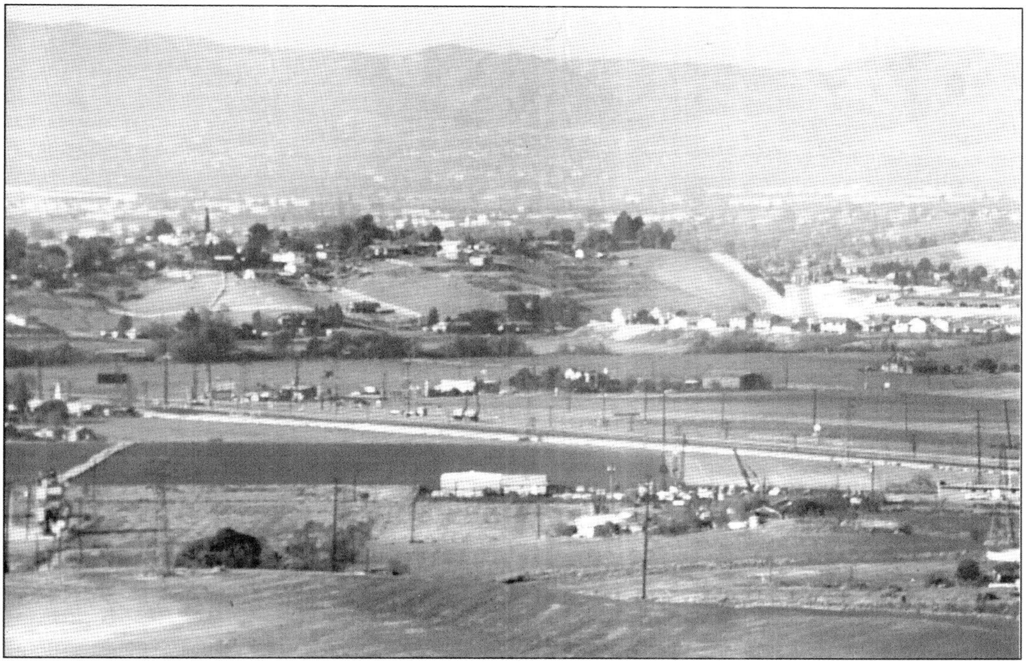

THE COMMERCE CENTER, 1970S. Until this time, the industrial area off Valley Boulevard and Lemon Avenue was occupied by the Comino family. Giuseppe and Blanco Comino's entrance to their home was off Valley Boulevard.

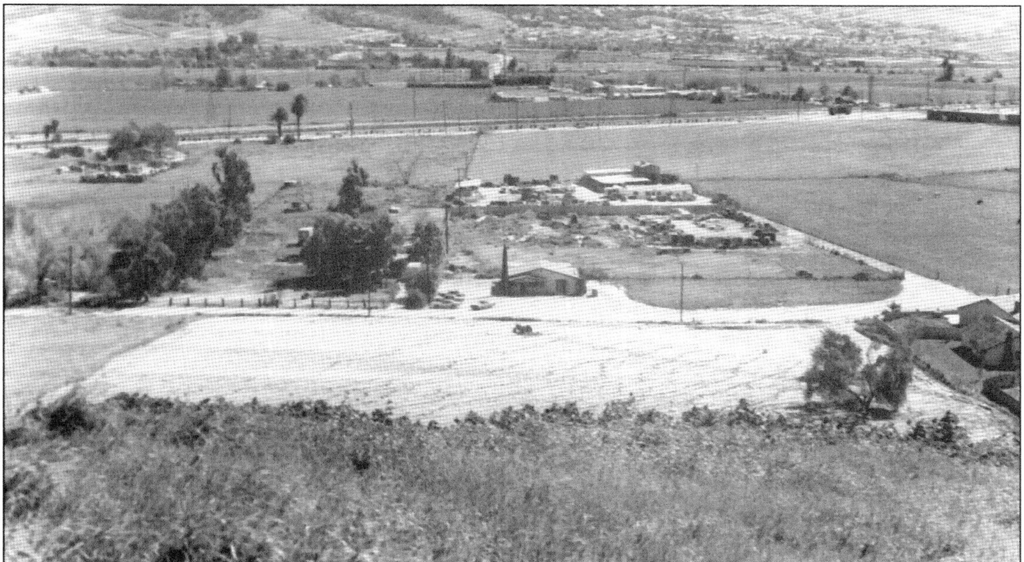

CARREY ROAD COUNCIL HOME, 1970S. During the 1970s, the council planned the future of Walnut in this small home. Important decisions made and adopted include Walnut's code book and general plan. Mayor Joe Hahn, Bill Wentworth, Bill Cotton, Bill Daley, and Jim Zamary adopted the general plan in July 12, 1978. During the 1970s, the residents on the council decided to make Walnut a single-family residential community. The higher the elevation of the land, the less density the developer was allowed.

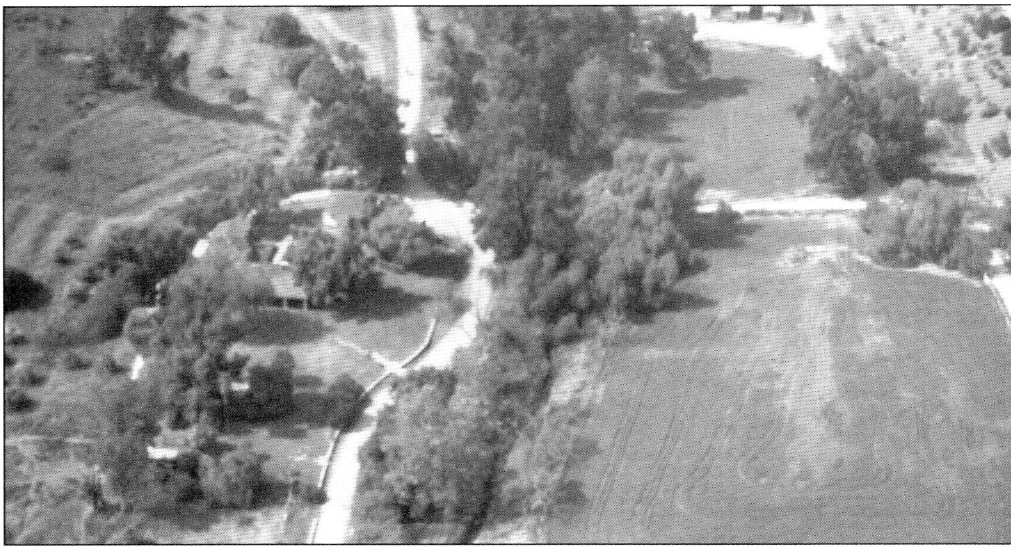

Winnett Ranch, 1930s. The property was once a part of an 1,800-acre ranch owned by Exupere Sentous from the late 1880s until 1935. At this time, the parcel was reduced to 80 acres and sold to wealthy businessman J.P. Winnett. Winnett cofounded Bullocks department stores, and during the week, he lived on Wilshire Boulevard. He used the ranch off La Puente Road on weekends to host parties and special events, including annual foxhunts. Ranch activities were frequently featured in the *Los Angeles Times* society section between 1930 and 1956. In 1944, the movie *National Velvet* with Elizabeth Taylor was produced in the lush hills on the property.

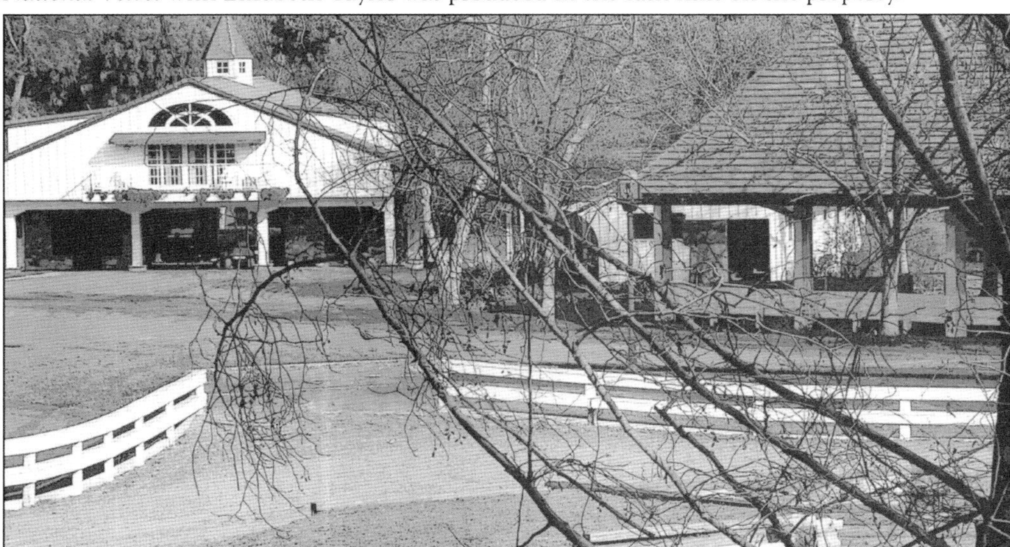

Brookside Equestrian, 1968. The equestrian center was part of the Winnett Ranch. When Winnett died in 1968, Claremont Colleges inherited the 80 acres and Keith Walton bought 28 acres, which he restored, keeping the original barns authentic to the 1930s. Today, the ranch serves as the training headquarters for the US Olympic equestrian team. The Waltons also have dressage training, board horses, and host special events such as movies and television shows, commercials, weddings, corporate events, and private parties.

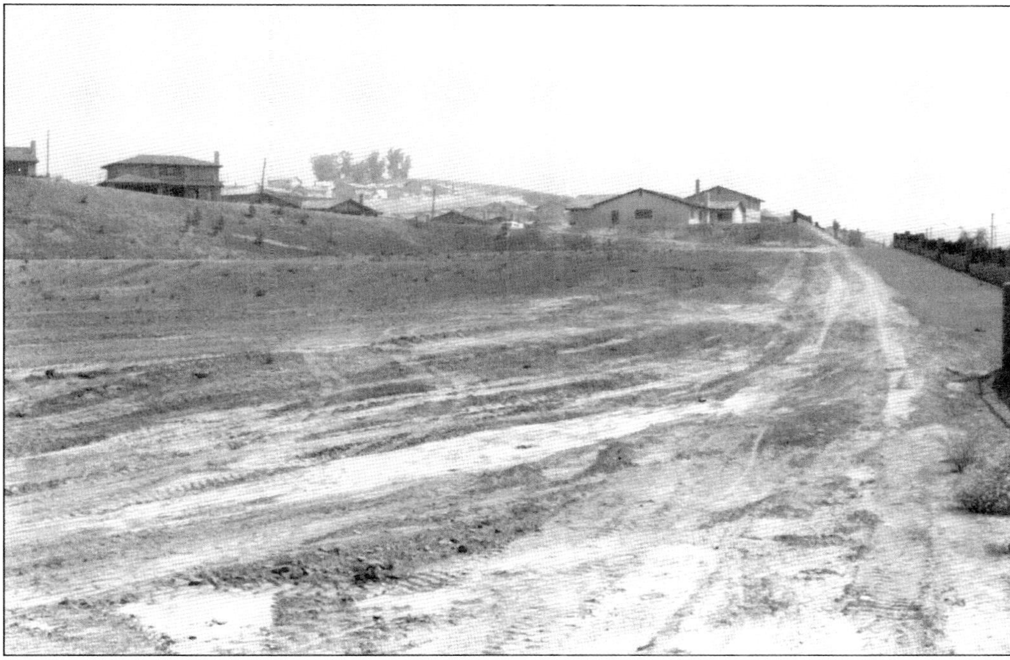

COUNTRY VIEW TRACT, 1973. Located off La Puente Road, this development was built by the La Solana Corporation. The single-family home development began construction before the general plan was adopted in 1978. Until this time, La Puente Road was a small, two-lane street with few homes, and the developer had to build bridle trails along the front of the development. This was the start of the 26-mile bridle trail system in the city. After this, all developers had to put bridle trails in front of developments.

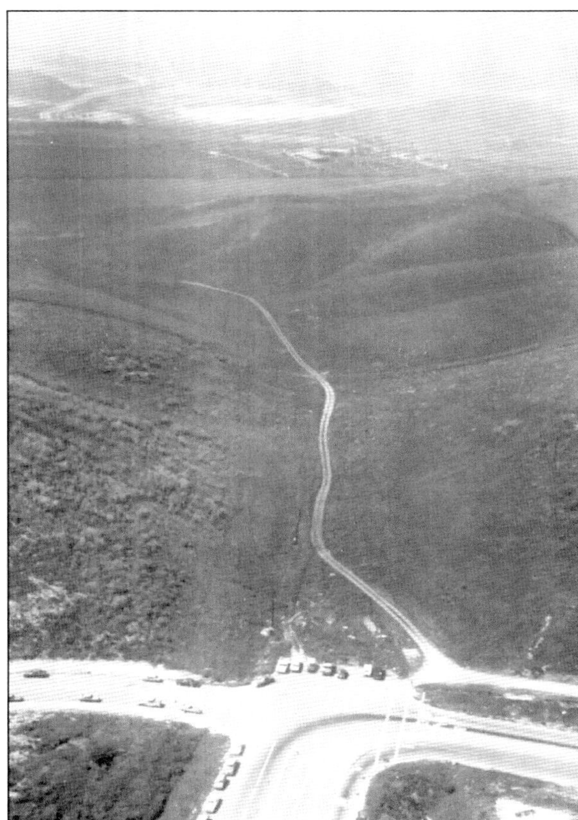

ROLLING HILLS, 1980S. This photograph shows the beautiful hills of Walnut before massive grading took place in the 1980s. As one resident said, "Living in Walnut before the big developers came in was like living in paradise."

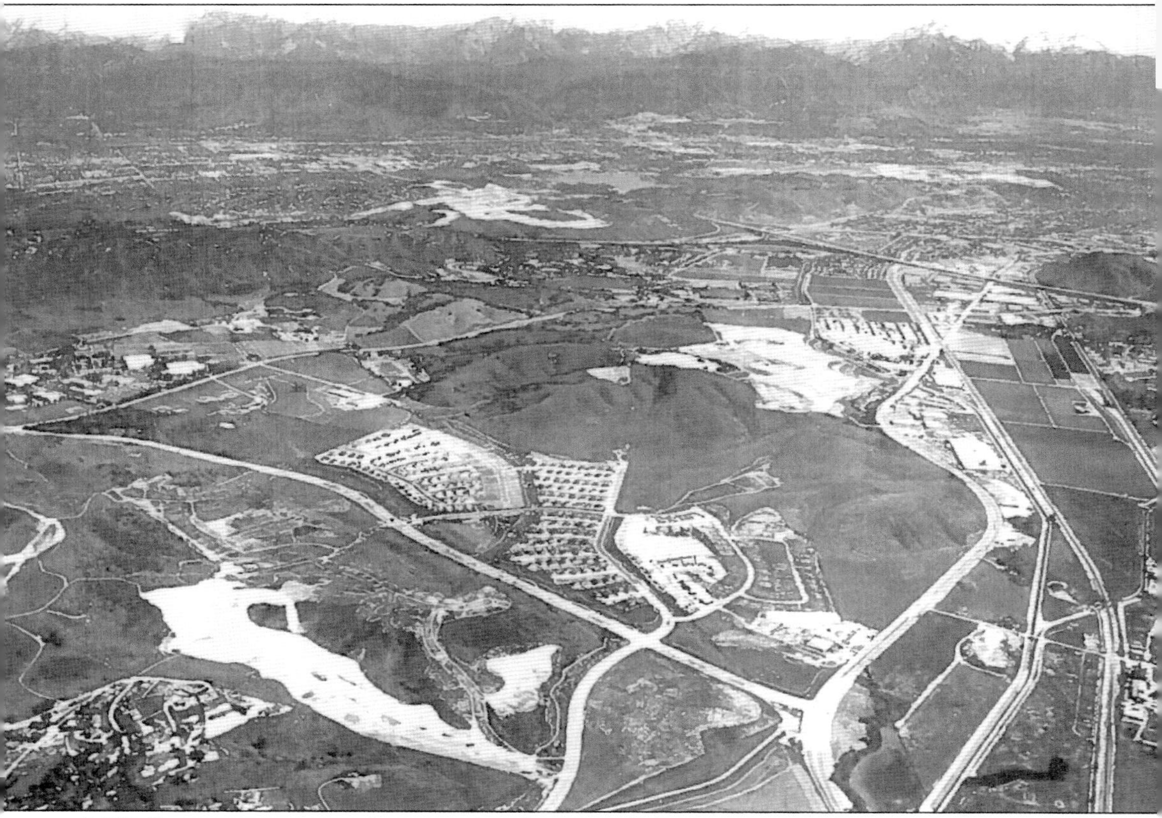

RDP Ordinance, 1970s. In 1979, after the general plan was approved, zoning became a widely discussed and controversial issue. The council prepared an RDP ordinance that would permit a developer to cluster single-family homes on less than the lot size required by the zoning, provided the balance of the land was used for a school site, parks, recreational areas, or open space held in common or granted to the city. After a bitter fight to approve an initial ordinance that would limit the development of clustering, an election was held to decide which plan to adopt. When neither passed, the RDP that was later adopted by the council stipulated housing density would be limited to the number of lots allowed in each zone per the general plan. The homes east of Grand Avenue were built on smaller lots that left many acres of open space, including Snow Creek stream and Snow Creek Park, which was built as part of the developer's Park and Lieu fees.

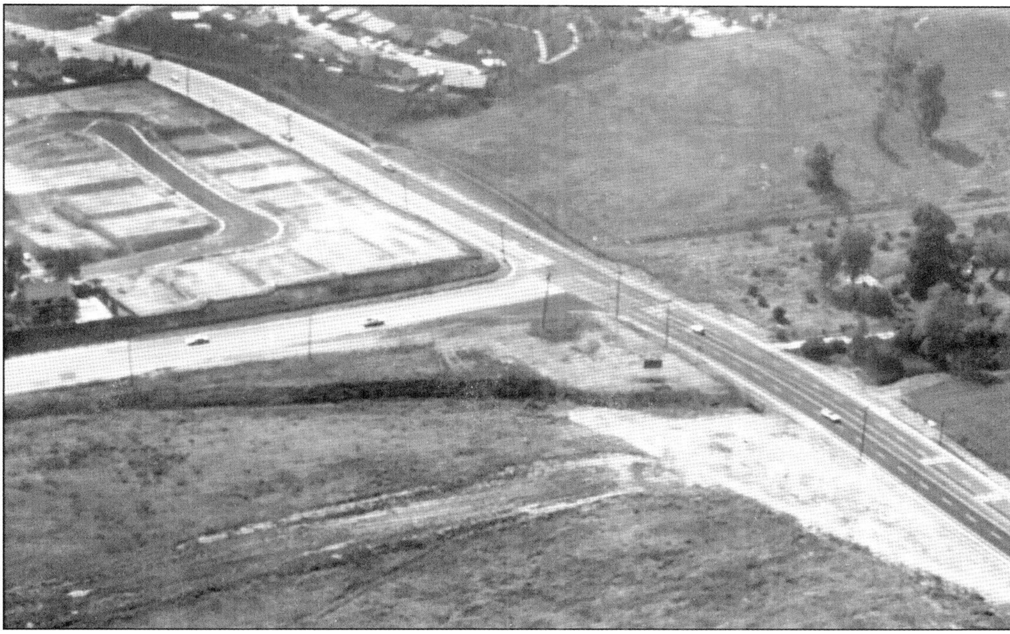

LEMON AVENUE AND LA PUENTE ROAD, LATE 1970s. This photograph shows building pads for a housing development off La Puente Road. Lemon Avenue ends at La Puente Road. Von's shopping center is not yet built in the bottom left of the photograph, and the Winnett Ranch is visible on the right.

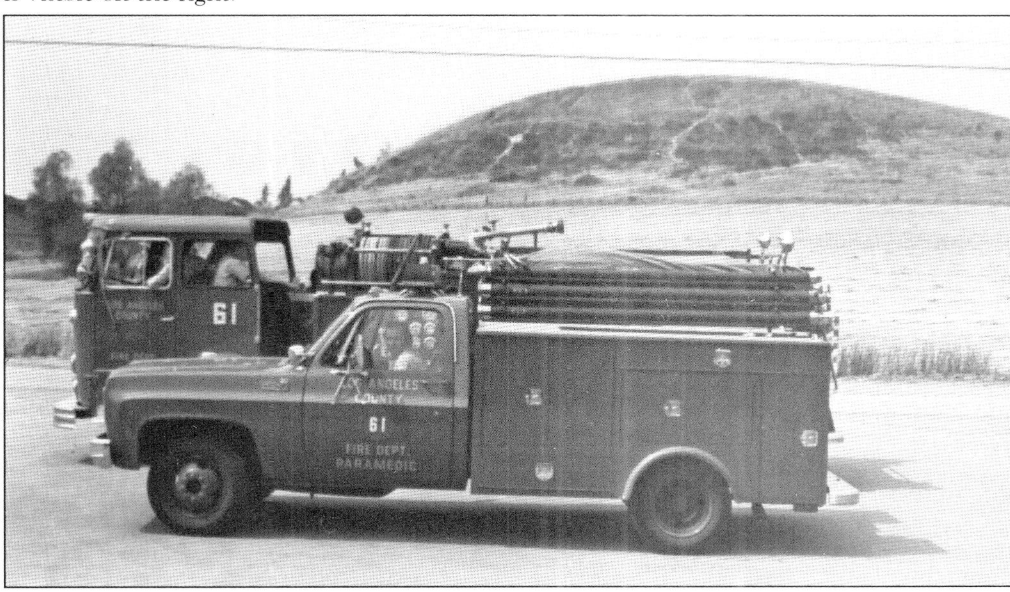

LA PUENTE ROAD, 1970s. The view from Cantel Place in the Gartel area shows La Puente Road. It was home to farmhouses, cows, horses, and a scattering of tract homes built in the 1970s. In the past, the city's isolation and uneven terrain made it unattractive to developers, who preferred sites that were flatter and easier to build. Walnut was an anomaly, since city officials saw nothing wrong with the city remaining a single-family town, which was supported by all the residents who lived within Walnut's borders.

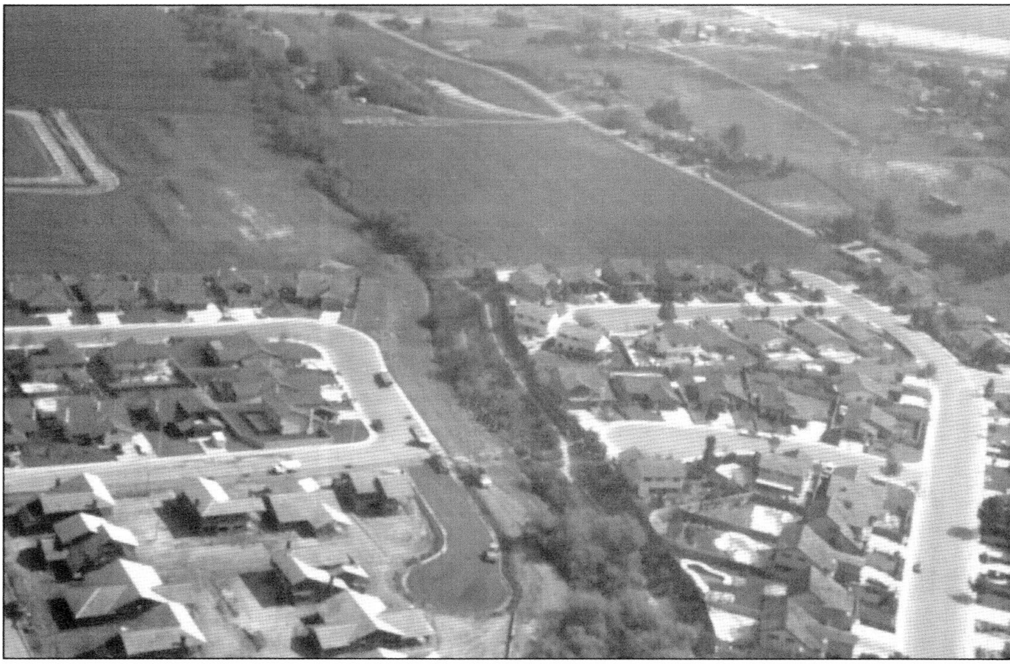

LARWIN HOMES, LATE 1970S. Here, the Larwin Homes off Avenida Alipaz border Lemon Creek, which flows between two subdivisions. The open fields stretch to Valley Boulevard, and the creek was left in its natural form and is part of a major storm drain system for the city.

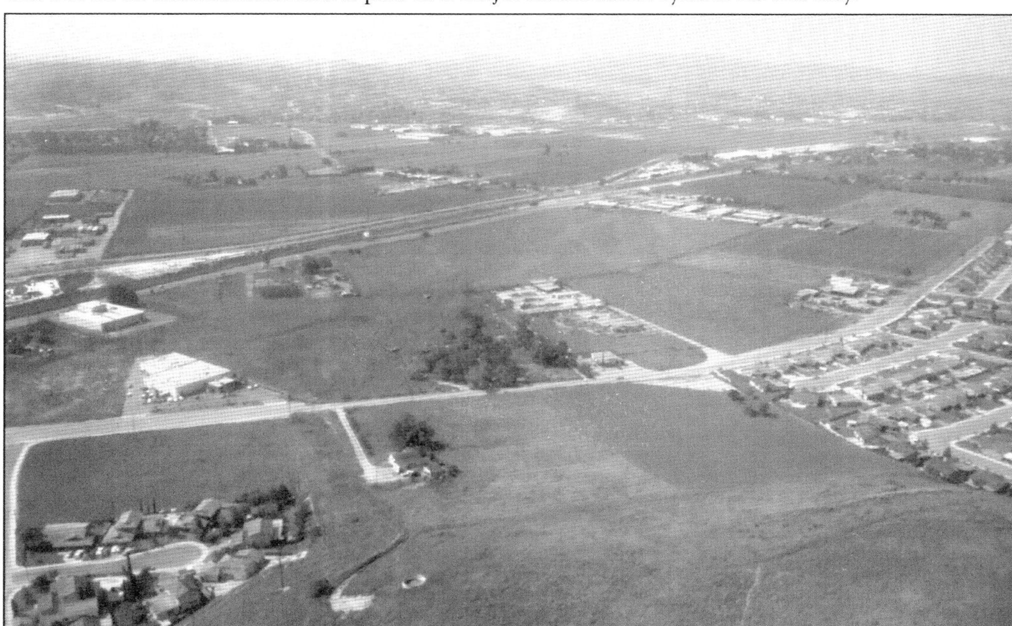

CARREY ROAD AND VALLEY BOULEVARD, LATE 1970S. A road goes west to the Carrey farm in front of Walnut's second city hall. A small house in the bottom left of the photograph had a 150-year-old pepper tree on the property. Citrus trees and dry farming were practiced well into the late 1970s and early 1980s.

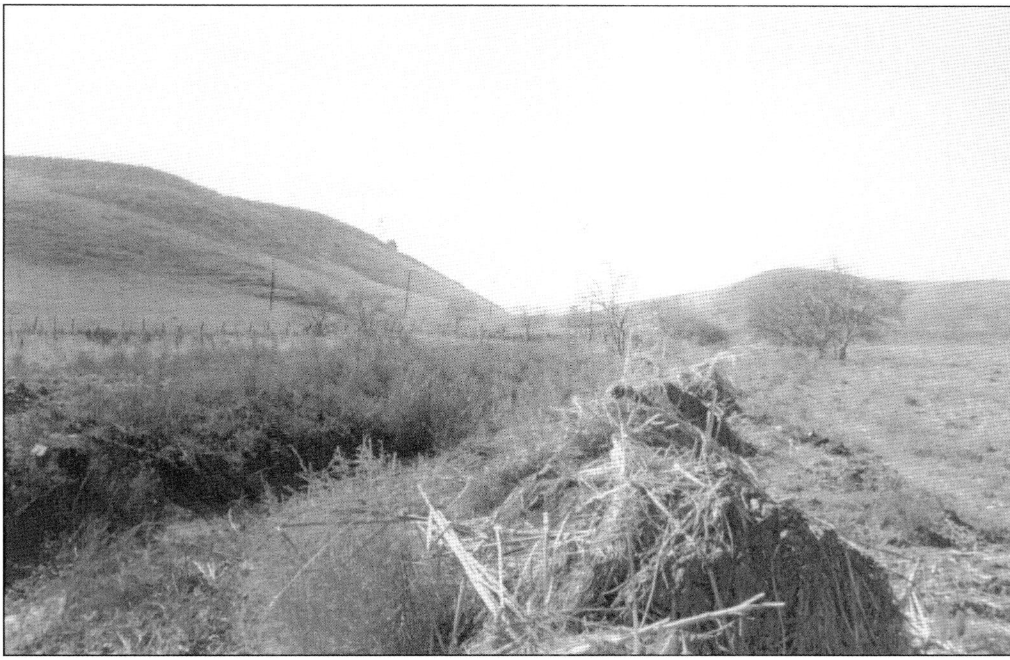

AMAR ROAD, 1960S. This photograph shows the proposed location of Amar Road. The road was not built until the 1980s, and slow early growth made it possible for Walnut youngsters to roam hills, build forts, and hunt for snakes, frogs, lizards, and fish in the streams.

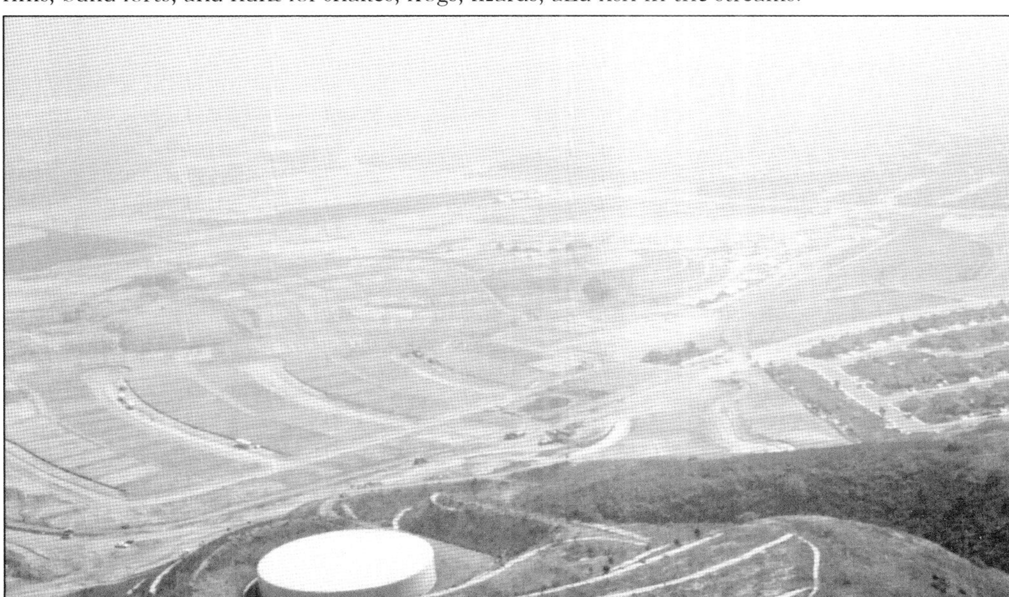

SNOW CREEK DEVELOPMENT, 1980S. The grading that had begun to take place when Walnut started to grow in the 1980s is shown. Pictured here is the Snow Creek development built by Shea off Grand Avenue and the Marlborough development on the west side of Amar Road. When the grading started, Amar Road did not exist. Developers were finally building single-family homes in the hills.

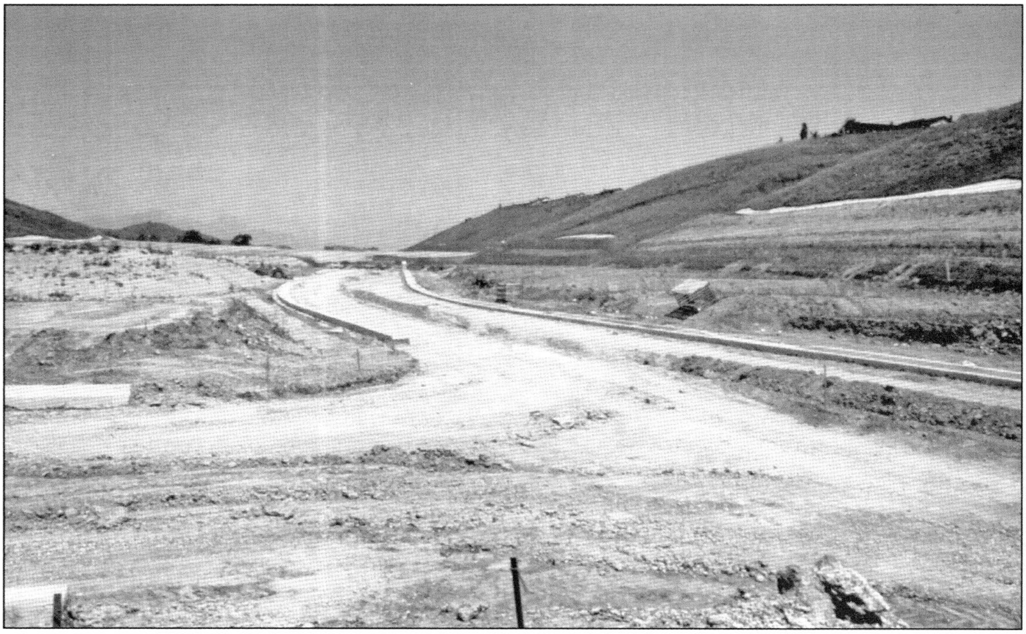

LAST OF THE RURAL AREAS. Looking north in the San Gabriel Valley, before homes and Amar Road were constructed, people could see the beautiful hills of Walnut. With its small population and slow growth, Walnut was kept as a rural area longer than neighboring cities.

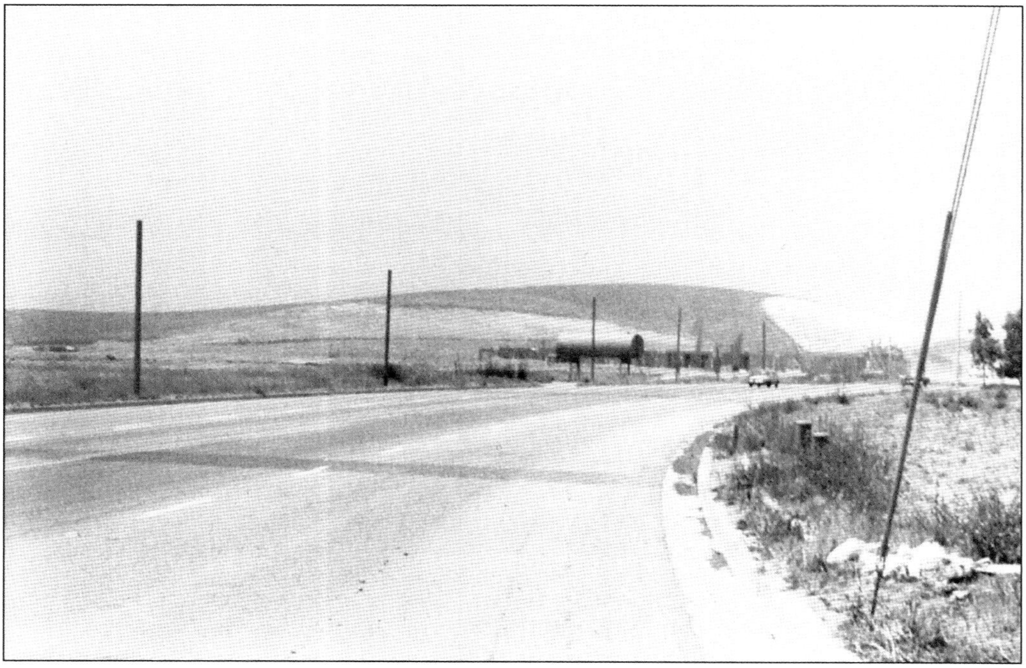

LA PUENTE ROAD, 1980S. Before home construction in the area, Walnut was still a city of gently rolling hills and a scattering of early developments, along with meandering roads, farmhouses, cows, and horses. This lasted until 1986, when Lewis Homes were built across the street from city hall and north of Valley Boulevard.

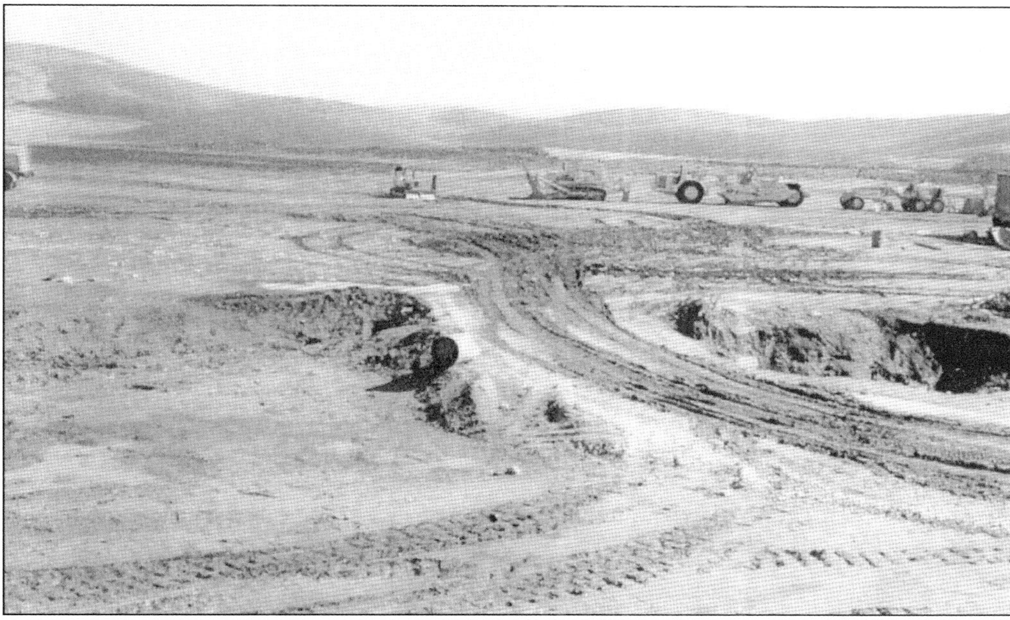

COUNTRY HOLLOW ROAD CONSTRUCTION, 1985. Upon completion, this road led to Westhoff Elementary School and the Marlborough Ridge homes. Located on the northeastern side of the city, the subdivision includes Walnut Ranch Park. The project included 210 single-family homes and opened in 1986, overlooking the San Gabriel Valley. In previous years, this large area had been an open field—home to coyotes, snakes, lizards, and an occasional deer. This photograph shows the initial grading of Country Hollow Road.

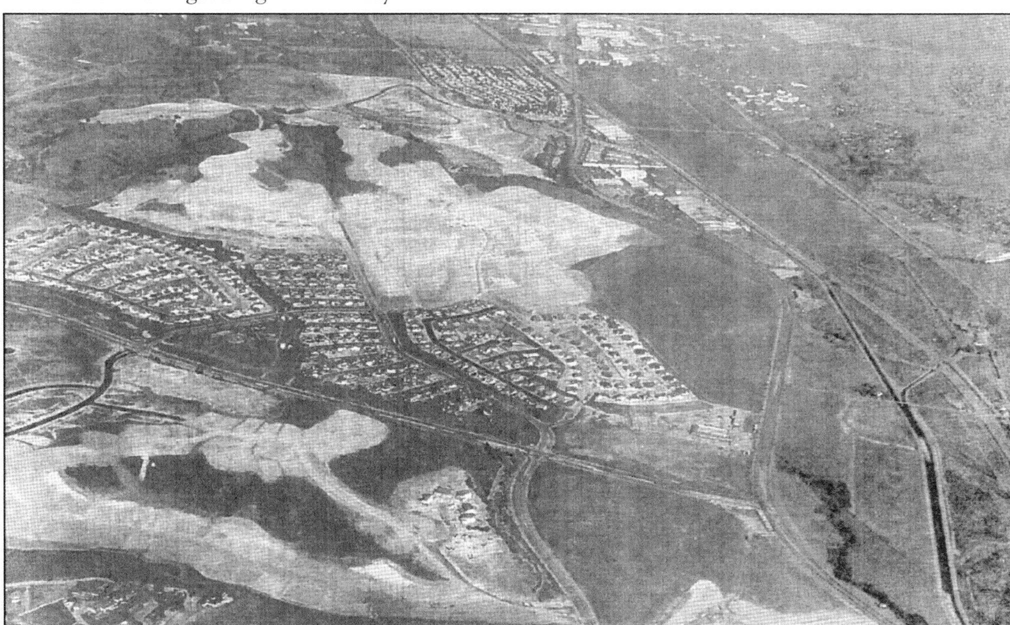

CITY AERIAL VIEW, 1988. Before the Lewis Development Company began construction across the street from city hall, this photograph shows Snow Creek only constructed halfway.

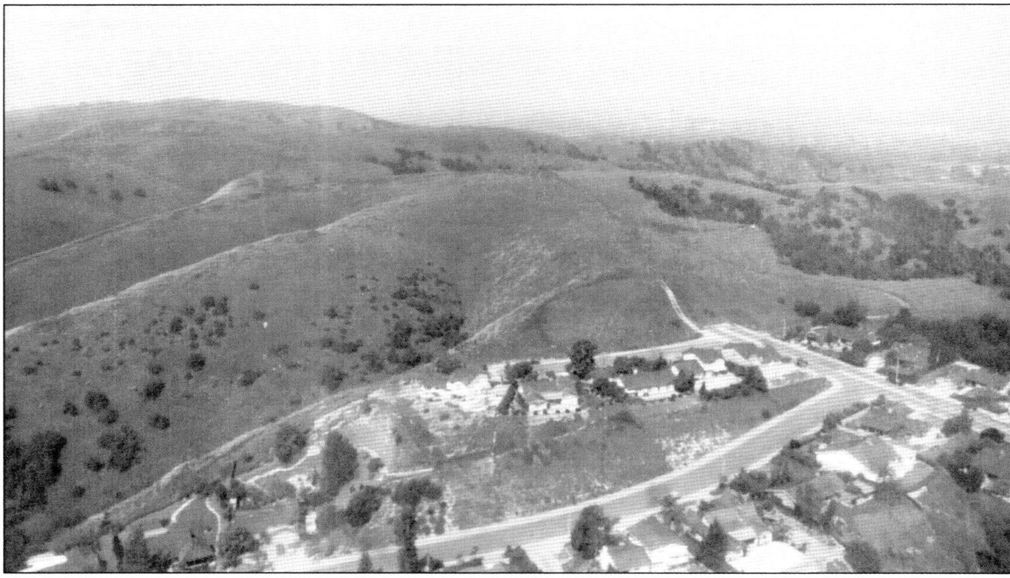

SHADOW MOUNTAIN ROAD, 1980S AND EARLY 1990S. Located in the northwest area of the city, the hills to the north remained undeveloped. During this time, when development of homes began on hills, large amounts of land were owned by Marlborough Development Company, which went bankrupt and was bought by Bramalea in 1989. In 1995, Bramalea went bankrupt, and J.M. Peters began developing single-family homes on half-acre lots. Today, the Belgate Estate homes sell for more than $1 million.

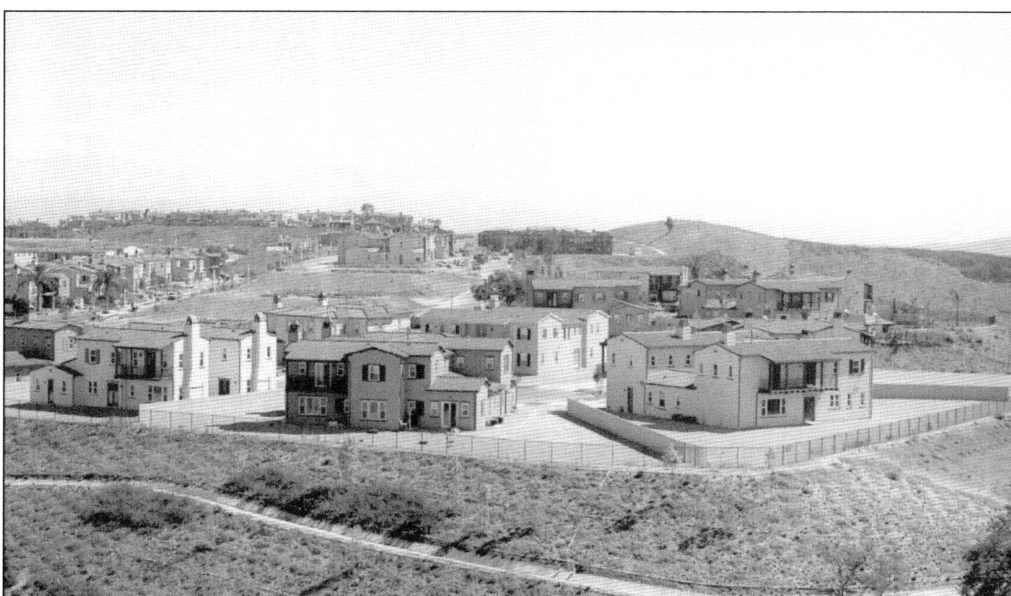

HOMES ON MEADOWPASS ROAD, 1990S. Recent developments have transformed homes into big, spacious, and beautiful places. In another area of the city, Standard Pacific is building on the last open space remaining. The Three Oaks development was named after the many oak trees that surround the property. Three Oaks has over 240 acres of open space and spectacular views. In 2011, Walnut is a quiet, peaceful, and family-oriented community.

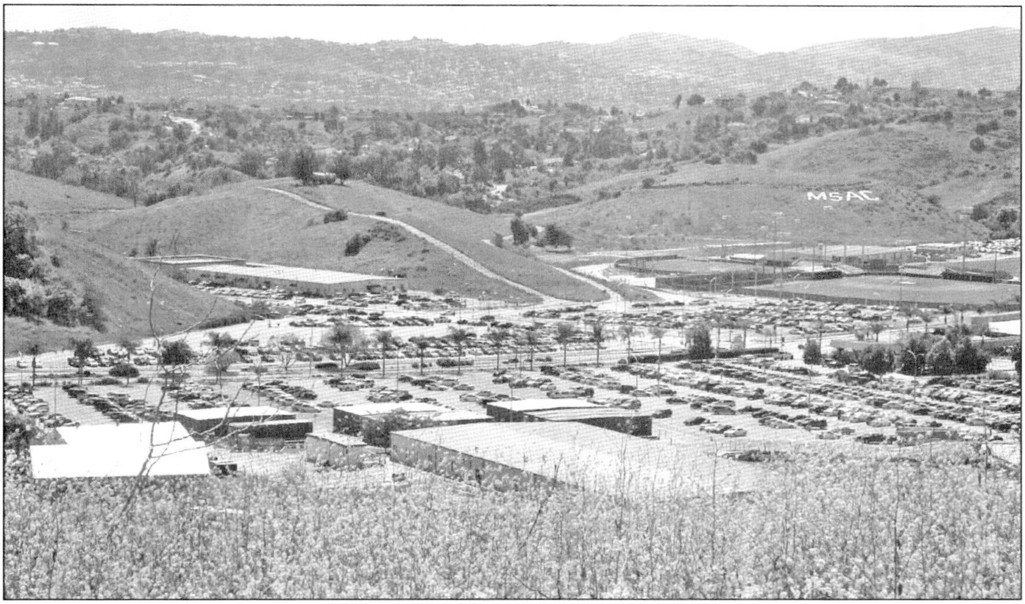

Black Walnut Groves, Present. Known as mission walnuts, walnut trees were originally brought from Spain by the missionaries and planted by the Native Americans. On a hill overlooking Mount San Antonio College is an old covered wagon and several walnut trees as a memorial to remind residents that this area was once planted with black walnut trees. Walnut is home to one of the largest remaining black walnut groves.

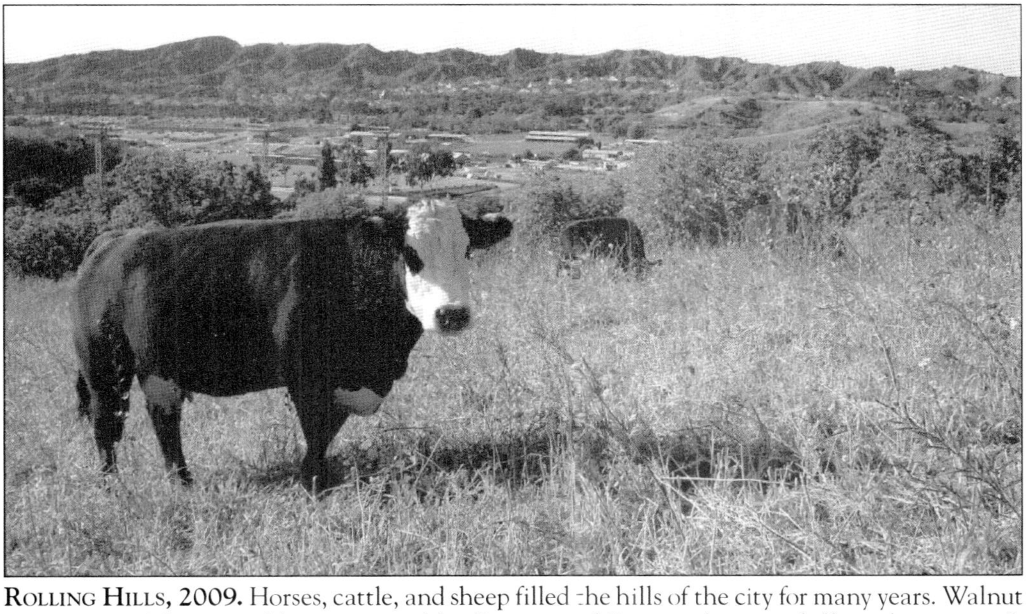

Rolling Hills, 2009. Horses, cattle, and sheep filled the hills of the city for many years. Walnut was separated from neighboring cities like Covina and Pomona by steep hills and canyons. It remained a rural area while surrounding cities were growing. In the 1940s, Walnut consisted of dirt roads, cacti, and grasslands covered in the spring with wild mustard seed. It was not until the late 1980s that Walnut began to grow. The area around Mount San Antonio College retains some of the past.

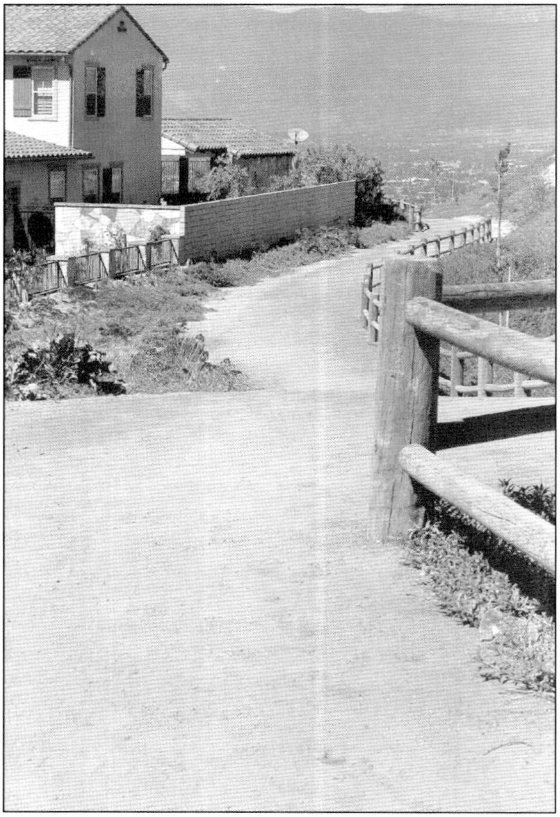

Schabarum Trail, 2000s. The Schabarum Trail begins at the city limits to the north and winds across a grove of walnut trees to Skyline Drive and down to Walnut Ranch Park. It then proceeds west on Amar Road to the Three Oaks housing development. Inside Three Oaks, it travels north across the property to the eastern city limits. The trail, built by Standard Pacific through Three Oaks, provides scenic views as well as beautiful rest stops.

Walnut Ranch Park, 1987. Part of the Marlborough housing development, the park has provided the American Youth Soccer Organization (AYSO) Region 624 a home for over 20 years. Every year, more than 1,000 young people sign up to play soccer on the four fields. Walnut Ranch Park is adjacent to Westhoff Elementary School and nestled in the scenic hillside.

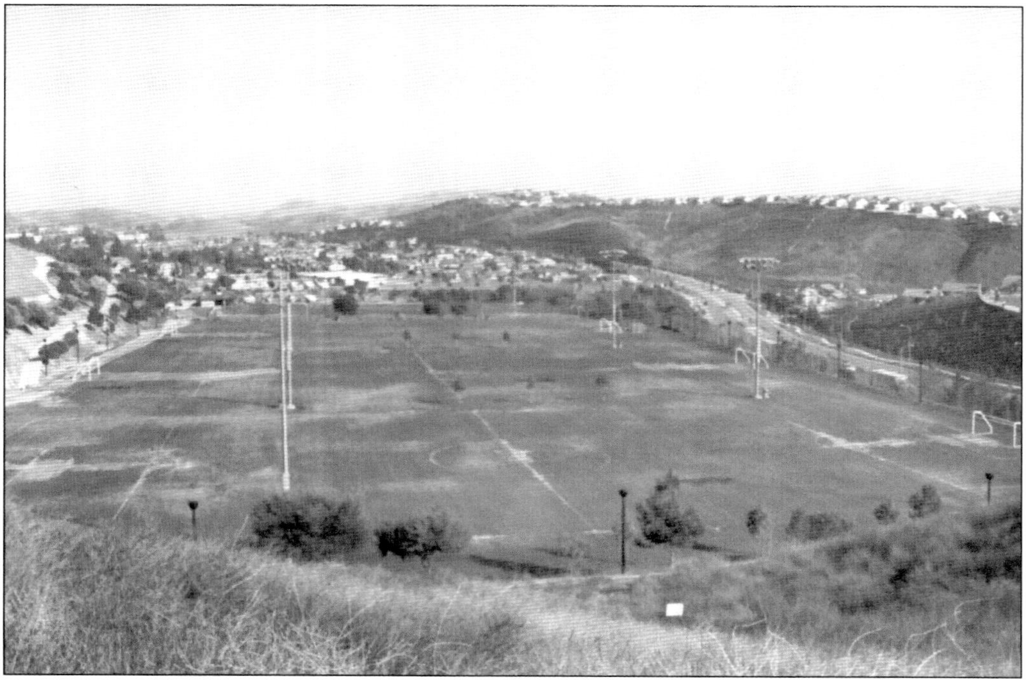

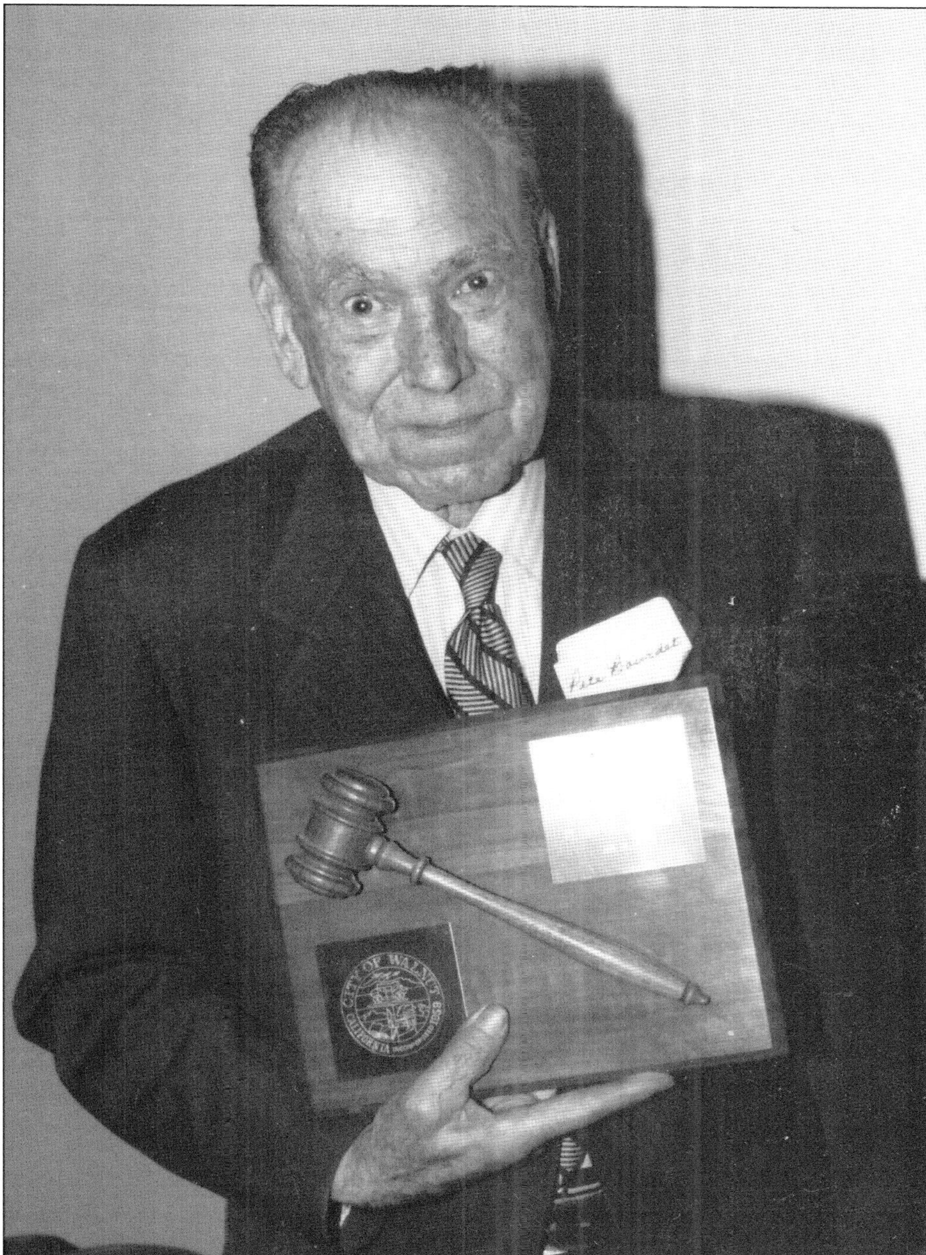

Water District, Early 1950s. In order to obtain a reliable water supply for the area, landowners (ranchers, farmers, and residents) in the local area voted in July 1952 to form the Walnut Valley Water District. Louis Bourdet and Ernest Carrey from the Walnut area were elected directors on the first board. At this time, the district provided water to a population of less than 800. Pete Bourdet, pictured here, was the second director, serving Walnut from 1957 to 1987. Until the 1980s, landowners voted for a director to represent a district for a four-year term. Bill Wentworth, who served from 1987 to 2003, was the first director elected by popular vote. Allen Wu was elected in 2003.

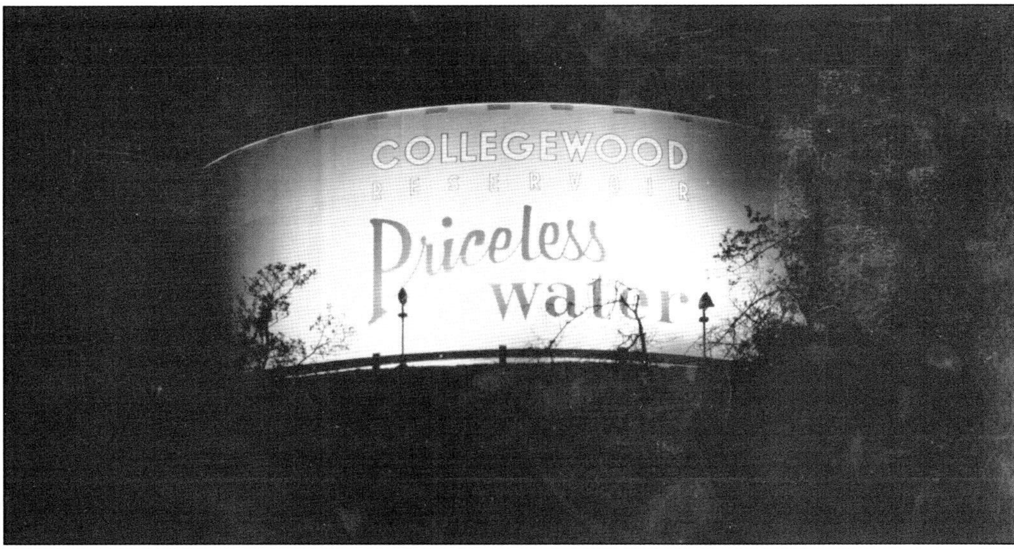

First Water Tank, 1965. In 1964, Walnut Valley Water District manager Ed Biederman reported that a water plan had been completed and that work had begun on the project. The water district completed Walnut's first water tank in the northern area of the city, above the Collegewood tract. Following completion, Biederman painted the tank—causing local residents to object and the sign to come down. Today, Walnut has 10 water storage tanks in the city in addition to a recycled pump station on Grand Avenue and Valley Boulevard.

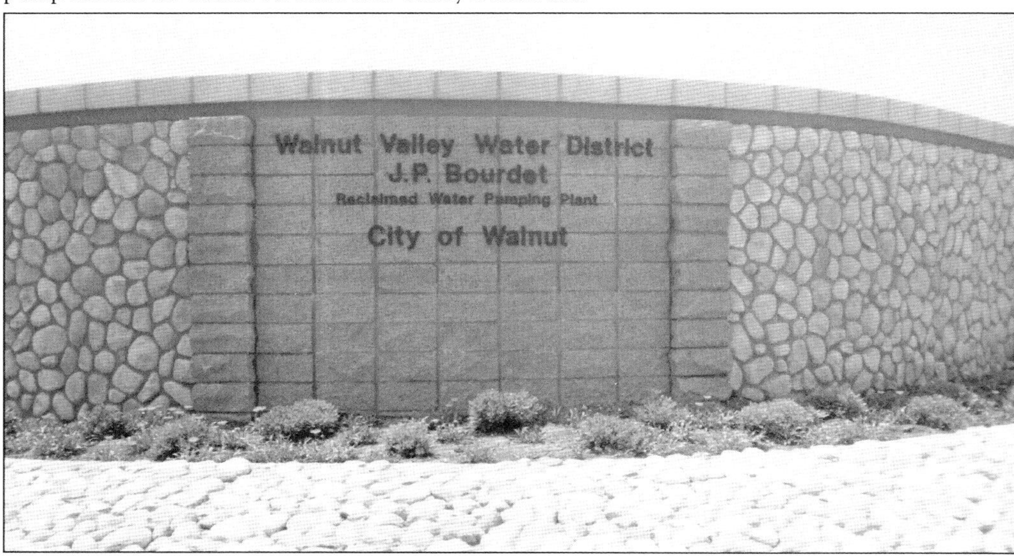

Recycled Water System, 1986. Providing water for irrigating the landscaped areas of parks, schools, and other private and public areas, the recycled pumping station sits on the corner of Valley Boulevard and Grand Avenue. The facility was named in honor of Pete Bourdet, longtime director of the district. The district's first recycled water system was completed at a cost of $8.5 million. The system included 17 miles of pipeline, a two-million-gallon storage tank, and the main pump station. It originally had 21 customers serving 340 acres of land. Over the years, the recycled water system has grown to 227 connections serving 600 acres in 2011. The city of Walnut enjoys lush landscaping year-round due to this water system.

Eight

Beautification of Walnut

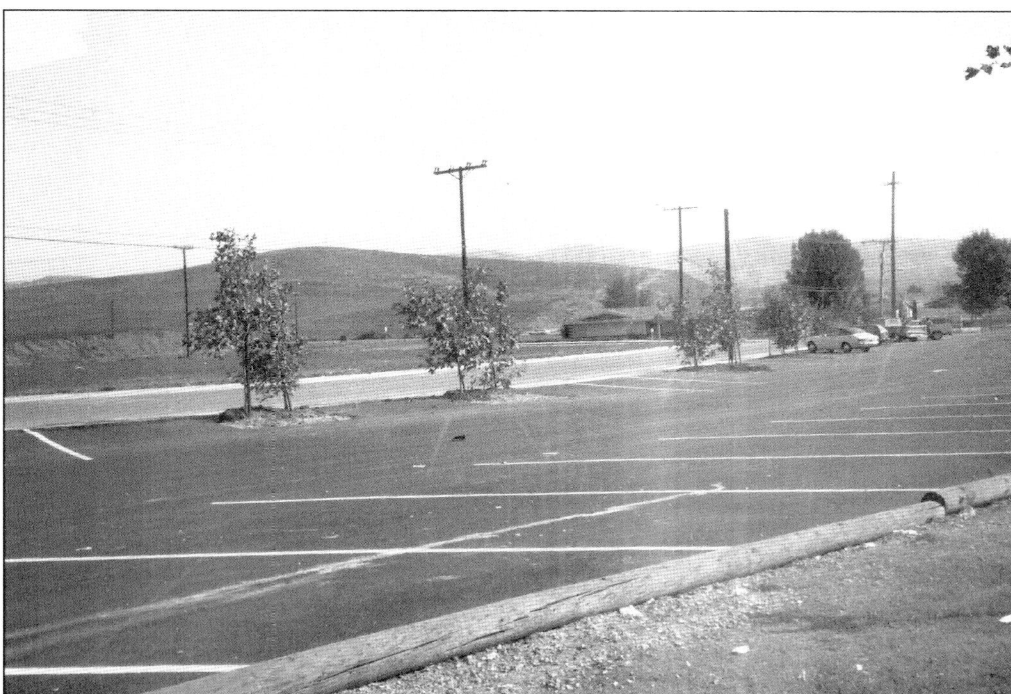

Suzanne Park, 1959. Los Angeles County gave Suzanne Park to the City of Walnut in 1959. The 12-acre park was to be maintained as a park with no expense to the county. The area originally held orange groves; in 1959, six acres were still orange groves. For many years, the park was named Walnut City Park; the name was changed in the 1960s to Suzanne Park.

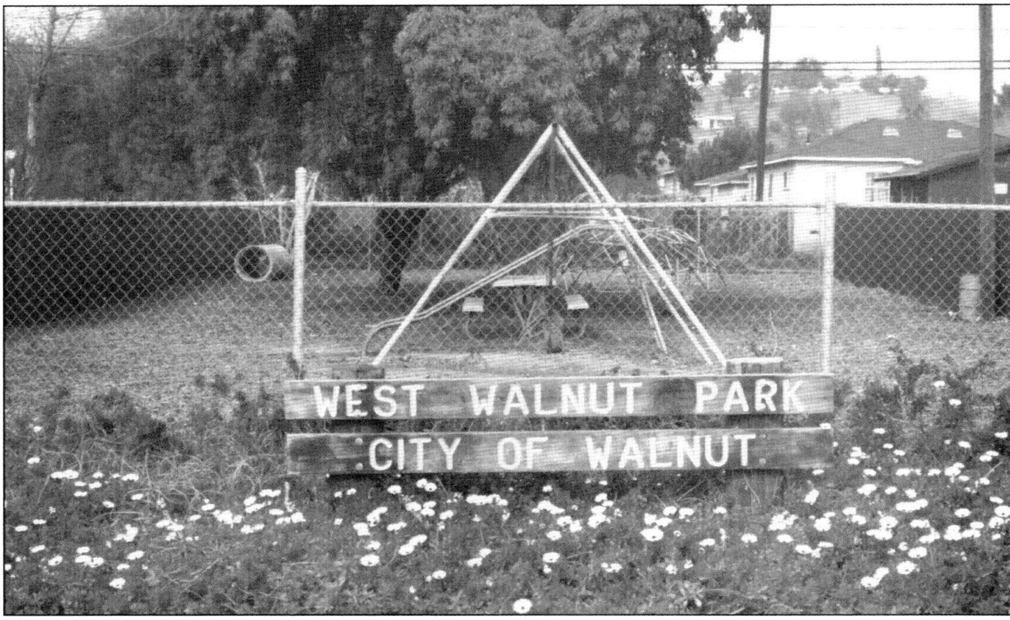

West Walnut Park, 1960s. During the 1960s, the city had an empty lot on Valley Boulevard. The council decided to make a small park for the southwest area of the city. A slide and swings were put in, but it was not a top priority for the city, and it was not well used or maintained. The park was then closed during the 1990s.

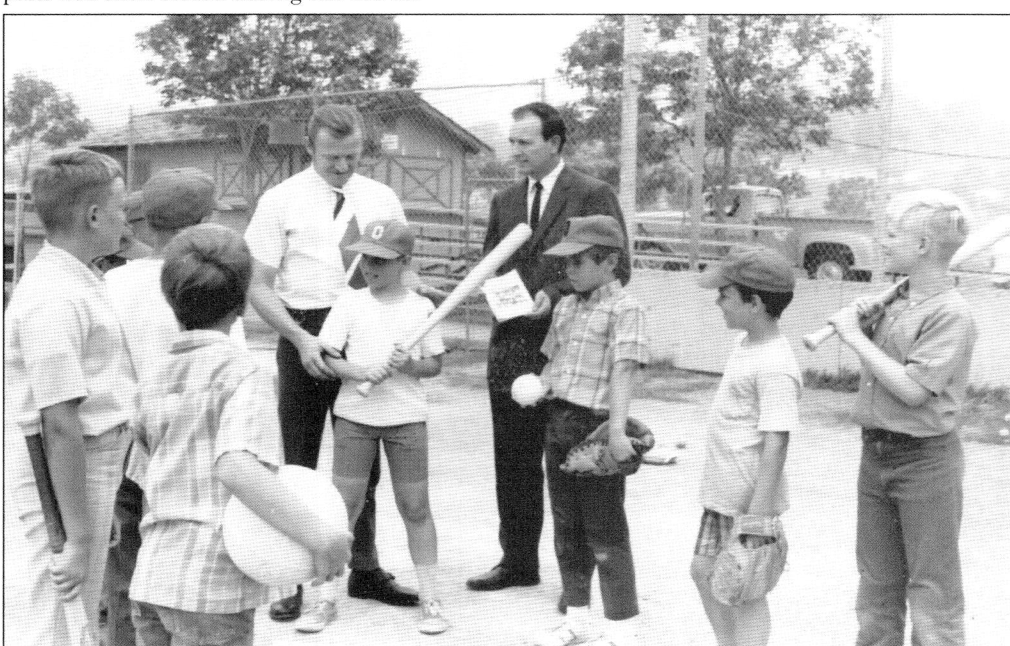

Pony Baseball, 1974. Suzanne Park served as the official field for Pony Baseball until the league moved to Creekside Park and Snow Creek Park in 1987. Mayor Dick Laughter joins residents and throws out the first ball for Walnut Valley Pony Baseball.

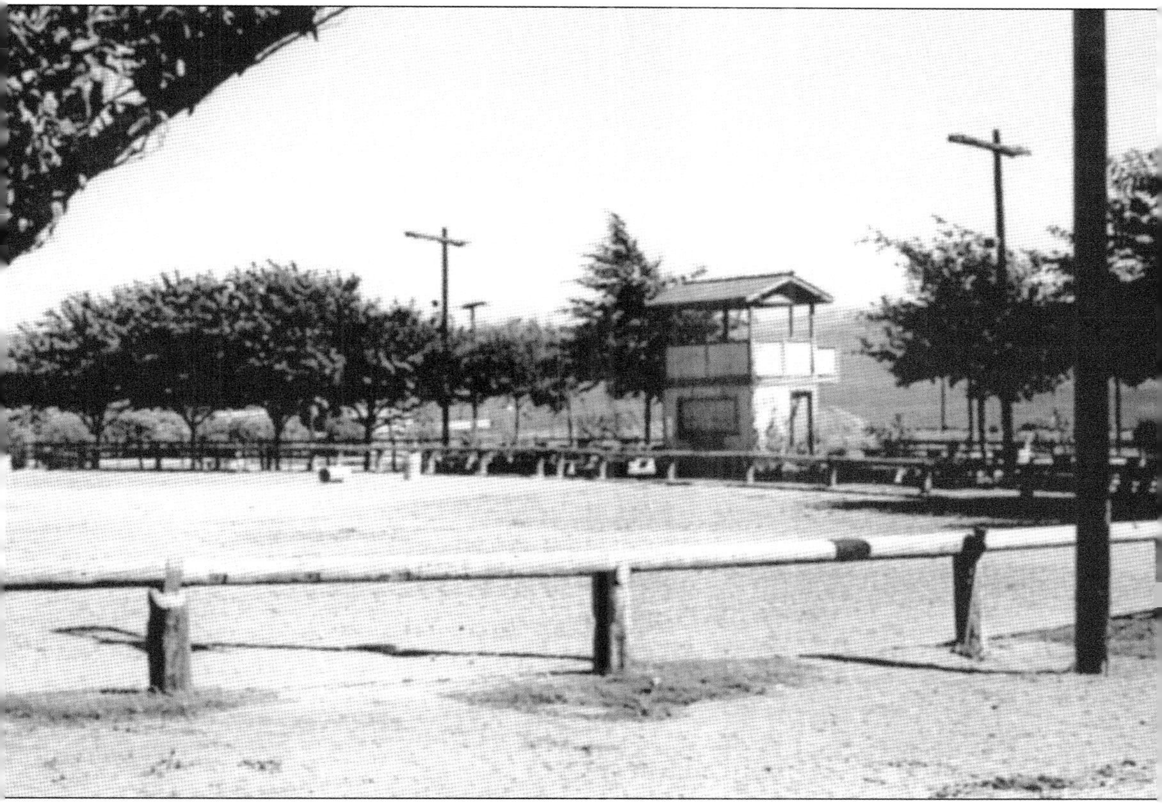

SUZANNE PARK UPGRADED, 1960S. Residents donated labor and materials to build a small baseball diamond, picnic area, archery range, and horse ring. A road was graded for access to the baseball diamond, and the entrance was also paved. From 1963 to 1964, the budget allotted $700 for park maintenance and $300 for maintenance supplies. There was a reserve fund of $2,032.57 over the previous five years from the sale of oranges. The new contract for oranges would yield a smaller fund for oranges; therefore, the council voted to give park budgets $2,000 more. The park is located at Suzanne Road and Fuerte Road.

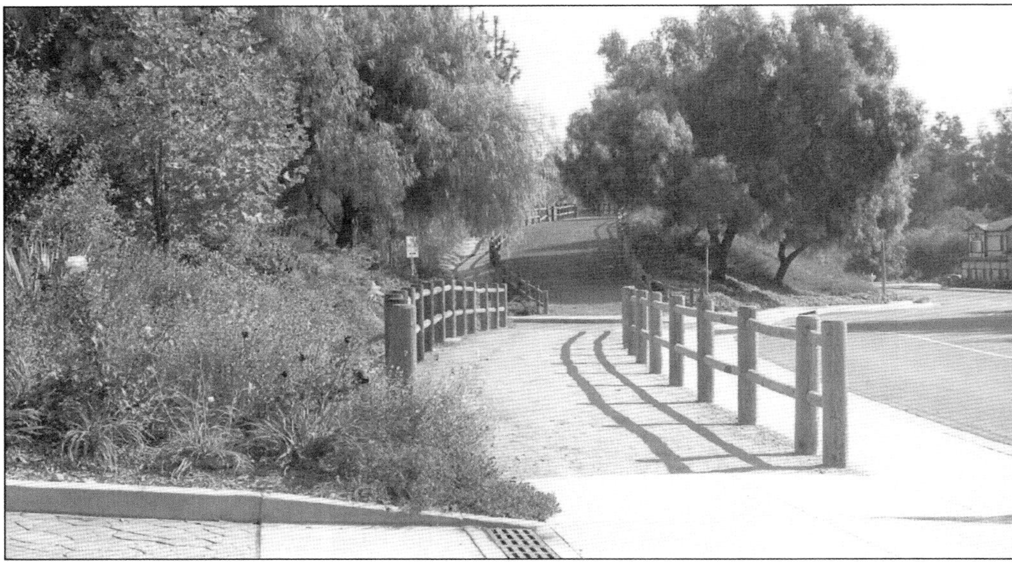

MONEY MAGAZINE, AUGUST 2011. Ranked 57th in the nation and first in California, Walnut was one of "The best 100 places to live in the United States with a population of 50,000 and under." *Money Magazine* reported, "With its 90 acres of parks, sports fields, trails and open space, Walnut offers relief from urban congestion—and the weather to take advantage of. Walnut is a community of single-family homes and has one of the strictest open space requirements in the area. Equestrian trails, parks, and lush landscaping will continue to be the city's most prominent features. Easy access to major freeways and the beaches are less than an hour away, and because of its high-performing schools."

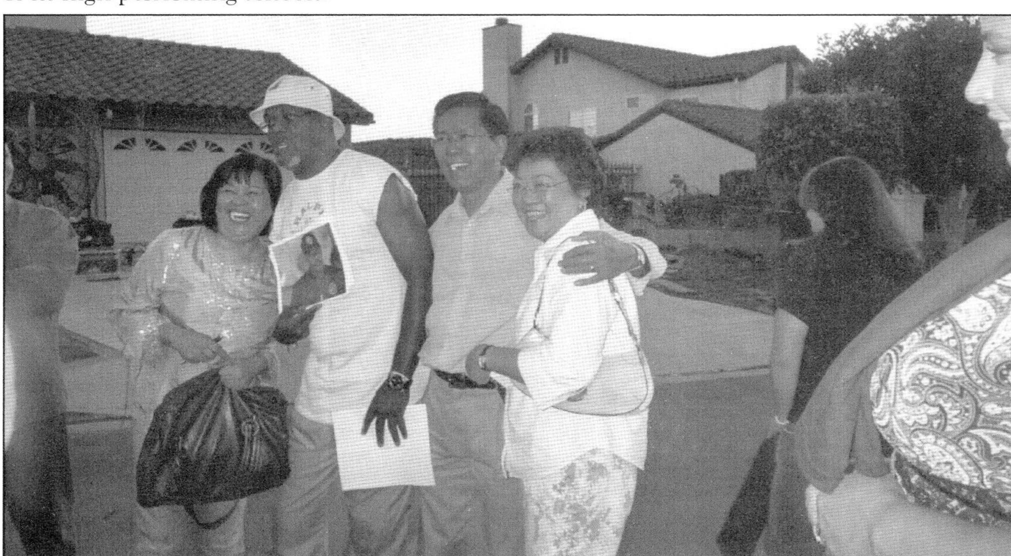

MOVIE MAKING, 2007. On the set of *Lakeview Terrace* in 2007, Walnut resident and council member Tony Cartagena (center) and Norie Cartagena (right) are in the picture with movie star Samuel L. Jackson between takes. Producers of *Lakeview Terrace* chose the city of Walnut because of its rural character within a suburban community and also for its single-family homes and small-town charm. This movie was released in 2008 worldwide.

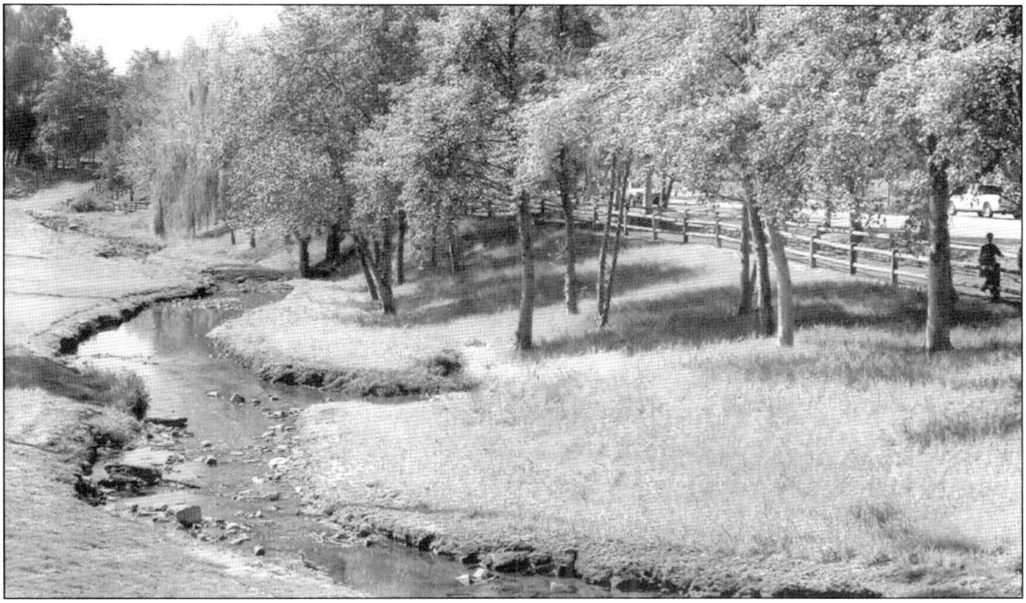

Snow Creek Stream, Late 1970s. The council decided to keep the natural creek that flowed through the Snow Creek development. A large area around the creek was dedicated as open space. Today, the creek serves as one of the major storm drain systems in the city. Walking by the creek, residents can observe crawdads, fish, herons, and other wildlife in the stream and surrounding areas.

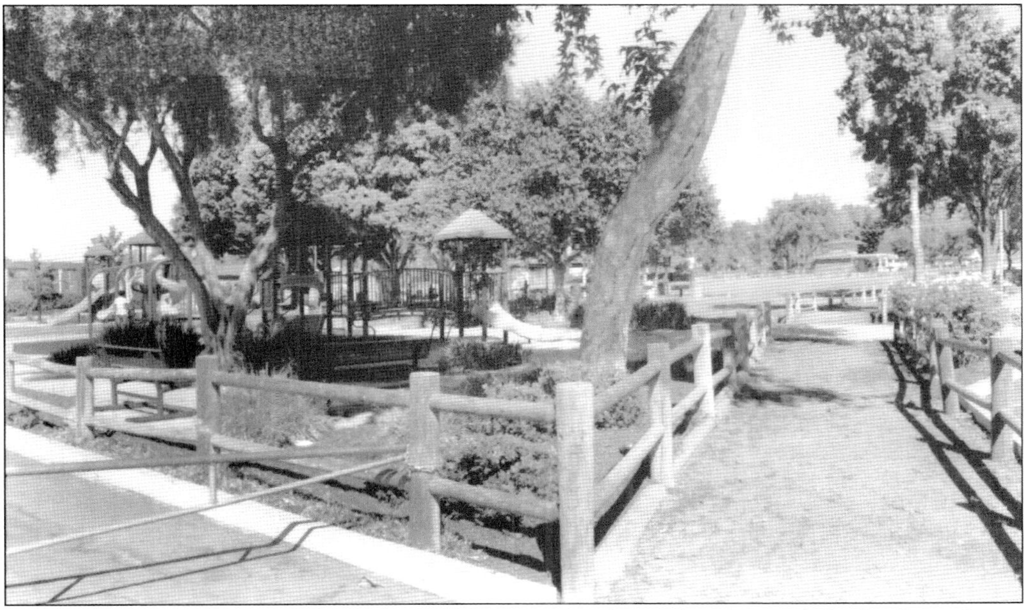

Suzanne Park Renovation, 2001. The picnic area was changed and upgraded; a bridle trail runs along the parking lot; a new children's play area was added; and the softball fields were redone. A new building was constructed for the horse ring announcer's booth. The Walnut Softball League now plays on all three fields. Some of the original trees were left as a reminder to the past. It is still home to the annual Family Festival and is frequently used by residents for family picnics.

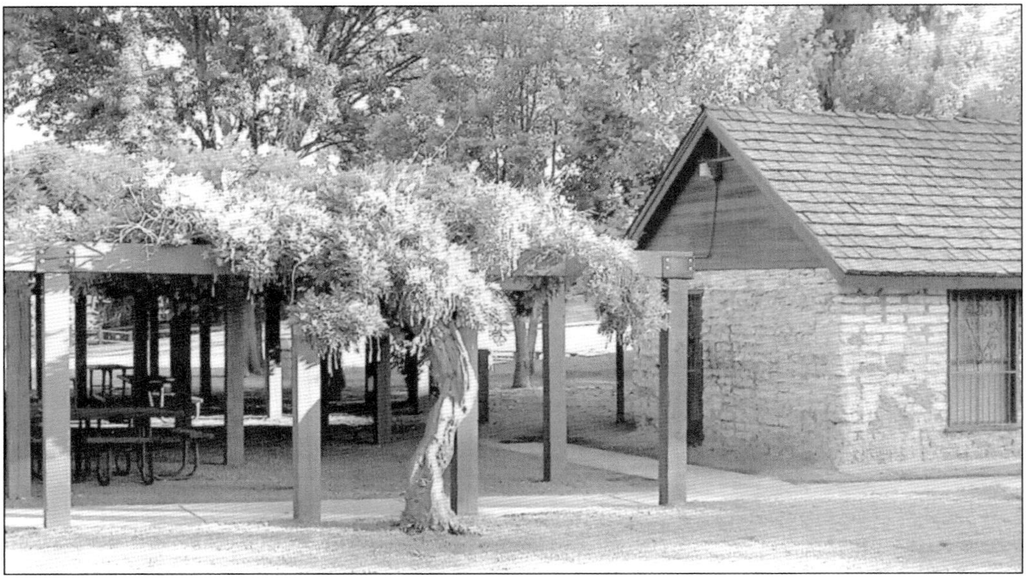

Lemon Creek Park, 1976. Lemon Creek Park was a bicentennial gift to the city from the residents of Walnut. Restoration of the W.R. Rowland Adobe Redwood Ranch House was the most difficult project. Under the direction of naval officer and resident Ron Way, a local naval construction brigade restored the park. The Walnut Valley Women's Club collected antiques from local donors to furnish the inside of the structure. The Walnut Junior Women's Club donated money to build the barbecue; the Walnut Lions Club donated the surveying and landscaping; and the Walnut Kiwanis Club built the fire pit.

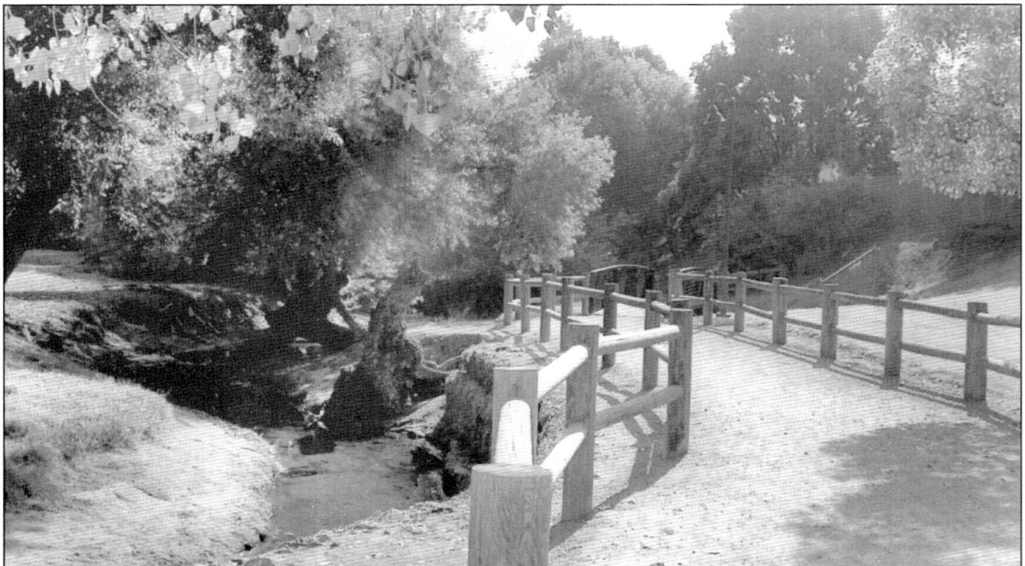

Lemon Creek, 2000s. The creek still flows in 2011 as it did hundreds of years ago. In 1974, the city left the creek in its natural state. Many adobes built by the Gabrielinos surrounded the creek in the 1800s. When secularization occurred in the 1830s, Native Americans continued to live in the area and were employed by the Mexicans on their ranchos.

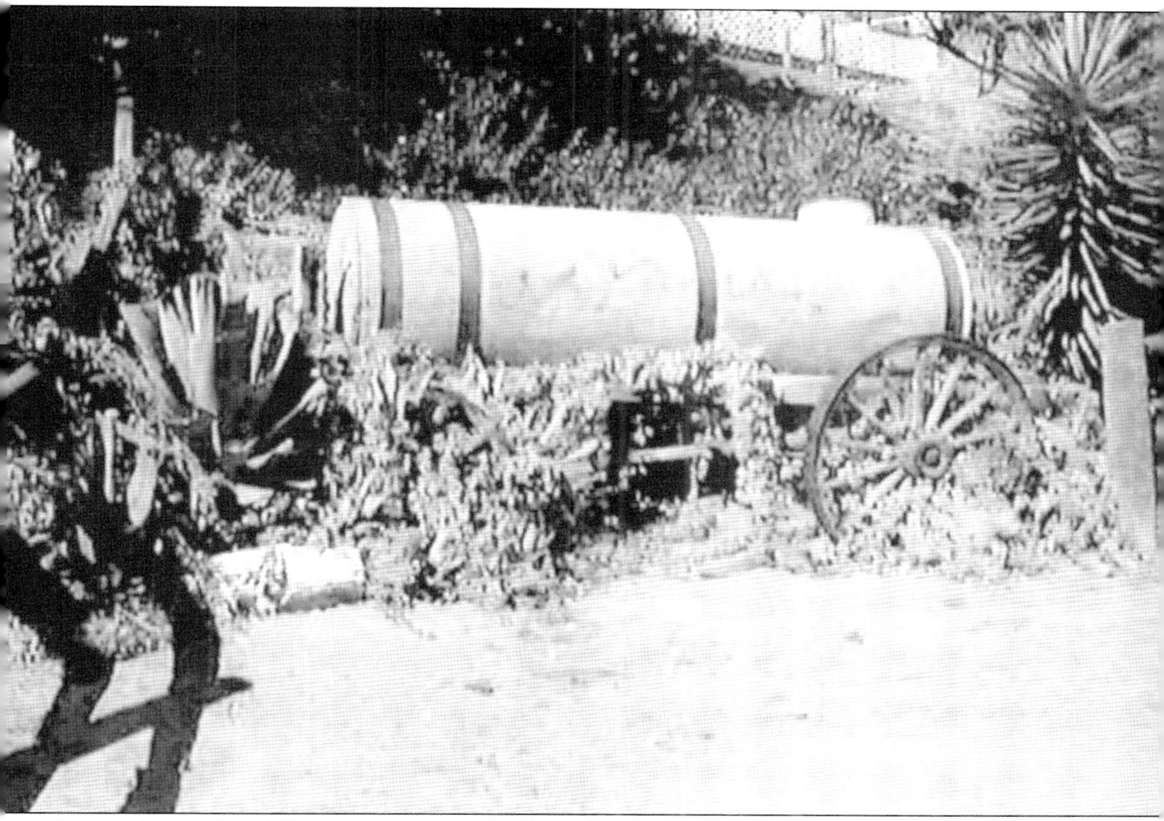

LEMON CREEK PARK WATER TANK, 1900S. The park is home to an old water tank used by farmers in the late 1890s and early 1900s to provide water while they worked on the fields. The 19th-century water tank was part of a horse-drawn vehicle. The park is also home to a 175-year-old wisteria vine that covers the patio next to the W.R. Rowland Adobe Redwood Ranch House.

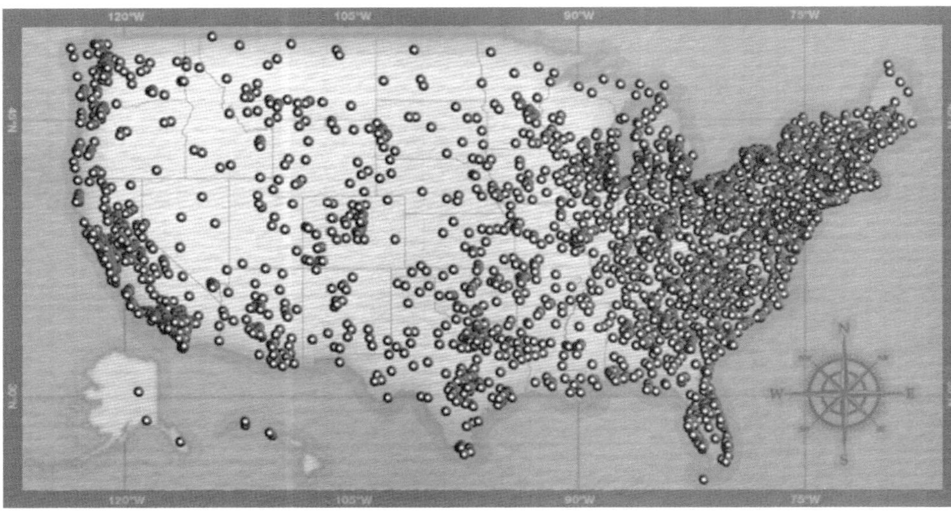